Blow My Head Off

CW01402177

THE AUTOBIOGRAPHY OF

Jeff Mason

COPYRIGHT NOTICE

Copyright © 2022 Hyfrydle Publishing. All rights reserved.

The moral rights of Jeff Mason to be identified as the author of this work have been asserted by him in accordance with the Copyright, Designs and Patents Act of 1988.
All rights reserved under International and Pan-American Copyright Conventions.
No part of the text or images in this book may be copied, reproduced, transmitted, downloaded or stored in or introduced into any information storage system, in any form or by any means, whether electronic or mechanical, now known or hereinafter invented, without the express written permission of the author and the publisher.
English edition: Published in Great Britain in 2022 by Hyfrydle Publishing
Paperback ISBN: 978-1-7395940-0-8

ACKNOWLEDGEMENTS

All material is used under licence and permission from the understood copyright holders, including Sue Spencer for material from her private archives and The Glenn Miller Orchestra UK.

PREFACE

In some countries, this book would be deemed inappropriate for minors.

CONTENTS

FOREWORD

My wife, Penny and I met Jeff in November 2020, on a naturist holiday in the Canary Islands. Over dinner, we exchanged anecdotes, as we became acquainted. We had an initial insight into his interesting life as a saxophonist and clarinetist. He discovered that Penny and I had met HRH Prince Philip, Duke of Edinburgh a few times. Jeff told us that he had played at Prince Philip's 70th birthday. We said that we had been at his 80th and how the wonderful Dame Shirley Bassey went right up to the Duke of Edinburgh, singing "Big Spender". Jeff then recalled how he had been flown out to Monte Carlo, especially to play for her.

Like Jeff had often been told, we too suggested that he should write his autobiography. He wanted to, but knew that he needed help, so I volunteered. After returning home, it took a few months before he got into the project. I never envisaged how much I would look forward to each new chapter emerging.

What developed has proven to be a record of an even more amazing life than I had ever imagined, and that the book is likely to have a significantly wider appeal than just from fellow musicians. Rather like with jazz, themes recur in different places but with varying colour and character.

His book epitomises something which I deduced a while ago, namely that the majority of naturists are not just comfortable about shedding their clothes in the company of others; they are also much more open than many people in baring their souls and revealing their mistakes and failures in life, their financial ups and downs and what would typically be called their private lives.

It is no surprise therefore, that Jeff's book delivers a refreshing 'warts and all' chronicle of his fascinating life, including coming to terms with his homosexuality at a time before the law and public understanding matured.

From humble childhood beginnings, the brilliant talent of the young Jeff soon achieved the recognition that took him on adventures around the world, playing both clarinet, saxophone, flute and other instruments in the well-known big bands.

I am humbled by the talent that makes possible not just mastering a variety of musical instruments with passion but drawing upon a vast repertoire, played perfectly from memory.

Chris Crook

1

PROLOGUE

As I start this book, in the early spring of 2020, we are in the middle of the worldwide coronavirus pandemic, something the human race has never experienced before. This will surely go down in the history books of the future, along with the Black Death in 1348.

We are in lock-down in our own homes and only allowed to go out to buy food, medicines and to exercise locally. Fortunately for me, we have lots of nice walks in the Bournemouth area, including along the promenade but we are currently prohibited from the actual beach.

We have been advised to wear face masks when out; about 50% did so, including me. Later it became mandatory indoors. A lot of people are also wearing gloves, because the virus can allegedly also be transmitted by touch. While shopping for food, everyone must queue outside, also keeping well apart from one another, while still wearing masks. We are only allowed inside the supermarkets a few at a time. The floors have been marked out as one-way systems, to help to keep us at a safe distance from one another.

One day, when walking to the supermarket, I passed an older lady sitting on a seat; we were both wearing our masks, which I found quite amusing, because if we had been walking around wearing a mask before lock-down we would probably have been arrested as potential robbers.

I stopped and said to the lady, "What do we all look like in these masks?"
Her quick response was to say,
"I think my mask is an improvement".

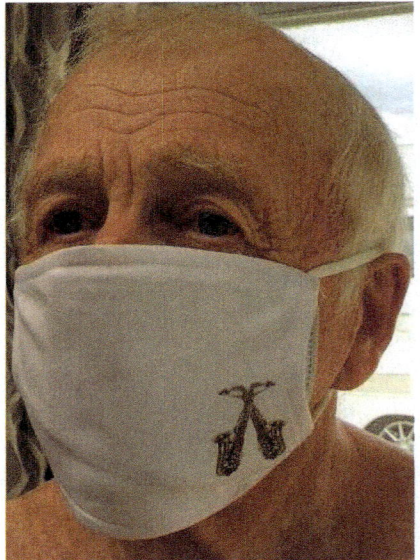

At this time, people worldwide are dying in their thousands every day. I am one of the lucky ones, as I have a garden where I can go outside, to do some gardening or have a spot of sunbathing during the summer. I feel so sorry for families in flats and apartments who can't even go outside, except for a daily walk or to shop.

2

It's also proving to be the hottest April on record, which only makes it even worse for those people in flats. I live in Bournemouth, which is on the coast, but as previously mentioned, no one is allowed on the beaches at this time.

One really good thing that has happened has been the coming together of communities through this period. People throughout the country were asked to go to their doorsteps or windows and clap their hands at 8pm on Thursday evenings, in appreciation of the doctors and nurses in the hospitals, treating patients with this terrible virus. People in my community have stood in their front gardens or hung from windows of their flats to clap their hands together. As my contribution, I thought it would be nice to play my saxophone for them. Every Thursday, I'd sit on my garden wall, to play a different tune each week. The sound carried a long way and soon people were coming round from other roads to listen and to clap along.

Eventually, it was announced nationally that the next Thursday should be the final ritual of clapping and making other noise, such as banging pots and pans.

On that last evening, I played "We'll Meet Again" and stood in the middle of the road to play the National Anthem. Since then, so many people have stopped and have spoken over the garden wall, thanking me. It definitely helped to bring our little community together.

In the past, lots of my friends who have listened to my stories and little adventures throughout the years seemed to find them interesting, so much so, that they have repeatedly said, "You should write a book."

I have continually been putting it off.

"Now I have to stay at home, whether or not I like it", I thought, "This is the time to start writing about all my little adventures."

So, here goes:

INTRODUCTION

I was born on the 27th of June 1943, towards the end of the Second World War, at a Hospital in a Derbyshire town called Heanor, but I lived and was brought up with my parents in the village of Kimberley, Nottinghamshire, which is just over the county border of Derbyshire, and about five miles from the City Of Nottingham, which is probably best known for the stories of Robin Hood and his merry men, in Sherwood Forest. There is also Nottingham Castle, the famous annual Goose Fair, along with the Raleigh cycle factory, Player's cigarettes and the home of Boots the Chemists. Little of the original castle remains.

Another son of Kimberley, who was nine years older than me lived three doors away from my parents and represented Great Britain as a cyclist in the 1952 Olympic Games in Helsinki and the 1960 Olympic Games in Rome. His name was Lloyd Binch. He worked at the Raleigh cycle factory in Nottingham during the day and no doubt rode one of their bikes during the Olympics. He lent me his road bike once, when I was a teenager. I felt like the king of the road on that bike.

With regards to Kimberley, I often wondered if there are any connections with the famous Kimberley Diamond Mines in South Africa. Many towns in America and Australia have English names given by early settlers from their home country. Names in America such as New England, New Hampshire, New York and New Jersey spring to mind, so why not Kimberley in South Africa as well? In fact, the connection is with Kimberley in Norfolk and with the 1st Earl of Kimberley.

Our two main employers for the men in the area were the coal mines and the local Nottinghamshire Brewery, Hardy & Hanson's Kimberley Ales. For the women of the area, it was a huge Wolsey stocking factory, which unfortunately was demolished in the 1960s, to make way for a shopping precinct.

My mother nearly died that hot June summer's day, giving birth to an overdue nine-pound bouncing boy and was warned by the doctor not to have another child, as there was a strong possibility it could kill her. Consequentially I didn't have any siblings. I seem to remember her asking me on more than one occasion if I would like a brother or sister. Fortunately for her, I always said, "No".

My maternal grandparents lived in Holbrook Street, Heanor. They ran a very successful bakery business, selling from both their premises and a van, for a door-to-door delivery service, which was driven by my mother during the war. My grandmother was born of farming stock; her parents having owned their own farm, called Daisy Farm in Heanor. I somehow feel that there is still farming in my blood somewhere, as when I was a boy, my heart was set on being a farmer when I grew up. I really loved animals and still do, to this day.

As a young man, my grandfather was a butcher by trade, which also has a tenuous connection to farming. Later on, life was to lead me in a completely different direction away from my desire to be a farmer, and this turned out to be more suited to me than farming. My father's mother and his sister, Dorothy lived together in the family house in Eastwood, which is halfway between Heanor and Kimberley. Eastwood was also the birthplace of the author, D. H. Lawrence. I don't know much about my paternal grandfather Percy, as my grandparents had been divorced before I was born and Percy wasn't spoken about. My Aunt Dorothy was also divorced and had a son one year younger than me. He was called Peter, who came more into my life during our teenage years together.

1 - MY CHILDHOOD - OH! THE INNOCENCE OF A CHILD!

I don't really remember anything much before the age of four or five but as I reached the age of around five or six years old, I became aware that my father was at work during the day, then came home, had his evening meal, changed into his black evening suit, that my mother had warming by the open coal fire and went out again at night.

This meant I didn't see much of him during those early years, as one way or another, he seemed to always be working. My mother explained to me that to earn extra money, Daddy had a band that played music for dancing during the evenings. Of course, this was just after the war, and money was still hard to come by. The extra money would have been very handy.

This identified him as a semi-professional musician, something which is different to being an amateur; amateurs give their time for free, whereas semi-professional people are paid for their labours.

My father's main job during the day was working in the Rolls-Royce experimental department, which was situated in a factory in Hucknall, not far from where we lived in Kimberley.

He had also been working there during the war, helping to re-build Spitfires that had been damaged in combat. The factory had an exceptionally long runway that could accept the large planes like the Avro Vulcan bomber and later, the Boeing 747 Jumbo jets. Both had Rolls-Royce engines, and this was where the engines were developed and tested to destruction on a test-bed before they were put into any aircraft, where they had many more test flights before going into production.

This was also the place where they built and tested the first vertical take-off and landing (VTOL) technology in the 1950s, which eventually went

6

into the Hawker Siddeley Harrier jump-jet. The first tests for this were done on a test-bed known as the 'flying bedstead' which consisted of four large metal gantries, one in each of the four corners of the whole structure, which resembled a four-poster bed, hence the nickname. A Rolls-Royce RB.41 Nene engine was attached to each corner by some sort of tether which could slide up and down the gantries when the engine was powered up. The pilot would sit somehow on the top and try to control the lift. At the time, this was a completely new concept and very, very dangerous for the test pilot.

I remember his name was Tom Shepherd. I didn't see any of these things myself; it was relatively secret stuff at the time, and I was still only a small boy. I could only base my knowledge on what my father told me about it all. However, after I retired, I visited the Science Museum in London and hanging from the ceiling in one room was the original flying bedstead, officially called the Rolls-Royce Thrust Measuring Rig (TMR). I have to admit, it brought a lump to my throat, knowing that my father had worked on that very same machine. An internet search on 'name of test pilot of Flying Bedstead' will come up with the details, picture and more information.

As you might expect, there were a lot of local dances after the war (or 'hops' as they were called in those days.) Going to a dance in the evening was one of the opportunities to meet members of the opposite sex, at the same time, being able to let your hair down, in those early days after the war.

At the age of five, I started to attend the local primary school, which was just across a field from our house. My mother would stand at my bedroom window and watch me cross the field containing a herd of cows. I had no fear; it seemed a perfectly normal thing for me to do. I wasn't at school for long that year, as during the winter, I developed bronchitis which, incidentally, continues to dog my health every winter to this day. The bronchitis kept me at home until the following spring. This had far reaching consequences regarding my education which will become apparent later.

In an effort to protect me during my first few years before I started school, the only person with whom I played was the boy next door, who was two years younger than me. We were both isolated from the world and from the common illnesses such as measles, mumps and whooping cough - the usual things kids pick up. As I hadn't built up any immunity to any of these viruses, I came in for a few of those as well as my bronchitis. Needless to say, I didn't attend school or learn much at all during that first year.

During that winter, I spent a lot of time at home. My mother had the radio on one day, listening to some band playing the popular music of the era, while she did the housework. I remember to this day, asking her if Daddy ever played on the radio. Her reply was, "No he's not good enough." That was shattering news for a little boy to hear at the age of five. That simple sentence quashed my interest in music altogether, taking the next five or six years to get over it. That was the first of two things my mother said to me that stuck in my mind. Later, I will mention her second comment, the significance of which I didn't understand until I was fifteen. Instead of developing any enthusiasm for music, I showed more interest in animals and farming, which is also in my blood. My mother's grandparents owned their own farm in the Derbyshire town of Heanor. At that young age, I had romantic thoughts of becoming a farmer, like my great grandparents.

As the only son of an only daughter, my grandfather doted on me. He was well aware of my interest in farming and animals, particularly horses and ponies. Once a year, my grandparents would take me with them to Mablethorpe, because my grandfather's sister had a holiday home there. I loved to ride the donkeys and Shetland ponies; I was always on them.

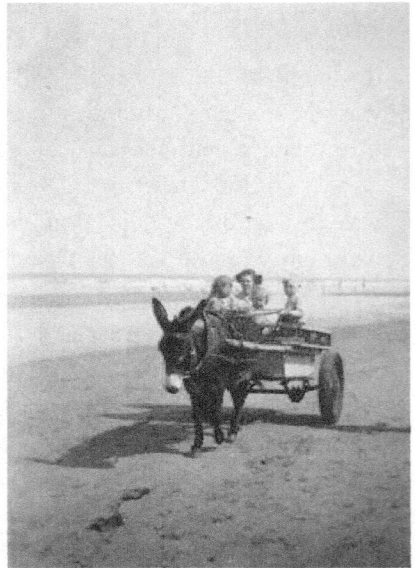

Although I didn't realise it at the time, my grandfather would pay the donkey man for me to have rides and to help lead them up and down the beach most of every day.

I loved it and thought I was a bit special to be doing that. Of course, I wasn't aware at the time that the animals aren't stupid and they knew exactly how far they had to go down the beach, before turning back and although I may have been leading them, they would have turned themselves back without me being there.

As I have already mentioned in the Introduction, my grandfather had his own bakery business. He wasn't a rich man but he wasn't exactly poor either. He must have wanted to treat his only grandson, so he bought a pony for me. I could have only been four going on five years old at the time because I remember it was before my parents separated and mother taking me away, to stay with my grandparents. He was a lovely looking pony, a light chestnut colour with silver main and tail. We called him Ginger. It turned out that he was an ex-circus pony and could perform certain circus tricks such as standing on an upturned half-barrel and rearing up on his hind legs on command.

My dad could make him do his tricks, but, of course, I was too young. However, it was fascinating for me to watch. On the next page, I have a picture of me, sitting on his bare back while the pony stands on a half-barrel or tub; no saddle, no bridle. It looks great.

The problem was that Ginger was still a young gelding and far too strong-willed for me. For anyone who isn't familiar with the word gelding, it means a male horse or pony that has been castrated to stop it breeding, which also calms them down. Sometimes, travellers and circus showmen would only do half the job which had the effect of it not being able to breed, while still keeping the strong stallion traits. Anyone who has ever watched a stallion in full flow, chasing after a mare in season will know exactly what I mean. They can be totally wild, un-controllable and dangerous, but my dad could do anything with Ginger.

We used to borrow a trap from the farmer and go out on Sunday drives in the pony and trap. I enjoyed that, but really I was far too young to have a pony anyway. I couldn't handle him, but a young teenage girl could ride him without any problem. He definitely took a dislike to me; he must have sensed my fear.

Ginger
(In the picture below, Ginger's front legs are on a half-barrel)

The final straw came when I was riding him alone from the farm to our house one day. Just as we turned the corner into our road, he threw me off and onto the road, and then turned back on me with his teeth bared and fury in his eyes. He bit me on the shoulder and carried on to the house on his own. I can still see that face baring down on me now. I had teeth marks on my shoulder for some time after that. He could be nasty and that's probably why the circus got rid of him anyway. That was the end of him as far as I was concerned. I wasn't going anywhere near to him again, so he had to go.

Looking back, I think Ginger must have been a half-castrated stallion; he had all the traits. Neither my grandfather nor my dad could have known at the time, because they wouldn't have any idea about anything that had taken place in Ginger's past life as a circus pony. My dad knew of a local riding school and I went there for a few riding lessons, where I was allowed to ride a lovely placid Dartmoor pony, named Dinah. Naturally, I fell in love with her and negotiations took place, with a bit of arm twisting and the crossing of palms with gold. She became mine and Ginger went to the Riding School. Dinah was great. I could do anything with her; I could crawl under her belly, between her legs and she wouldn't kick or bite - a real sweetie. She had a foal, but it had yellow jaundice and unfortunately didn't survive.

Dinah with foal

      The toy I played with the most was my model farm. I had sheep, cows, horses and most of the other animals found on a farm. However, as I grew up, I began to realise what a hard life it was and there was more to farming than just animals. Looking back at things now, perhaps the alternative would have been studying to become a zoo keeper rather than a farmer, as that only requires looking after animals, without the agriculture.

My parents bought me a set of books called Newnes' *Pictorial Knowledge*, in the hope that I would get interested in more academic things, but to their dismay, the only book I constantly read was one about animals of the world - *Volume 1 Story of the Natural World* - the story of animal and plant life.

The next few years were pretty uneventful although very enjoyable just the same. I had my playmate next door and we did the usual young boys things together. His father built him a sandpit, in which we would play. They also had a disused air raid shelter at the bottom of their garden, which made a great den. We had to make our own entertainment in those days. They were good and happy times for us. We played in the field behind our house, and went scrumping apples and bird nesting in the allotments that were at the back of our two houses. However, we only observed the bird nests (not taking eggs), because I was a great lover of animals, which I still am.

We would play cowboys and Indians in the field, climb trees and on one occasion, we went on our own pretend safari, hunting for swallowtail butterflies in the local woods with our butterfly nets and with sandwiches in our back-packs. There was also a pond in the field, where we could find frogs and frogspawn in the spring, along with the common newt and the now much rarer great crested newt. The pond was also teeming with other wild life, such as dragon flies, pond skaters and water boatman.   The latter was a black beetle with a pair of legs that resembled a pair of rowing boat oars, that made it move like someone rowing a boat. I have already mentioned I am a great animal lover and even at that young age, I knew many species.

In the winter, the field gave us even more entertainment when the snow came and we could go out sledging or tobogganing, as it's also called. I remember going out in the dark evenings on my own, to meet my friends at the sledge run, coming back to change my wet clothes while my mother had another dry set warming by the fire, ready for me to change into and off to do it all again.

On their way home for tea after school, some of the boys would pee at the top of the sledge run, so that when it froze, the top of the run became like a sheet of ice, in order to give us more speed down the hill. More speed = more distance. The goal was to reach the hedge at the bottom of the field where the pond was. We steered the sledge by putting either our left or right leg out depending in which direction we wanted to go. Some of boys would lay flat, face down on the sledge with another boy on top to give more weight which made it even faster downhill, it was really fast and exhilarating like that, but the only problem was towards the bottom of the field where the snow became deeper the sledge would come to a sudden stop because of the extra weight, but boy did we have fun?

Those were the days when we could go out and play with our school pals without any supervision or fear of any danger. Compared with the children of today, we were, in essence 'Free Range Kids'. We didn't have any money, computers or mobile phones to distract us, but for us, those days were the best of times; we didn't know anything else.

A year or two later, one morning after breakfast, I was in my pyjamas, sitting on my stool by the coal fire and reading my comic, at the same time unconsciously touching my privates. My mother then said, "Don't play with that - you might need it one day."   That was the second thing my mother said that I will never ever forget. It seems amusing now, but at the time I didn't fully understand what she meant.

At the age of around five and a half, my parents parted, my mother and I went to stay with my grandparents. This went on for roughly two years, before things got patched up and we returned to the family unit. My dad used to say, "Even a bad experience is an experience" and this was an over all bad experience, but one which also helped to shape my future life. Not only did I miss most of my first year at school when aged five, but I now had two changes of school between the ages of five and ten, plus another one at twelve, all of which put me behind with my schooling, never to recover academically.

2 - SKELETONS IN THE CUPBOARD

My parents met at a dance, where my father was playing in the band, of which he was the leader. I know by my own experiences that some young ladies are attracted to what they think is a glamorous life. Later in her life, my mother told me that one of the reasons she was attracted to my father was because he didn't drink alcohol like her father. Apparently my grandfather would come home from the pub in the evening, quite drunk and he then abused my grandmother. My own mother didn't want to go through that, so she married a teetotaler instead. Little did she know that there was something much worse for her, down the line.

My bedroom was above the lounge and I would often hear my parents airing their grievances in loud voices, having heated arguments and generally shouting at one another. This would keep me awake, wondering what was going on downstairs. I could only have been four or five and wondered if that was what all parents did.

At the age of five, I started at the local infant's school. I missed most of that first year, as in the winter, I came down with bronchitis which kept me at home until the following spring. This loss of early education had far-reaching consequences in later life.

One day, my mother met me at the school gate. She told me we were going to live with Grandma and Granddad. When I asked why, all she said was, "Daddy's been naughty."

I didn't know the real reason until I was about fourteen; it was then that things began to fall into place.

During the time that we lived with my grandparents in Heanor, I had to go to a new school there. Later in life, I realised how disruptive to my education that had been, and that in due course, I was to pay the price.

As for the social side - I had a great time. There was much more freedom than I'd had before; there were lots of other boys to play with, a recreation ground with swings, a slide and roundabouts to push around ourselves. The swimming pool was open in the summer. It was also during the summer that I learned to ride a bike.

My best friend and I built a den under a thick holly tree which was in one corner of my grandparent's garden. Also under the holly tree were some large barrels containing petrol. I later deduced that my grandfather must have bought them on the black market during the war, to help to keep the bread van on the road, given that petrol was rationed during those times. By the time we two boys discovered them they were contaminated with water and no longer useable. They would have been hidden in that corner of the garden under the holly tree, to keep them from the prying eyes of the authorities, who would come round from time to time, checking up on things. I understand there was a lot of black-market bartering taking place with certain commodities during the war.

During late October / early November, our gang would go out under the cover of darkness, hunting for wood for bonfire night on November the 5th. I was having a great time, I'd never been in a gang before.

One day, the girl next door asked me round to play with her. We went into their shed and she made the classic statement, "I'll show you mine if you show me yours" - which, at that age, seemed a normal suggestion, so that's what we did.

When I went back home, my mother asked me if I had enjoyed playing with my new friend. I told her in all innocence what we had done. She then told me in no uncertain terms that I must stay away from girls in future and just play with the boys. That was exactly what happened until I met my first girlfriend when I was eighteen.

On Sundays, my father would come and pick me up from my grandparent's house and take me back to Kimberley for the day. He had bought a huge Meccano set and proceeded to encourage me to build things but I wasn't really interested in those kinds of things. We would also do jigsaw puzzles.

Because he was always working both day and night, during my early infant days, when we were all still living together, he really didn't have a clue what my interests were and I hated spending those Sundays with him, possibly because I knew he'd been naughty.

Eventually there must have been talks between all the parties concerned, (except me, of course) and perhaps my mother had thought my grandparents were spoiling me. Maybe she thought I needed a father figure? I don't know. Another factor may have come into play, as during the 1940s, single mothers were still very much frowned on in society, so perhaps she was feeling pressure from that direction, but one thing I did realise in later years was that she had sacrificed her happiness for my sake. (That became clear many years later, when she had died, and her best friend who lived next door said to me, "Your mother lived and died for you.")

My father promised my mother he would never be naughty again and that he would buy her a washing machine, as an incentive for us go back to Kimberley. Up until to that point, all previous washing in the house had been done by hand; in those days, a washing machine was quite a luxury. I asked him if I could keep some pigeons in the shed at the bottom of the garden, he agreed at the time. Differences were patched up, so, with that promise, mother and I moved back to Kimberley. My mother got her washing machine but I never got my pigeons. He was my father and we lived in the same house together, but for me, things were never the same again. He was just there, as far as I was concerned and that was it. I always did as I was asked to do but I didn't ever really accept him again. That entire trauma damaged me to some extent, but at the same time it's all part of life and we have to get on with it.

Time passed. By now I would be around 14-15 years old. One Sunday morning, my father took my cousin Peter and me to buy an engine for our model aircraft. On the way home, my father parked the car in a village called Kirkby-in-Ashfield and said,
"I'm just going in this shop, I won't be long".

He walked a few yards down the road and disappeared into a shop. Peter and I amused ourselves for a while in the car, playing about with this new engine but my dad didn't come back for what seemed like ages, so I got out of the car to look for him. I walked to the shop to see if I could see him. It was a sweet shop which had a 'closed' sign on the door, so I returned to the car, and there we waited till he eventually came back.

Some time after we got home, my mother must have waited until she and I were alone, and then she must have asked me how we had got on that morning. I told her in all innocence about the shop. One thing I definitely remember is her saying, "I know where the shop is". Some months later, she told me that she knew about the shop and the woman who owned it and had been to Kirkby-in-Ashfield in order to confront her. That's when I began to realise what all the shouting had been about downstairs, when I was a little boy of five years old, upstairs in bed, listening. Despite his promises, it would seem that, "Daddy was still being naughty".

My father seemed to be totally unaware of my reluctance to accept him again but, to be fair, he did his best by taking me to big band concerts and generally running me about, to help to further my music education. However, he still seemed unable to show me any affection or show any interest in my hobbies or things I liked to do, which were the things I really wanted from him more than anything. I know he was proud of me but there was something missing. My mother told me once that he got his pleasure through showing me off to his friends, but that wasn't what I required. What I needed was some way to let me see that he loved me, but that just wasn't forthcoming.

All things seemed to be quiet on the 'naughty' front for the time being, until I was 19 or 20, by when I was a professional musician, and was playing at the Locarno in Nottingham. One Sunday morning, I decided to go to my dad's usual band rehearsal. He seemed overly keen to introduce me to his girl singer. She was sitting on a table with her legs crossed in a provocative pose. I was a bit more worldly-wise by this time; I knew right away that there was more to this than met the eye. This time, in order to keep the peace, I decided to keep my mouth shut and not to go telling tales to Mum.

By the time I was 20, the band I was with was moving to Bournemouth to take up a residency in the Pavilion ballroom. It was there that I spent my 21st birthday, in 1964. In the meantime, my grandfather had passed away and my grandmother had moved into our house, after suffering a stroke. That meant that my parents were unable to come to Bournemouth to celebrate my 21st together, so my dad suggested he would come on his own, while my mother stayed at home, in order to look after grandmother.

I met him at teatime and we walked together to the Pavilion in the evening, as he was coming to listen to the band. I thought it was just a bit odd when he insisted in approaching the Pavilion from a certain direction. We climbed some steps and there, at the top, sat the girl singer from his band. As we approached he said, "Fancy seeing you here". You can imagine how I felt when I realised he'd brought her down with him for a dirty weekend, on the pretext of seeing me, while my mother was stuck at home, looking after her own mother. I was furious, but what made it even worse was that I had to sit on the stage all night watching him having fun, dancing with her. Can you imagine how damaging that was for my brain? These were the sorts of reasons I didn't have any respect for him. I don't remember whether or not I told my mother, but by this time she was stuck with the situation and was unable to do anything about it anyway. There were other occasions when, in later years, they came to visit me in Brixham, Devon where I was playing at a holiday camp. He would go off to phone his floozy, while leaving my mother and me talking. She knew what he was up to, but didn't want to make waves while on holiday.

Once when I was back at home for a visit, an argument broke out, my mother took my side and he went for her throat with a carving knife. I put my arm round his neck and threw him on the floor. He was a broken man but it still didn't stop him seeing his 'bit on the side'.

At one stage my mother decided she wanted to change her style of furniture from G Plan to Ercol and was selling the G Plan. My dad said, "There's a young couple at work, soon to be getting married and who would love to buy the furniture to start their home."

That way, my mother got her Ercol and the couple got their G Plan. More time passed. I was now working in London. Some time later, I returned home again for a few days visiting my parents. I had been using my dad's car for some reason or other. On the Sunday, when it was time for me to return to London, I realised I had left something in the boot of his car. The problem was that he was at work, doing overtime, so off I went to Hucknall where he worked, only to find the car park completely empty. I walked over to the commissionaire on the gate, to be told nobody works on Sundays.

I returned home, where my mother said, "I know where he is." She had the address and off we went to the floozy's flat. Sure enough, my dad's car was outside. I parked close behind him to make sure he couldn't get out, bearing in mind that he had once boasted to my mother,
"You'll never catch me".

Up we went, to a first floor flat. Mother hid round the corner, while I rang the bell. There was a short time before he opened the door, giving him the chance to look out of the window and see my car. Eventually he came to the door, wearing only a pair of under pants. My mother appeared from behind me and I pushed him into the flat where all hell broke loose. It was like something out of a film. Mother found the girl, who was hiding behind the bed. She was literally hitting her with her handbag and I couldn't believe the language that was spewing from her mouth; I did not know that my mother knew such words. I left my mother to it and went into the lounge where my father was looking very sheepish, to say the least. I was finally able to give him something back for what he had put my mother through for all those years. Eventually my mother came into the lounge to join us. The final straw to pour salt into her wounds was to find her G Plan furniture sitting on her old carpet in this woman's apartment. Mother's shock was plain to see; what a bastard he was.

He ended up with cancer and Alzheimer's. After all he had put her through, my mother still nursed and looked after him, right to the end. She had to take him to the toilet and wash him; the whole works. I honestly don't know how she did it. If that wasn't sacrificing herself, I don't know what is. Through most of my life, I blamed him for their marital problems. As far as I was concerned, he was always the one who was in the wrong. However, one day, I remembered something I had overheard him telling one of his band members, years before, when, as a boy, he had started to take me to play with his band, to learn the ropes. All I had overheard was that their sexual life was non-existent. I had absolutely no idea at that age what he was talking about. I'm not sure if I am right, even now, but earlier in the book I recalled how my mother nearly died giving birth to me and that the doctor had told her if she had another child it could possibly kill her. Maybe she was so very scared of having another child that she became frigid and didn't respond to his advances, so he had to look elsewhere. That's something I'll never know.

Immediately after my father died, my mother asked me if I would go to see an old friend of theirs, Walter Campion and his wife, Elsie, to let them know my father had died. I had known Walter from a little boy, as sometimes on Saturday morning, my dad would take me into Nottingham, presumably to give my mother a break. We would go to Sneinton Market and call round to see Walter Campion in his shop, for a chat. In those days, I was a quiet, shy, little boy, who did as he was told. Those were the days when little boys were told that they should be seen but not heard. When I saw Walter and Elsie, after my dad died, he made a strange comment that set me thinking. He said, "I can't believe how different you are now. When you were a boy, you were very slow."

I thought what does he mean, 'slow'? I pondered on that for some time. Then I began to think. Maybe he had a point. To some people, I may have seemed a bit slow and dim, but, a good comparison to me is the Hare and the Tortoise. I tend to be a bit slow off the mark, however, I get there in the end, but it has to be at my pace. This led me to start thinking about school exams and how I had left school without any qualifications. I now know why that was. It was because I don't work well under pressure. School exams are pressure and so, for that matter are recording sessions. Although I did my share of recording sessions, it was not something in which I excelled, because of the pressure. I recall my dad telling me that he also left school without any qualifications, but he ended up as an engineer for Rolls-Royce, and eventually I made it as a top professional musician.

On the day of his funeral, his mates from Rolls-Royce sent a wreath containing the words, 'TAKE FOUR BARS REST LEN.' In order to fully understand the meaning behind those words, I will have to try to explain. Because my dad was working during the day, as well as many nights playing in his band, he was prone to take a nap during his dinner break at Rolls-

Royce. He would clear his workbench, tell the boys he would take four bars rest and have his nap. Here is a picture of him, asleep on his bench.

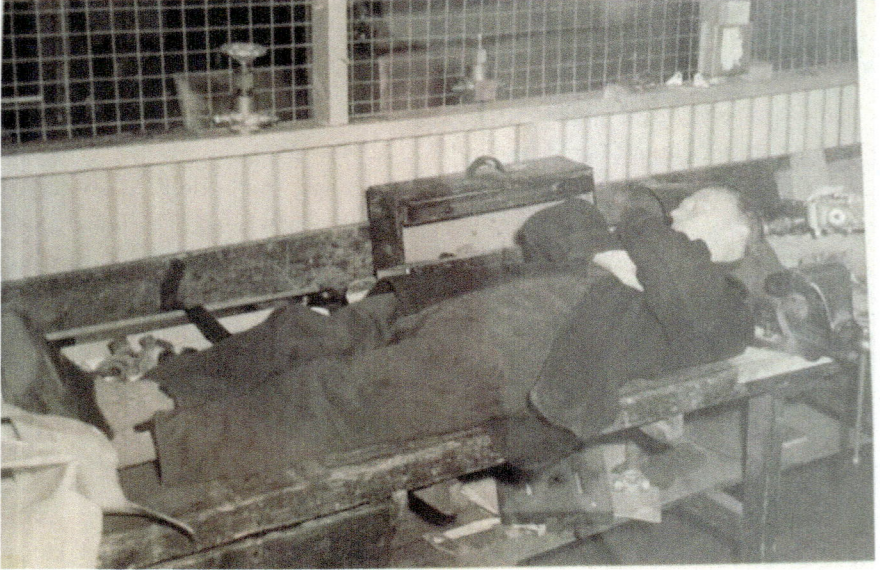

Despite all the bad feelings I'd had in the past, those few words hit me like a sledge hammer. I had to run to the shed at the bottom of the garden, to sob my heart out in private. Even today, as I write these words I feel that lump in my throat and a slight tear well up.

As will be recounted in the next chapters, he had, after all, tried hard to encourage me and to help me to develop my musical ability.

3 - MY FIRST INSTRUMENT

I would have been nine or ten years old when my father came home from work one evening with a black case which he put on the table. He opened it up to show me what seemed to be a very strange object which turned out to be an alto saxophone. He said,

"I'm going to give you the chance to learn to play this instrument. If you don't try, you won't be able to turn round to me in the future and say you didn't have the opportunity".

He gave me a bit of a challenge. After all, I didn't have any interest in music whatsoever, remembering what my mother had said those few years earlier about daddy not being good enough to play on the radio. Despite all that, I decided to give it a go anyway. As it turned out it was the best decision I ever made.

How many times in my career have I had people come to me and tell me that they used to play the piano when they were a child, but regrettably gave it up, saying they wished they'd kept it up and could play now?

The make and model of this silver-plated alto saxophone was a Besson International. By sheer coincidence, it had belonged to my godfather, Fred, who was my dad's best friend and who had played Lead Alto in my father's band in the 1940s, many years before. In a shop, my dad had recognised the case when he saw it, opened it and bought it for me.

My father was a drummer. He didn't play the saxophone himself, so he arranged for me to have lessons with another of his pals, whose name was Wink Meer. I'm sure Wink was just his nickname, but he was always referred to as Wink. Sunday mornings were the day for my lessons, so off we went for my first lesson on the saxophone. Wink suggested I should start on the clarinet, as it is a requirement for all alto sax players to be able to play the clarinet as well as the saxophone. He also told me that the clarinet is harder to play than a saxophone at first, but once playing the clarinet has been accomplished, the saxophone will come more easily.

OK, so it then became twice the challenge, but there was no getting out of it at that stage! The next thing was when my father turned up with a second-hand clarinet, of a French-sounding make called Buisson.

I started my first lesson one Sunday morning; the tutor book I would be using for the next three years was called *Otto Langey's Clarinet*, first published in 1890 and still going strong. I slogged at it for those three years, for one hour a night and I hated every minute of practising. I don't really like practising, even now, but it has to be done.

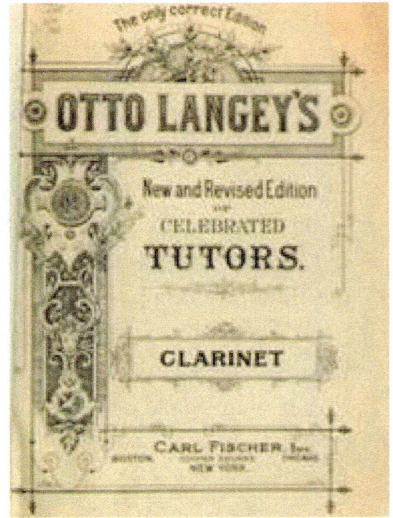

I just don't know how classical pianists can practise eight hours a day; it would kill me. I don't have those powers of concentration, I'm afraid. I would practise in my bedroom, while my dad lay on the sofa downstairs, listening. He must have realised after a while, that I had some kind of natural talent, which wasn't apparent to me at the time. For me, it was just a slog and something I had to do. If I wasn't practising properly and was just messing about, wasting time, he would be up the stairs in a flash and say, "I'll break that bloody thing over your neck, if you don't get on with it." This was tough love, but my goodness, did it pay off in the end!

I progressed and began to play the high notes, which can be a bit loud and screechy at first. One evening, during this period, we had a knock on the door. When my father opened it, there stood a policeman to tell us that our next door neighbours had contacted the police complaining about the noise. But my father was told,

"As long as I didn't practise past 9pm, we were not breaking the law" but, by law, they still had to report the complaint to us anyway.

My mother became anxious and would go out of her way to not get on the wrong side of the old biddy next door. So it was decided I would have to go and practise in the shed at the bottom of the garden. My father had an old coal-fired pipe stove there and in the winter he would light it when he came home from work, so the shed would be warm for my practice. I didn't have a wrist-watch then, so when my hour was up, my dad would switch the shed lights off and on via the fuse box in the house to let me know that my hour was up and I could finish my practice. I remember a time, when I had a particular piece of music to learn. One day, while I was in the house where there was a clock, I timed it to see how long it took to play the piece just once. I then worked out that if I played it 'X' number of times, the hour would be up. Thereafter, when I had finished playing that number of times, I was back in the house before my dad had time to switch off the lights in the shed. He was flabbergasted but never did know how I did it.

Around this time, my parents took my cousin, Peter and me to Nottingham for the day. While we were in a café having lunch, a strange and weird thing happened. An elderly lady came to our table, (mistaking Peter and me for brothers) and said to my mother,

"Excuse me, but I've been watching your two boys" and, pointing to my cousin, she said, "This one will have to wear glasses before too long but if he wears them as instructed, he will grow out of them and won't need them again."

Then she turned her attention to me and said,

"This one is going to be a policeman".

My mother thanked her and off she went back to her table. Nothing happened for a while after that, but it turned out later that she was right on both counts.

4 - MY FIRST PUBLIC PERFORMANCES

In 1954, I was aged eleven and in my final year of the junior school. The class for the final year of the school was traditionally taken by the head master, who was known by the boys as being a bit of a strict taskmaster, particularly if you were badly behaved in class. The punishment was to be taken by the side of his desk, where you were told that his little dog was going to bite you, as he proceeded to put his hand up our short trousers and nip your bottom. We didn't think anything of it at the time; it was just the punishment we expected, and it didn't do us any harm. This was the year we took the important Eleven-plus (11+) exam, which decided whether we went to the Grammar School or the Secondary Modern. But before that, we had the school Christmas party to look forward to.

Even though, at the time, I had only been playing my clarinet for about eighteen months, at the most, I was now able to play a few simple tunes like Christmas carols, hymns and a couple of folk songs, so it was time for my debut as a solo performer, with piano accompaniment provided by the head master. We played some Christmas carols for the school to sing along with, followed by "Bless This House", a clarinet solo. I was very nervous, particularly as the head master was playing the piano.

Also that year, I did the same thing again at the Rolls-Royce factory Christmas party where my dad worked. The L. M. on the drum-head stands for Len Mason, my father.

After all the excitement of Christmas, it was back to normal. I carried on with my practice and continued to make progress, although I still found practising a bit of a chore. During the final summer term at the junior school, we took the Eleven-plus exams. I passed the first part but unfortunately didn't make it through the second part. This meant that I was destined to attend the Secondary Modern school. Even the word 'secondary' infers second best.

I would have been totally out of my depth and comfort zone at the Grammar School. It proves to me at my present age of 76, that academic prowess is not for everyone, and those who are not academically inclined can still have a very successful working life without needing to excel academically.

I can't remember exactly when I started to play the saxophone as well as the clarinet but I do have pictures of me playing the sax, still wearing short trousers. I don't think I was having sax lessons at that time so I must have been delving into the saxophone by myself.

Round about age 12, my father managed to get me into the Junior Harmonic Orchestra in Nottingham, on Second Clarinet. As the name suggests it was a classical orchestra, which wasn't really my interest. The Secondary Modern did have its advantages though. Firstly, it was closer to home, which meant I didn't have to have school dinners or travel into Nottingham, for the grammar school and back home to Kimberley on the bus every day.

Secondly, it was just as well as it turned out, because I am not an academic swot; I have a leaning towards the artistic temperament, hence the music.

27

My parents were only interested in the popular music of the day - mainly the big bands, to which we all listened most of the time on the radio at home. When anything remotely classical such as a classical orchestra or ballet came on the radio or television, my dad would say,

"Turn that rubbish off."

Consequently I wasn't exposed to any classical or ballet music. However, being in the orchestra was a good experience never the less. I did that for about two years and performed in a couple of concerts with them at the Nottingham Concert Hall. But when they managed to get a trip to play in Germany, I was excluded, which angered my dad, particularly as I was right at the front on their publicity photo. Consequently I didn't do that any more. My last concert with them was in March 1956 at age 13. I wasn't destined to be a classical player anyway.

I have a programme in my album, telling me that I played three clarinet pieces in a school concert on the 15th November 1956 during the second year of my secondary school education.

It's more than difficult for me to remember exactly how my clarinet playing had improved over those past two years since the Christmas concert at the junior school, but judging by the pieces of music I was playing in that secondary school concert, I must have been playing pretty well by that time. One of the pieces was called "Clarinet Cadenza" by a well-known British clarinet player and bandleader called Sid Phillips. I won a talent contest with the same piece, during the summer of 1957 in Great Yarmouth, one year after the school concert.

I'd memorised "Clarinet Cadenza" especially for that day. There was another young clarinetist in the same contest, who in my opinion, produced a better sound than me, but, even at that age, I was a bit of a showman and I think that swung it for me.

That same year, I went to my first proper concert in Nottingham. It was Bill Haley and the Comets. That was when Rock and Roll first started. Who can forget their hit records like "Rock Around The Clock" and "Shake Rattle and Roll"? I was hooked; no more Glenn Miller for me!   (As I write this, the phrase, 'famous last words' hovers over my brain.)

The first record I bought was "Diana" by Paul Anka, because it included a repeating sax solo that I loved to listen to. I was also a fan of Cliff Richard and the Shadows at the time. My father took me to see the Count Basie band at the De Montfort Hall in Leicester. At another time, we went to see and hear the Duke Ellington band, also at the De Montfort Hall.

It would have been during the summer holidays, before I went back to school for my final year, that my parents took me for a weekend in London to look for a better sax. We part-exchanged my Besson for a second-hand Selmer Cigar Cutter. Selmer saxophones are top of the range and I still play a Selmer sax to this day; it's a much later model, called the Mark VII (Mark Seven). Incidentally, the Selmer Cigar Cutter is now very much sought after by collectors and aficionados.

29

While my father and I were shopping for a saxophone, my mother went shopping in Oxford Street. She also wanted to walk down Park Lane. So it was arranged that we would meet her at a certain time at the bottom of Park Lane on the pavement outside the front of the Hilton Hotel. We arrived on time to find mother waiting there. When she got in the car she told us that while she was standing there, a man had pulled up in a car and tried to accost her. Not being familiar with London, my parents didn't know that behind the Hilton is Shepherd Market, which at one time had a bit of a reputation as a 'red light' area. I found the thought of someone trying to pick up my mother slightly amusing; it was not that she wasn't a good-looking woman, but the fact that she was my mother.

My dad hated driving in London and although this was about 50 years ago, the traffic was still overwhelming for him and he didn't know his way around. I still remember him trying to go the wrong way down a one-way street near Trafalgar Square. The buses were coming straight at us. It was quite scary and those bus drivers don't take any prisoners. (But in fairness, he was only going one way!)

Also, while in London, my parents took me to the Empire in Leicester Square, to hear Ken Mackintosh & His Orchestra. The ballroom is found underneath the Empire Cinema. Now, as I write this book, it no longer functions as a ballroom. Unfortunately the Ken Mackintosh band didn't play in the afternoons. I was slightly disappointed at the time, because Ken had a hit record called "Raunchy" which was an alto sax feature I'd heard on the radio and I was hoping to hear him play it live. However, there was another band on stage instead. They were called the Johnny Howard band. We sat on the balcony, watching and listening. All I can remember about the band is that they had five saxes and that the Lead Alto had a great sound. I'd never heard of Johnny Howard before. During their interval, Johnny came onto the balcony for his coffee. My dad went over to speak to him and he came over to speak with us. He seemed a nice person and I was impressed with the band. (It was there and then that I decided that I was going to be in that band one day; and so it was to be, some years later.)

After that trip to London, I started to hear the name Johnny Howard on the radio. He had his own show on Sunday mornings, called *Easy Beat*. The band also did other radio broadcasts such as *Music While You Work*. It was then that I found out his Lead Alto's name at the time was Barry Robinson. He had such a great sound, and I tried to model my own sound on his. Later on, Barry became the Lead Alto with the BBC Radio Orchestra.

I was now a teenager and my interests were changing; it was no longer all about playing with my toys and practising; hobbies started to creep in.

My cousin Peter and I developed an interest in model aircraft flying. We would buy the kits, build the aircraft and fly them by control lines in the field at the back of the house on Sunday afternoons. Peter had a Spitfire and I had an Auster, with high wings. They were powered by engines using special fuel available from the model shop. There were two engines available at that time - both with the prefix ED. Peter's engine was an ED Racer, mine was an ED Bee. Mine was a smaller engine with a very high pitched sound (just like a bee.) They were flown by control wires which enabled us to make the tail wing flaps go up and down. By having just two lines to make them go up or down, we could also perform lots of manoeuvres, including looping the loop.

During one particular summer, we would be flying in the field with our model aircraft, at the same time that the Avro Vulcan bomber, from Rolls-Royce, Hucknall was also buzzing round on its constant test flights. The noise was ear-splitting because Hucknall was so close to Kimberley and it was still low in the sky as it went over. This was just another example of the fun that the field afforded us as youngsters.

Unfortunately, the pond in the field that gave us so much pleasure as boys is now part of a huge Sainsbury's supermarket car-park, along with what were the allotments at the bottom of the garden. The field in which we had so much fun as youngsters is now a small housing estate and they call that progress!

In September of that year (1957), I returned to school for my final year. Studying for the final exams was to be the main focus for the time being. As with the Eleven-plus, I managed to flunk every part of those exams and left school without any qualifications whatsoever. In the end, I didn't need them anyway, as I ended up having a very successful career, despite not having any pieces of paper to say I had passed X, Y or Z. All of my knowledge comes from the 'University of Life'. As far as I'm personally concerned, it's the best university of all.

Also, at about the same time, my cousin Peter started to wear glasses, just as the old lady in the café had predicted some years before. She also predicted that he wouldn't need them for long, if he persevered. She was correct on that count. Peter was also about to leave school. He did better than me in his final exams and managed to achieve an apprenticeship to Rolls-

Royce, the company his uncle worked for. My part of the old lady's prediction was to come true eighteen months later, after I started work.

As I didn't have any academic qualifications and I wasn't yet proficient enough to turn professional, I had to look elsewhere. I managed to get a job at a music shop in Nottingham instead, which was the next best thing, until I could achieve my goal. The wages in the shop were £3.12s/6d – 3 pounds, twelve shillings and sixpence a week with a 2 shillings and 6 pence (2/6) rise every year. (The pre-decimal currency was known as £sd or Lsd, these abbreviations originating from the Latin currency denominations *librae*, *solidi*, and *denarii*). In 'old money' (pre-decimal) there were 240 pence or 20 shillings to the £1.

During my time in the shop, I would go to the same café each day for lunch. One day I overheard a couple of men at the next table talking about music. I spoke up and told them I was a budding musician. We began talking and I told them that I played the clarinet. One of the men told me he was conductor of the Nottingham City Police Band. They were looking for clarinet players and asked if I would like to come along and to join the band. I did just that, and although I was never officially a policeman, I had the uniform, which was worn for concerts. So the old lady was also right on the second count too.

I was to stay at the shop for about three years before I got my first break as a professional musician.

There is also another side to my life which starts to manifest itself at about the same time, which I will reveal in the next chapter.

At the end of the last term at school, I was invited to form a band to play at the end of term dance. My dad fixed me up with the trumpet player and the pianist from his band and played drums himself so that was to be my swan song to my school life.

Jeff

Jeffrey Mason
————————and his Band

★   HEAT WINNERS, HALL FINALISTS, AND
AREA FINALISTS MECCA NATIONAL BAND
CHAMPIONSHIPS 1958.

14 Broomhill Road - Kimberley - Nottingham
Tel. Kimberley 3165

33

5 - ON A PERSONAL NOTE

During my last year at school at the age of 15, one of my school pals, along with another boy took me to the potting shed in the school gardens. We all took our trousers off and my pal proceeded to massage my private parts until I climaxed. That was a first time experience for me. Then I knew exactly what my mother was referring to, when some years earlier she had said to me, "Leave that alone, you may need it one day."

Sometime between the period of starting my daytime job at 15 and becoming a professional musician at 18, I gradually began to realise that I seemed to be more attracted to older men than to girls. As you might imagine, I was very confused and bothered by this. I had a picture in my head of the archetypal Christmas card scene, with me sitting by a fireside, smoking a pipe, Golden Labrador at my feet and my wife sitting opposite. To have a wife and children was what everybody did, or so I thought at the time.

I was so disturbed by my feelings that it seemed that my only option was to seek some advice from our family doctor. I told him of my problem. He decided I should see a psychiatrist, so it was arranged for me to see one in Nottingham. By this time, I was a professional musician, working at night in the Sherwood Rooms, a Mecca ballroom in Nottingham, so I was free during the day. I made an appointment to see the psychiatrist.

The appointments were to be at the same time, on the same day, once a week. I don't think the psychiatrist had any idea how to help with my particular problem; most men in those days wouldn't be prepared to seek his advice because of the stigma attached to homosexuality, given that it was still illegal at that time. He probably wouldn't have had the experience anyway. All we did during those sessions was to try to see pictures in ink blots and put wooden blocks into their correct holes, anything a child could have done. It was an absolutely complete waste of time, as far as I could see. At the end of my last appointment, the psychiatrist said to me,
"Whatever you do, don't ever give in to your feelings."
I did as he asked and I managed to hold out until I was around 22 or 23; I can't remember exactly.

The immediate problem for me was my mother. She was so curious to know why I was going into Nottingham at the same time on the same day once a week. Unbeknown to me, she decided to go through my pockets, only to discover my appointment card. She must have gone to see the doctor immediately, to ask him what it was all about. The doctor told my mother what my problem was. Because I was still under the age of 21 at the time, it is possible that the doctor may have been legally obliged to tell her. When she confronted me, I was furious that she felt the need to go through my clothes to pry into my life. My plan had been to keep it under wraps for as long as I could, but now the cat was out of the bag. She told me that I must never tell my dad or he would kill me. So that was how it was left for a long time.

I hadn't had any experience with girls before (or boys for that matter) except, as I have mentioned in Chapter 2, when I was about eight or nine years old, and I had that classic experience of "I'll show you mine, if you show me yours", after which my mother told me to stay away from girls in future. Except for a few isolated experiences, that's very much how it still remains today.

However, I did have a girlfriend when I was 18, and another at twenty-one, but that's covered in another chapter. At the age of 20, the band in which I was working at the time moved to Bournemouth for a summer season in the Pavilion Ballroom. I had my files from the Nottingham psychiatrist moved to Bournemouth. At the first opportunity, I made an appointment and duly went to see the psychiatrist there. He read through the notes, asked a few questions, wrote out a prescription, told me to take it to the hospital pharmacy, then to go home, take one tablet a day and to go back and see him again when I'd finished them all.

I did as he asked and after a short while, I started to grow breasts and my penis started to become smaller and solid. For any man who might be reading this, I can best describe the feeling of my penis as like being in a cold swimming pool before puberty. After I had finished the tablets, I went back to see him again and I asked him,
"What were the tablets you prescribed for me?"

He told me they were female hormone tablets, and then said,
"I can't make you into a heterosexual but these tablets will stop you wanting sex completely. You have an imbalance of hormones; these tablets are obviously too strong, so go home, just take half of one a day, then come back and see me again when you've finished them."
That would have meant I would not be heterosexual. I would not be homosexual but I would be asexual. So back it was to my flat, where I threw the tablets away, because by this time I had decided I didn't want to go through life not experiencing love of any kind. If I was to continue being attracted to older men, then that's the path I would take, but that wasn't the

path I was expected to have to follow, the day I had set out to see our family doctor.

Taking the pills was bad enough, but in a way I was lucky, because I later found out that the other option would have been electric shock aversion treatment. I once met someone whose mother had this form of treatment for mental health problems. He told me he was once present when his mother had one of these treatments and had to sit while she was foaming at the mouth. He said it was painful to watch. That was 55 years ago and I'm sure they didn't know as much about human genes as they do now. I'm older and hopefully wiser, having had experience on the front line, so to speak.

From my various experiences, along with the knowledge that I have gleaned by talking to people, I am now of the opinion that homosexuality is present in some people's genes, even if it is not out in the open. This opinion is borne out by what I've heard from others, who have uncles, brothers, aunts and even a grandfather, who were either gay or bi-sexual. (The person who was later to become my partner, told me that when he was still a little boy, he caught his own father having sex in the stables with the male groom.)

This is all purely my theory and supposition, based on my knowledge and hearsay, plus the knowledge gleaned over the years. How often have we heard phrases such as he takes after his father, it runs in the family or it's in his blood? Well, I think it's in the genes. We know that some diseases are hereditary so why not homosexuality also.

Only recently, a scientific article was brought to my attention. The title is, "We may know why younger brothers are more likely to be gay".

The psychiatrist was perfectly correct about the imbalance of hormones, as some homosexuals are more effeminate than others. There are two types of homosexuals. One of them is effeminate, and the other type is masculine. Personally speaking, I like to think that I fall into the second category, that's why the psychiatrist told me the tablets were too strong for me and to take half instead of a whole one, because my imbalance was on the lower or masculine side of the scale.

The gay men that most people notice are the effeminate ones, who walk and talk like women, gesticulate a lot with their arms and have limp wrists. Those types are known as 'mincing queens'. They're the only type noticed by most people, including my mother. She was probably afraid I would turn out to be like that.

Believe me, for everyone who behaves in an effeminate manner there are at the very least twenty or thirty homosexuals or bisexuals walking down the street that you would never recognise as such in a million years unless you knew. Everyone knows the phrase 'it takes one to know one'. For twenty-three and a half hours a day I behave, and do everything a heterosexual man would do and nobody would know I was different from any Tom, Dick or Harry. In the past, I have painted and decorated three houses, both inside and out. I love gardening, tinkering with cars, and once, I even built a flat pack kitchen. If you are a DIY person and have ever attempted something like that, you will know how hard it is. The name of the flat pack company was MFI. I had another name for it, which was: 'Mother F***ing Impossible'.

However, what goes on behind closed doors isn't anybody else's business and from what I have read and heard, some heterosexual couples perform more sexual deviations in the bedroom than I would ever consider and they have the gall to call us 'queer'! I use the term 'homosexual', because I don't like either of the British slang terms of 'puff', 'poof' or 'queer.' Personally I don't think I fit either of those descriptions. Nowadays, the word everyone uses to describe homosexual men and women and sometimes other orientations is 'gay.'

Gay is the American slang term that has crept into our vocabulary, so from now on in this chapter I will refer to homosexuals as gay. I was later to discover that, in the same year as me at school there were at least three other boys and one teacher who were also gay and yet I never knew. I did have a schoolboy crush on the science teacher, but he wasn't the one who was gay.

You may remember that in the Introduction to this book, I mentioned that my grandmother was born on a farm. She also had a sister who married the owner of a factory in Derbyshire. They had three children. Although it was never spoken about, I'm 95% sure that two of those three children were gay, a boy and a girl, which I think bears out my theory that it's in the genes.

Deciding to go with my feelings was the best decision I ever made. I've had a wonderful life and I wouldn't change a thing. Given the same options, I'd make the same decision again.

During the early part of my career, I was working in Grimsby. My current bandleader had also been my saxophone teacher, when I was a teenager. After the first rehearsal, we found some 'digs' and for the first night I had to share a room with Art, my teacher/bandleader and he had the double bed, while I had a single in the corner. I couldn't get to sleep and neither could he. After a while, he started masturbating. I got so aroused myself that I had to do the same. Nothing was said the next day, but following that experience, I began to have feelings for him as more of a father figure, but it wasn't long before he dashed those thoughts, when he did exactly the same as my real father had done and that was to have a relationship with the girl singer.

After that, the pedestal I had put him on came crashing to the ground. I was angry with him and maybe a little jealous that I couldn't have what the girl singer had. On the very last morning before we all left Grimsby, I knocked on Art's bedroom door and went to tell him I was sorry for being such a pain in the neck and tried to explain why. I was so cold in my pyjamas and he said it's cold, get into bed with me. I was so close and wanted to get even closer to him. I explained my problem and he was very understanding, but that was as far as it went.

I will include parts of this side of my life later in other chapters, because my sexuality eventually became more intertwined with my work after I was 'outed', and also because it plays a big part of who I am. In the meantime, I was trying to keep my private life separated from my working life, because I knew that the musical world was a relatively small one and as I began to know more people, I didn't want the word to get around in those circles that I was gay, in case they would say, "Don't book him, he's a puff" and I would be out of work in a flash. However, by the time I was in my early to middle thirties, I was getting established in London and was finally 'outed' by a tenor player in the band I was in at the time. From then on, there was no going back into the closet. The details of this are revealed in a later chapter.

Until the age of twenty-two, I managed to do as the psychiatrist told me. He had said, "Never to give in to your feelings." At this point, the only other person who was aware of those feeling was my mother. I managed to keep things under wraps as far as my work was concerned until I was 'outed' (as they say) when I was around thirty-five, but more of that later.

If a person is keeping things under wraps, it's known as being in the closet. This is an American word for wardrobe or cupboard, so if a person is in the closet, it means that they are hiding their sexuality. So when I said 'outed' in the earlier paragraph, what I was actually implying was that I had been forced out of the place from where I was hiding and that then my sexuality had been revealed for everyone to know.

My first gay encounter was soon after I started work in London at the age of 21 or 22. I had a bedsit in Notting Hill. One afternoon, I decided to go to the Gate cinema to see Zorba the Greek. The film had already started. I found a seat on the end of a row and sat down. After a while, I felt the knee of the person sitting next to me pressing against mine, I moved my knee away slightly, but the other person's knee came back again. I half-turned to look at this person sitting next to me. It was an older man. I began to think, so this is how it's done, and this is how people meet.

Eventually he leaned over to me and said,

"I've seen this film before; would you like to come back to my place?"

In for a penny in for a pound, we left. When we got out of the cinema and I was able to see him in the daylight, I saw that he was shabbily dressed and was decidedly unwholesome. I was horrified, and made the excuse that it was my first time (which, of course, it was) and scuttled back to my bedsit. It was enough to put me off for years, which in actual fact it did.

It was when I was with the Eric Delaney band and we were doing a summer season at the Winter Gardens theatre in Bournemouth, (my favourite town). Sundays were our day off, so one evening I decided to go back to the bar under the Norfolk Hotel, where I'd watched a band some years before and to try the bar next door which I'd been told was full of queers. It was the first time I'd been in a gay bar, so I just sat with a beer and observed. Eventually an older gentleman with white hair came and sat down at the same table and we started chatting. He was from Wales and was in Bournemouth on holiday. He was staying at the Norfolk Hotel, so after the public bar closed he invited me up to the Hotel bar for one more drink. He asked me if I had ever been to the beach at Studland Bay. I hadn't, so he offered to take me the next day. Studland is a naturist beach. Once there, we took our clothes off and went for a swim. Afterwards we lay in the dunes at the back of the beach. Needless to say, I learned a lot that day. I saw him a few times over the next week. After his holiday was over, he would often come down from Wales for the weekend, to see me. We saw quite a bit of one another over the next couple of years. I also visited his apartment in Wales a couple of times. His name was Stan. However he was a possessive and extremely jealous man, continually twisting things around, telling me,

"You said this and you did that" when I knew I hadn't. I became so confused that I began to think I was going mad, so he had to go. As some Americans say, "I don't take no shit from nobody".

It's odd that right from the start, when I began to realise that I might be gay, I have always been attracted to older men and not to men my own age or younger. Looking back, even as a young boy of eight or nine, I always wanted to sit on the garden seat with the old man next door. He was a well-built man and very patient with me. I adored him without realising it at the time. In hindsight, I also had a crush on the man two doors away. It may be because I didn't receive any affection from my father as a child; I don't know, but the fact remains to this day, that I'm only attracted to older men. I was probably looking for the kind of father I never had.

During the time I was in my middle teens and playing sax in my dad's band, I was asked to deputise for two nights with another band and when I got there, I was immediately attracted to the bandleader but thought no more about it at the time. Several years later, after joining the Eric Delaney band, I was at home for a few days and decided to go into Nottingham one evening, as I'd been told there was a gay bar in the Flying Horse, an old coaching inn, just off the main square. I went in and bought a drink at the bar and looked around the room. My eyes spotted a good-looking older man, standing by himself. I looked at him for a while and thought that he looked like that bandleader I once worked for years ago, so I went up to him and said,

"Are you a bandleader by any chance?"

He confirmed my thoughts and we started chatting. After a while, he asked me if I'd like to go back to his house.

He told me his wife worked nights and she wouldn't be there, so I went back with him and we had some fun on his lounge carpet before I went home. I saw him a few times after that. The last time we went back to his house as usual and a few days later, I was sitting on stage during a performance and I started to get an itch in my groin under the hot stage lights. I couldn't scratch in full view of a few hundred people, so surreptitiously, in the hope that no one would notice, I slowly rubbed my saxophone up and down between my legs in order to try to ease the itch. The next morning when I awoke, I still had an itch so decided to investigate the problem. I saw three little black spots and realised they must be pubic lice, commonly called genital crabs. I'd heard about these things before but never experienced them. I also knew I had to crack them between my thumb nails to kill them. Needless to say, I never saw him again. I was still very inexperienced and didn't really have much chance to meet anyone while I was on the road with the band, constantly moving about and in any case, I try not to mix business with pleasure. I'm not a particularly promiscuous person anyway, but when you are travelling, like we were, moving on every week, there isn't much chance of meeting anyone, particularly now, as we all had our caravans parked in close proximity. We could easily see what one another was doing. It was a bit like living on *Coronation Street*.

This particular week we were playing in a club in Brighouse. One morning, I went into the club to have my usual wash in hot water and to have a pee, to save using the toilet in the van. The cleaner was in the gent's, mopping the floor. We got talking and he told me he did the cleaning job in the mornings but at night he operated the switchboard in the small local telephone exchange. Some 40 years ago, it wasn't all automated like it is today. Some of the telephone exchanges in the smaller towns were still manually operated. I was invited to meet him in the telephone exchange that night, after we had done the show. I rang the doorbell of the telephone exchange. He let me in and up the stairs to where the telephone exchange switchboard was, and in we went. He had a bed up there, so he could have a rest when the phones were quiet. Needless to say, we ended up on the bed; it was bizarre to say the least. The phone would ring in the middle of things and he would have to go and plug someone in, to make a connection and then it was back to the business at hand. It was a night to remember. I saw him a few times after that. He came down to Bournemouth on the train one weekend, while we were doing a summer season there. He booked a hotel and we stayed together for a couple of nights before he had to go back. What was about to happen the next time we met was even more bizarre than my visit to the telephone exchange.

On one occasion the band was coming back on a ferry from Ireland. We all had our own cars and I was on my way back to Nottingham. I phoned my friend in Brighouse to see if he could put me up for the night. It was a long way from Ireland to Nottingham. I had been travelling all day and I couldn't make it home in one go. I knew he was married and his son was still at home and that they also had a lodger. I'd met them before when I'd been invited to tea one afternoon when we were working at the club, so I knew they had a full house When I arrived at the house, he had made a bed up on the sofa for his wife, telling her that I needed a good night's rest in a proper bed. So the wife slept on the sofa downstairs while I slept in one of the twin beds in his room. I've had a few strange experiences during my life but that's up there with the most bizarre.

During one period, I took a break from the Eric Delaney band and at that time, I did a variety of different jobs. In December 1968, I took a job playing in the pit orchestra in the Pantomime at the Nottingham Theatre Royal, mainly because I knew a couple of friends who were also in the pantomime, which was *The Pied Piper*, with Freddie 'Parrot Face' Davies and one of the young pop idols of the time, Mark Wynter as Mark.

THEATRE ROYAL · NOTTINGHAM
PANTOMIME SEASON OPENS 24th DECEMBER at 7.0
TOM ARNOLD & BERNARD DELFONT present
THE SPECTACULAR COMEDY PANTOMIME

FREDDIE DAVIES
MR. PARROT FACE
AS THE 'PIED PIPER'

MARK WYNTER
AS 'MARK'
THE POPULAR SINGING STAR

The Pied Piper

BIG
COMPANY INCLUDES

DON SMOOTHEY
ANNA-LOU and MARIA
BETTY EMERY   FULL CORPS DE BALLET

THE FINEST and FUNNIEST PANTOMIME in the MIDLANDS

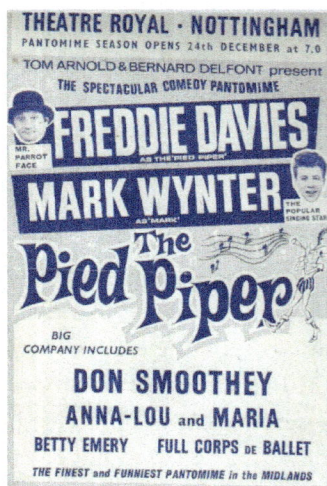

I was able to stay at home during the pantomime which was very convenient for me. I didn't see an awful lot of my parents, as we had matinées in the afternoons, followed swiftly by the evening show and they were asleep by the time I arrived home at night. I would talk to the man who played the Burgomaster in the pantomime, over a drink in the pub afterwards and we got to know one another quite well. Sometimes, I would go back to his accommodation for a 'drink with benefits', before going home.

One particular night it was snowing and icy.

He thought I should stay the night rather than risk the elements.

I rang my mother to tell her what I was doing, so she wouldn't worry and think I'd had an accident in the snow if I didn't come home. When I told her I was staying in Nottingham, she just slammed the phone down on me!

The next morning I drove home. Although I obviously had a key to the house, on this occasion, I chose to ring the front door bell. When my mother came to the door, I said,

"Don't you ever do that to me again after I had the decency to phone you to let you know my reasons for staying in Nottingham last night".

My Dad was retired by this time, and I presumed he was lying on the sofa downstairs. Mother and I went upstairs into the bathroom, where a fierce argument ensued. I think mother thought she had some sort of hold on me because my father still didn't know anything about my sexuality. Suddenly my father shouted, "What's going on upstairs?"

I said to my mother,

"I'm going down to tell him. I'm not having any more of this."

So, down I went, to break the news. Much to my surprise, he just said,

"I don't know anything about these things apart from what I hear on the shop floor at work and I don't want to know, but your mother will never say another word" and she didn't, so life just carried on as usual. I think the main thing my mother was worried about more than anything, was me getting into bad company and ending up in the river Thames or worse. That was never going to happen. One thing she did say to me in later life was,

"I'll accept your lifestyle, but I'll never understand. The one thing I regret is that I will never have any grandchildren."

I felt very sad for her, but it's my life and I have to live it my way.

As far as my private life was concerned, things were on the quiet side until the following spring. I saw an advert for musicians to audition for the Ice Show in Bournemouth, my favourite town. I came down to do the audition but I wasn't what the musical director was looking for. As I was already in Bournemouth, I thought I may as well call into the bar at the Norfolk hotel for a drink, while I was there. There were two or three men standing in a corner chatting. I knew one of them to talk to, so went over to say, "Hello". That night I was to meet the man that I would spend the next thirty-eight years with.

We chatted a while but I couldn't keep my eyes off this tall white-haired, well-dressed, distinguished older man. When I got a chance, I turned to the man I already knew and asked him if this elderly statesman was available. His reply was,

"You don't stand a chance there."

However, I stayed till closing time and engineered it so we both walked out together. As we walked towards the road, I introduced myself,

"I'm Jeff, by the way."

I asked if he had a car, otherwise I could offer him a lift home. He didn't drive, so I took him back to his flat. His name was Harold. I was invited in for a coffee. Thirty-eight years later and I still remember that I didn't ever get that coffee. I stayed the night instead. The next morning, Harold had to go to work. Coincidentally, it turned out he was a music teacher in a school. He said,

"You can stay here if you like and I'll be home about five o'clock this evening."

The place was full of antiques and he was taking a risk leaving a total stranger in that flat; I could have run away with some valuable things. Needless to say, I was still there when he got home at 5pm. I saw a lot of Harold during the next year or so. I would drive down to Bournemouth at every opportunity when I had a few days free but it was to be three years before I moved down to Bournemouth permanently and we bought our first house together.

6 - HAROLD SCOTT, MY PARTNER

I've mentioned before, that I am more attracted to older men, rather than men my own age or younger. I go for the white-haired, distinguished-looking older type and Harold had all of the qualities I like, including his age. I was 27 years old, while he was 57, some 30 years older. That definitely made Harold the father figure I had been waiting for.

Harold on Mount Titlis, Engelberg, Switzerland, August 1970

I think the reason my friend in the Norfolk hotel bar didn't think I had any chance with Harold was the fact he had never had a regular boyfriend before. He had only had casual friendships with people that were in Bournemouth for their holidays and were only there for a short while. But things were about to change for both of us. Harold was also a fine classical pianist with the letters LTCL after his name, which stands for Licentiate of Trinity College London. He also was a music teacher in one of the Bournemouth schools. We had our music in common from the very start.

Harold and I knew one another for three years before I moved in and we bought our first house together. I told him right from the beginning, that my music career came first, as I had known so many heterosexual marriages that had failed because the wives were sitting at home every evening alone while their husbands were out working. There wasn't any social night life together for either of them, which isn't good for a young married couple and even worse, when any children came along and the wife had to deal with things alone. So unless these things are explained from the start, in many cases it doesn't always work. From then on, I drove to Bournemouth whenever I had a few days free, to spend as much time as we could together. Harold didn't mind this arrangement, as he was used to being on his own and he was still working anyway.

He knew what I did for a living, and could always come and stay with me in the caravan during his school holidays. It worked quite well and gave each of us time to get to know one another before we took the plunge. Even though Harold and I met in Bournemouth, by sheer coincidence his mother lived in a village just the other side of Nottingham from Kimberley, called Burton Joyce. During one school holiday, Harold came up to see his mother in Burton Joyce. It just so happened I was also in Kimberley at the same time and I arranged to meet him in Nottingham for lunch. My mother said she would like a lift into town with me but didn't want to meet Harold. Mother and I were walking down Long Row which is one of the streets leading to the main square in Nottingham. It was another day for fate to lend a hand, as I saw Harold walking toward us. I swear on my life, it wasn't planned; it was just fate. My mother was 'having kittens', when I told her Harold was coming towards us; she couldn't get out of it now

I made the introductions; we all had a few words and went our separate ways. Later when I caught up with mother at home she said
"Well, if it has to be somebody, I'd rather it be him, he's a gentleman", and so he was. As we were both in the Nottingham area at the same time. Harold invited me over to Burton Joyce to meet his mother, who was in her 90s by this time. She was an aristocratic old lady and while Harold was out of the room she said to me,
"Look after him for me, will you?"

And so I did, for 38 years. The subject of sexuality had never been talked about between Harold and his mother but it must have been a mother's intuition on her part.

I was in my second period with the Eric Delaney band. We were a small community on the road together and not mixing much with other musicians outside of that community. Most members of Eric's band were aware of my sexual preference, but it was never mentioned, except for just once when Hilson, the other drummer made some quip I didn't like and I poured my drink over his head. Then he told me he'd also had sex with another man and his remark hadn't meant to be derogatory. It would be later, when I was working in London that it was more important to try to keep things under wraps for as long as possible.

From this point onwards, I'll be including the two sides of my life as one, because it's more important to be who I am, rather than not what I am.

7 - THE FIRST STEP
~ The Semi-Professional Days ~

I was still taking clarinet lessons with Wink Meer. With his help, along with my father cracking the whip, and with my constant practising, I was starting to get somewhere. As I mentioned in an earlier chapter, I had been playing the saxophone without needing any special tuition. Wink had told me during my first lesson that if I learned the clarinet first, the saxophone would become easier. He was right about that, as I found it quite easy to work on the saxophone by myself, without needing any special lessons.

Then came the last time I had a clarinet lesson from Wink. Henceforth, I would work on my own, for the time being. On that same day, he told my father that there was a young trumpet player who lived in the same area, and who had a small band that was looking for a sax player. We went to this man's house and arranged to go down and have a practice with them. After that first practice, I was invited to join the band. It was my first band. I learned a lot during that time and we did the occasional paid job as well.

At the same time, my father started taking me to play Second Alto sax with his own band on Saturday nights, in order for me to learn the ropes, so to speak. For that, I was paid 10 shillings, when there were 20 shillings to the pound, so that was equivalent to 50 pence in today's money. Taking inflation into account that 10 shillings would have gone much further 50 years ago than 50 pence does today.

This turned things completely around for me. I went from finding practising to be an effort and a chore to absolutely loving being on the stage, performing. From that moment on, I knew what I wanted to do when I left school. That was, to be a professional musician.

Around this time, a professional sax player from London came to live in Nottingham, to run a corner shop with his wife and daughter. During his time spent in London, he had worked with famous British bands of the time such as Stanley Black, Sid Phillips and the Joe Loss Orchestra, with whom I also did a lot of work in later years but through choice never actually joined the band as a full time member. My father got to hear about this man and arranged for me to have lessons with him on sax. His name was Arthur Lester, known as Art. I learned how to produce a good sound, or tone as it's called. I also learned how to play modern swing and jazz as well as learning how to phrase music.

The simplest way I can explain phrasing in music is that it's pretty much the same as we phrase and say words when we are speaking, such as by accentuating some words or syllables more than others and by the use of punctuation.

This took me to a whole new level. Before forming his own band in Mansfield, Nottinghamshire, Art was currently playing at one of the three Mecca dance halls in Nottingham called the Palais-de-Dance. I was still working in the music shop at the time. Thursdays were half-day closing for the shop, so Art arranged for me to sit in with the professional band there in his place during the afternoon tea dance. That was good experience for me. The name of the leader of that band was Gene Mayo. Years later, I was to meet Gene again in Sunderland. He was getting on in years by this time and had retired from the music business and was a sad old man, selling cigarettes in a kiosk.

It must have been around this time that Art, my saxophone teacher was offered a job to form his band on the Mecca circuit in Manchester, which was a step up from Mansfield, where his band was currently working. Art and his family moved to Manchester, so that was the end of my saxophone lessons. He was a good teacher and I respected him. I didn't hear from him for a while but he must have had to come back to Nottingham one time on business and called in to see me. It was the first time I had heard from him since he went to Manchester and I had been disappointed about that. I remember saying to him,

"You know Arthur, as far as you're concerned, I'm out of sight out of mind."

His reply was,

"In the music business, you make lots of acquaintances but make very few friends." I found that to be a good piece of advice and very true.

My father's band rehearsed on Sunday mornings and as I was now available I went along to the rehearsals. I was playing First Alto sax with the band by this time. We had five saxes, (two altos, two tenors and one baritone), three trumpets, one trombone, piano, bass and drums. This was traditionally the typical size and line up for a big band. The First Trumpet player was also the band coach. He had been professional himself and really knew what he wanted from the whole band. As a novice and still comparatively wet behind the ears, I came in for a lot of harsh words but it was all constructive criticism. I didn't best like him at the time but looking back, I have a lot to thank him for. Years later, after I had turned professional, I called to see him one day to thank him profusely. Later, I wondered if my dad had told him to give me a hard time in order to push me along. I am aware that sometimes I needed a kick up the backside to keep me motivated.

As the band progressed, my father managed to secure an engagement every Saturday night in the ballroom at Nottingham University. This was quite a prestigious position and that's where I earned my wings. I was still only 15 or 16 years old.

I also sang a couple of pop songs with the band. As I have already mentioned in a previous chapter, I am a bit of an extrovert and enjoy being in the limelight occasionally, which is just as well in the music business.

49

When I reached the age of sixteen I was able to have a motorbike. It was a Moto Gussi. It sounds exotic but it was only a small 98cc 2-stroke. I would go to work on it and enjoyed the freedom of being able to go further afield. Even though mine had the smaller capacity engine, it was capable of beating my pal's 125cc BSA Bantam anytime.

On the way into Nottingham there was a small traffic island and if there wasn't any traffic about, I used to be able to ride straight across it, instead of going round. I was a bit of a devil even then. The picture is of me and Robert Row, an old school friend, on his scrambler bike next to my dad's Dormobile, which he used for carrying some of the band members and the equipment around.

Just one year later, in 1961, when I was eighteen, I became eligible to drive a car. The original Martin Walter Dormobile was a conversion of the Bedford CA van into a mini-bus, with rear side windows and seats. Later models, from 1957 included kitchen and beds and an elevating roof.

My dad tried to teach me, but I kept trying to take the big, wide Dormobile through the same gaps that I could get through on the motorbike. There were a few raised voices between us and some tearing out of the hair, so it was decided that the father-son relationship was not working and I should go to a professional driving school for lessons. I passed first time. When I got back from the test with the pass marks, my driving instructor told me he was despondent when he saw the man who was about to be my tester walk towards the car because he was the toughest tester of the lot and notorious at failing new drivers and my driving instructor didn't think I stood a cat in hell's chance of passing. But I did and the rest is history. My first car was a 1943 Morris Eight two-seater tourer.

It was the same age as me, and cost the princely sum of £50. It needed some restoration but my dad, being an engineer soon sorted that out. I loved that car. It would be worth quite a bit now. We took the engine out and ground the valves by hand and I drove it for a few years and sold it for £50, the same as its cost.

After a couple of years at the University ballroom, one of the tenor sax players left the band and was replaced by a professional tenor sax player, whose name was Jos. He was in between jobs and needed a bit of pocket money. His presence in the band improved the sax section even further and it was a pleasure to have him with us. It was inevitable that he would get another professional job, sooner rather than later. Sure enough, he managed to get a job at the Sherwood Rooms, a Mecca dance hall in Nottingham. Very soon after that, another position for Second Alto became vacant with the same band. Jos had heard me play and recommended me for the job. This was just the opportunity I had been waiting for and it was also In Nottingham, which was even better, as it meant I didn't have to leave home just yet. If Jos hadn't played in my dad's band, I may have had to wait longer before I achieved my goal.

Throughout my career, I always seemed to be in the right place at the right time; Jos being in my dad's band at the right time was one of those occasions. I will highlight those instances throughout the book, when they arise. I've said many times, I am sure, that I have a guardian angel looking over my shoulder and this was one of those occasions.

My father wasn't too happy about me becoming professional, for more than one reason. First and foremost, I think he was hoping that I would take over his band when he retired. Also, it is a very insecure profession and not always particularly well paid. It just so happened at this time that there was a new computerized aptitude test available in London. It was a very new technology then. Computers were still in their infancy. I persuaded my parents to let me take the test, on the condition that they would allow me to pursue whatever came up. The test was basically a box-ticking aptitude test, where one would choose between two answers. I can't remember any specific questions but I do know that I didn't necessarily answer all the music questions favourably.

For example, if one of the questions was, "Which would you rather do: conduct a symphony orchestra, or drive a racing car?" I would have chosen the racing car, on the grounds that I was more interested in racing cars than classical music. After the test, we went back to Nottingham and returned a week later to get the results and an interview. Surprise, surprise: music came top of the list. I explained to the interviewer that my parents were against me being a musician for my career. Was there an alternative? One of the alternatives was to train to be an osteopath, on the grounds that I had an aptitude to helping other people get better, which is very true.

Helping people is something I have inherited from my father; he was always the first there, to help other people if he could. The person interviewing me said,
"You should follow your heart. I can see your name up in lights one day."
Metaphorically speaking, she was right, not exactly in lights but very close to the top of the ladder in my field.

During my research for this book whilst looking for something else, I came across the report I had kept all these years and completely forgotten about. It would seem that I was 18 when I took the test on 10th May 1952. Now, as I read through the report I can look back through my life to be amazed how accurate the report was. It mentions aptitudes that are so correct. The graphs in the report are a bit crude by today's standards but one has to remember that it was fifty years ago and computers were still in their infancy at the time. The graphs indicate that my worst subjects are maths, writing, selling, accounts and art (as in pictures.)

In the written part of report it says,
"This report shows conclusively that your present work i.e. 'shop work' is not in the right field, so you would be advised to change your job immediately. Also, on no account should you be tied to a desk."
Interesting, don't you think?

Among some of my best subjects were farming, mechanical engineering, research and music, which came top. Comments on the plus side were as follows,

"Your self-sufficiency rating indicates that you are the kind of person who works better with other people, as a member of a team or group, i.e. a band." A computer big enough to handle something like this test 50 years ago would probably have taken up a complete room.

Reluctantly, my parents agreed to let me follow my ambition. So it was that, in 1961, I joined Benny Daniels band at the Sherwood Rooms in Nottingham, alongside Jos Taylor, the tenor sax player. This was my first professional job. I was still only eighteen at the time. During the nine months I was there, I was playing six nights a week, instead of just once a week with my father's band. I learned and improved a lot during those nine months.

I also did some singing with the band, as Benny didn't have any singers in his band. So, I got to add another string to my bow, which proved to be very useful during my career.

One day, out of the blue, Benny dropped a bombshell. He told the whole band he was about to retire to Spain. This meant we all had to look for yet another job.

During my time with Benny's band, I met my first girlfriend. Her pal was seeing the trumpet player and Liz had her eye on me.

Liz is the one on the left. The two of them would come every Saturday and dance in front of the stage. We began seeing one another quite a bit. I met her parents and she met mine. Our problem was that I was about to lose my job and to move away.

8 - THE SECOND STEP
~ Leaving home ~

When the time grew closer to Benny Daniel's retirement, I started to look for another job in the music paper, the *Melody Maker*. That was the paper where jobs were advertised on the back few pages. I'd made my choice to become a professional musician and now it was a case of 'do or die'; it was up to me. I was determined to make it work, I can be very determined when I put my mind to it. The alternative was possibly to end up living in a cardboard box on the streets. I was going to make sure that didn't happen. As well as looking at the *Melody Maker*, I also wrote to other people including the great Geraldo, who had been a famous bandleader of the '30s, '40s and early '50s. He was now an impresario, booking most of the musicians on the cruise liners, including the original *Queen Mary*, *Queen Elizabeth*, the *QE2* and the *Mauretania*. The musicians on those ships were known as 'Geraldo's Navy'.

I was invited to do an audition at his London office, 73 Bond Street, London. I turned up at the door bearing his name, so I knocked and was called in. I still remember now; Geraldo was sitting with his back to the window. It was a huge room. He was sitting behind a large impressive desk   He just asked me to play something. I was so nervous in the company of this music legend but somehow, I managed to play a few tunes for him. When I'd finished, he said,

"I haven't got anything for you at the moment but I'll contact you when I have."

I left the building, thinking of that well-known phrase,

"Don't ring me, I'll ring you."

I travelled back to Nottingham, feeling a bit down but, undaunted and I carried on looking elsewhere.   He was however, true to his word. A few weeks later, he sent a telegram asking me to report to the Mauritania.   I rang back to thank him and to say that in the meantime, I had found another job so I wasn't available at present. I have done a bit of research on Geraldo which turned up some information which I personally found fascinating.   I'd like to share some of it with you. His real name was Gerald Bright; that's where the Geraldo came from. His band was on the radio a lot during the 1940s; as a child I remember hearing his name then. Many of the big names in the music business passed through his band over the years. (Some of them I subsequently met and some of them I have played for, when I eventually reached London myself.)

Some of the names that passed through Geraldo's band were: Ted Heath, Johnny Dankworth, Ronnie Scott (of the world famous Ronnie Scott's Jazz Club in London), Nat Temple (I played with his band for a short time) and not forgetting Eric Delaney, the drummer, whose band I played with for five years, during my early twenties, some of the most exciting times of my life.

Geraldo also talked about a young music arranger who would do arrangements for his band which reminded me of a funny story I heard years ago. (The name has been changed so as not to offend anyone but the story is the same.) The said arranger was called 'Jack'. Jack became well-known and a respected person in the music business, not only as an arranger but also as a musical director on many records and radio broadcasts. It was known and accepted by the musicians who worked with him regularly that Jack was going through a sex change. One day, when the change was complete, he appeared on the conductor's rostrum as a good-looking woman and said to his friends,

"From now on I wish to be called 'Jacky.'"

So, one smart-arsed trumpet player stood up on the back row and shouted out,

"Hey Jack, I suppose a f**k's out of the question?"

Jacky continued to live at home with wife and family. One day, someone knocked at the door and when one of the kids opened it, the person said,

"Is Jacky in"?

The kid shouted down the hall in a loud voice,

"DAD, THERE'S SOMEONE AT THE DOOR FOR YOU."

Jacky eventually emigrated to the Unites States, where she was highly respected and I have seen her name come up as the musical director in the credits of some big American TV shows.

Trumpet players are renowned for being out-spoken characters. I think it must be the nature of the instrument they play. Here's another classic trumpet player's story, also true. This trumpet player was in court. The charges had been heard and the judge turned to him, standing in the dock and said,

"Have you anything to say in your defence, Mr Russell?"

to which his reply was,

"Yes, sir, beam me up, Scotty!"

Apart from contacting Geraldo, I had also written to Nat Allen, who previously had a band in Nottingham. I had met him while he was there. On that occasion he had said to me, "If ever you want a job, let me know." So this was another avenue I could explore; onwards and upwards. Nat Allen's band was now playing at the Locarno ballroom in Liverpool. I wrote to him there, at the same time reminding him of our previous meeting in Nottingham. I got a swift reply asking me when I could start. The opening was for a tenor sax player. I possessed a tenor sax, although I really preferred to play the alto but needs must and I needed the work, so off I went to Liverpool with my tenor sax. (Chapter 9 in this book deals with the saxophone family.)

I turned up for my first session with the band; the drummer said he had fixed up for me to stay at the same digs as him. When we got back to the digs that night, the landlady still hadn't got my room ready but said I could sleep in her mother's bed for one night and her mother would sleep somewhere else. Not only had she not got my own room ready but she hadn't even changed the sheets on her mother's bed. Her mother must have allowed her dog to sleep with her as well. The sheets were filthy, full of dog hairs and it stank. My first night away from home and I felt sick and slept on top of the bed, fully clothed. I will never forget that first night as long as I live. Things did get a bit better but I didn't ever feel comfortable there.

I was once told by my father that even a bad experience is an experience, and that was definitely a bad experience.

The style of Nat Allan's band was more on the pop side of music, rather than the dance bands I'd played with before. His band really wasn't for me, as I still preferred the dance bands. I hadn't been in Nat's band long when I heard a rumour that the bandleader next door at the Grafton Rooms was looking for a Lead Alto. I went to see him, he gave me the job and so it was that I gave my notice to Nat Allen and moved to the Grafton Rooms.

The Grafton façade over the entrance

The Grafton, as it was called, was a dance hall for private functions rather than for public dances and similar to the Sherwood Rooms in Nottingham and it was right next door to the Locarno.

Before I moved and was still at the Locarno, a local Liverpool group called The Beatles had been booked to do a slot, while the resident band had their break. The Beatles had just had their first hit record, "Love Me Do" and were still relatively unknown. We stood on the balcony listening to the first tune thinking they were three chord wonders, who wouldn't be around very long. Little did we know how wrong we were? As we all know now, The Beatles went on to write some great songs of our time; they will be written into history.

With the Benny Daniels band, I had played Second Alto, as Benny played First Alto, as well as leading the band at the same time. With Nat's band I was on tenor sax. When I joined Johnny Hilton's band at the Grafton Rooms, it was my first professional job as a Lead Alto, which was my aim in life. I was still only a young man, eighteen going on nineteen. Age was on my side. I think I was a good alto player then but had a lot to learn; these were still early days for me, as I was still a relative novice and we all have to start somewhere. During the time in that band, I heard that a previous trombone player had recently left to join the Joe Loss Orchestra. His name was Sam Watmough. I thought "lucky beggar". Little did I know that I would be working with him in the Joe Loss Orchestra one day!

Johnny Hilton was not too pleased with my Lead Alto playing and before long I was demoted to Baritone Sax. Being less than happy about being demoted, it was time to start looking elsewhere yet again. I wasn't too keen on Liverpool anyway. So once again, it was back to the *Melody Maker*'s back pages.

It wasn't long before I spotted an advert for a sax player to help form a new band at the Locarno, Nottingham. The Locarno was one of three Mecca dance halls in Nottingham. I applied for the job with my credentials. No CV was required in those days. I was given a date to start, and so back to Nottingham it was.

9 - ABOUT THE SAXOPHONE FAMILY

For the benefit of anyone reading this book, who isn't too familiar with the saxophone family, I will try to explain a bit about the instruments.

The saxophone was invented in the 1840s by a Belgian instrument maker called Adolf Sax. It's a hybrid instrument. The main body of the saxophone is made from brass, like a trumpet or trombone, along with all the other instruments in a brass band, but it's played with a mouthpiece and reed, similar to a clarinet and all the other woodwind instruments.

Brass players like to tease saxophonists by calling us 'Novelties' - because our instruments are neither one thing nor the other, but a mixture of both brass and woodwind.

There are at least nine different types of saxophone of which I can think at the moment but I won't confuse you with any details about that now.

The standard Big Band would consist of five saxes, but only three of the family are used. They are: alto sax, tenor sax and baritone sax. The names alto, tenor and baritone coincide with the voices in a choir. The highest voice in the choir is usually sung by the female soprano, followed by the altos. The tenors, baritones and bass voices are usually sung by males.

The highest saxophone is the soprano sax, followed by the alto, tenor and baritone. There is also a bass sax, which is rarely used these days in modern music.

You may have heard of the American soprano sax player, Kenny G. He has made the soprano very popular as a solo saxophone more recently. The soprano is also very popular for playing jazz, but not generally used in a saxophone section.

10 - BACK TO NOTTINGHAM

As I was leaving, after my last night at the Grafton Rooms in Liverpool, the bandleader, Johnny Hilton came up to me and said,

"Let me give you a bit of advice, son. Don't ever tell someone you can do something you can't".

That was a really nasty thing to say, but I got my own back a few years later when I was working with the Eric Delaney Band at the theatre in Liverpool. Frankie Vaughan was top of the bill. (Frankie was a son of Liverpool). The show finished around 10:30 in the evening and I knew Johnny Hilton's band would still be playing until at least 12 o'clock, so I jumped into my car and drove to the Grafton Rooms. The band was in the pub during their break. I went in and made my way over to Johnny Hilton and said,

"Hello John, I don't know if you remember me, I'm Jeff Mason, I thought I'd drop in to see you. I'm working at the theatre this week with the Eric Delaney Band."

He was so smarmy and gushing; he put his arm round my shoulder, called his new Lead Alto whipping boy over and turned to me, saying,

"This is Jeff. He's playing with Eric Delaney's band now. He was playing Lead Alto for me when he was only nineteen." This was not the kind of thing I would normally do, but he really wasn't a very nice man. Revenge was sweet, I thought, "Take that you pompous two-faced bastard."

Mum and Dad drove from Nottingham to Liverpool on my last night at the Grafton Rooms, to take me back home with all my belongings, ready to start my new job the following week. They had also brought my girlfriend, Liz with them. I hadn't seen much of her over the past year so it was nice to see her as well.

The following Monday, I arrived at the Locarno in Nottingham to start rehearsals for this newly-formed Don Jones band. The band was intended to be more of a rock and roll band, based on a popular instrumental group of the day called, Sounds Incorporated. Our line-up was organ, drums, guitar, bass guitar, tenor sax and baritone sax. Alan was the organist, with music arranger, Glyn Thomas on drums, another Glyn on bass guitar, (we called him 'Black'), Jim on guitar, Don Jones on tenor sax and me on baritone sax.

Don's nickname for me was, 'The Evil One.' I can't possibly think why, except that I do have a wicked sense of humour. One of my favourite things was to change the last word in the tittle of a tune to s**t. So for

60

example, Glenn Miller's "In The Mood" would become "In The S**t", with similar changes for "Little Brown Jug", "I'm in the Mood for Love" etc.

Whilst still playing with my dad's band, there was a pop song called "Hang Down Your Head Tom Dooley" which I changed to "Hang Down Your Leg Long Tooley". Coming more to the present, there is the song by the controversial George Michael (who was apprehended in America for importuning in a public toilet) "Wake me up, before you go-go" which becomes "ZIP me up before you go".

Black, the bass guitarist in the band had a beautiful Gibson stereo guitar. He claimed to have played with Joe Brown and the Bruvvers and with Sounds Incorporated but he was never able to substantiate either of these claims and was picked on mercilessly.

I was playing Baritone Sax yet again, but, at least, I was back home in Nottingham. The idea of the band was to try to emulate a Rock and Roll group, so rather than just standing on the stage, all on the same level, we each stood on a round plinth.

These plinths were at different heights for each instrument. I have to say it all looked very impressive and modern. This was not quite what I was expecting, but times were changing; Rock and Roll was all the rage and I was back, working in my home town again. It was now the 1960s, the Rock & Roll era but still in fashion were things from the 1950s era, such as Teddy boys, with their brightly-coloured jackets, drainpipe trousers, crepe-soled shoes (often with suede uppers) which we used to call 'brothel creepers' and fluorescent socks.

Wishing to look trendier myself, I bought myself a pair of lime green fluorescent socks, which my mother threw on the fire while I was out. Another time, mother and I were in Nottingham together and I bought a light green zip-up bomber jacket and she refused to go back home on the same bus as me. Now look what people wear; anything goes these days.

Don Jones was the bandleader and he played the tenor sax. His initials were D J which, also stands for Disc Jockey. The band was called The D J Six.

In general, the musicians in the big bands would supply their own black trousers, black socks and white shirt with a black bow tie, and all the bandleader supplied was a band jacket. But in order to look trendier, like a rock group, Don was splashing out on complete made-to-measure mohair suits.

In the big bands, musicians would sit behind music desks, reading their music but in the D J Six, being more of a rock group, we had to stand up and also memorise all the tunes, to simulate what other guitar groups were doing. Memorising a musical arrangement was a new concept for me and I found it quite hard to memorise at first but soon got the hang of it. Memorising turned out to be a good experience which served me well later in my career, when I found it easier to memorise instrumental features in front of other bands.

I had already seen The Beatles, live at the Liverpool Locarno. Now we had the Rolling Stones at the Nottingham Locarno, performing their first hit record, which was called "It's All Over Now".

I enjoyed my time with the D J Six. It was a very relaxed fun time; we all got on well socially as well as musically. It wasn't my aim in life to play in this kind of small combination but it was a good experience never the less. All of these different experiences were adding up to help me to make progress. I didn't go to a conventional university, but I was studying at the 'University of Life' and I was only in the equivalent of my second year. Graduation was yet to come.

Liz would come to the dance on Saturday nights but our relationship was not to be, as before long I was to be off again. Not the best of lives for a wife and family.

Attendance at the Locarno wasn't good, so Don Jones took the opportunity to take a job at the Bournemouth Pavilion Ballroom. The job would consist of six nights a week and three afternoon tea dances. Also, one of the evenings during the week was an 'old time' night. I had played old time dance music with my father's band but none of the present band had any experience, including the bandleader, so we had an older local musician to lead the band on those nights. He knew the correct tempos for the old time music. His name was Jack Dunkley. He also played violin and saxophone. I liked Jack; he was the first person to treat me as an equal adult and I never forgot that. We remained friends for many years, during my frequent visits to and from Bournemouth.

I must explain what is meant by old time music, as opposed to modern ballroom dancing. Some of the old time dances were 'The Saint Bernard's Waltz', gavottes, quadrilles, square tangos and the old time waltz. The old time waltz is little quicker than the modern waltz. These were just a few of the kinds of things we had to play on Old Time Nights.
The line-up for Don's band was a little different to the Nottingham band in so much as he added two more saxes, one more tenor and a baritone plus one trumpet. I played Lead Alto. The band was now a nine-piece band, much more to my liking.

During that summer, I decided it was a time for me to learn the flute. It was becoming more and more expected to be able to play the flute as well as the clarinet, as a double-up to the saxophone. Later on in my career, I was glad I had taken up the flute because it became necessary. I made enquiries, bought a flute and started lessons with a local flute teacher named Alan Melly. I continued lessons for the rest of the time the band was at the Pavilion.

In 1964, I spent my 21st birthday in Bournemouth and thought I would like to live there when I retired. I fell in love with Bournemouth. It's a lovely place to live. It has a nice town with lovely beaches, the New Forest, the beautiful Dorset countryside and not forgetting the seaside.

Sundays were our only night off from the Pavilion. One Sunday, I discovered a bar in the basement of the Norfolk Hotel. Here a small band played. I went in, to listen, and was intrigued when I found that they all seemed to be able to play one another's instruments. The pianist would go over to play the vibraphone, the bass player would play piano, the drummer would play the bass etc. It was amazing to watch. The place would be packed with holiday-makers and it was difficult to get a drink at the bar when the

63

band's interval came. One Sunday, when it was particularly difficult to get a drink at the bar, the chap sitting next to me said,

"There's another bar next door. It's easier to get a drink in there, but beware, it's full of queers".

I said, "Thanks for letting me know."

I didn't have any idea at that time that I would be setting up a permanent base in Bournemouth within the next six years and the Norfolk Hotel would become my local.

The engagement in Bournemouth was originally for a permanent all-year-round contract, but by the time the summer season was coming to an end, the Bournemouth Council decided not to renew the contract for the winter. So once again, we all had to start looking for other work. All good things come to an end, as they say. Hey Ho.

It was back to the drawing board, and the *Melody Maker*'s back pages. No wonder my dad said being a professional musician was a very precarious life. It wasn't many weeks before I spotted an advert for Tony Evans, looking for musicians, including an alto player, for Belfast. Auditions were to be held at the Mecca dance hall in Derby. I had met Tony before, so went along for an audition and secured the job on Lead Alto and prepared to go to Belfast.

I flew from Derby Airfield in an old Dakota twin-engine plane. At that time, the airstrip was no more than a bumpy, rutted field. This was my first flight I had taken on my own. I have to admit to having been a little nervous. My mother drove me to the airport to see me off, wondering when she would be seeing me again.

11 - BELFAST, HERE I COME

The summer in Bournemouth was over. Autumn was upon us, as I arrived at Belfast airport to be greeted by a cold, wet, miserable, grey day. That day was to set the scene for my time in Belfast. I turned up at the Plaza ballroom for a 'meet and greet' rehearsal, only to discover that Tony Evans had booked an older, more experienced alto player to play Lead Alto. Yet again, I was to play the baritone. I thought, "When am I ever going to get away from the bloody baritone and be able to play what I'd set out to play."

I was well and truly stuck in Belfast for the foreseeable future. Tony Evans had got me by the balls. I was not a happy boy. I wasn't prepared for this either, as I hadn't brought my baritone with me, so had to borrow one for the time being.

To make thing worse, Tony had fixed up the pianist and me in the same digs as himself, so I was stuck with him 24/7. Not only that, but the digs were on the Omagh Road, Belfast. However, the 'troubles' were not too bad during that time and I wasn't aware of any unrest.

Jim, the guitarist from Don Jones' band was also there so I had at least one friend to talk to. There wasn't much to do during the day except walk into town and look around the shops. I couldn't get out soon enough, so it was back once again to the *Melody Maker*.

In the meantime, whilst perusing the back pages of the *Melody Maker*, I noticed that Art Lester, my old teacher from Nottingham was taking a band to Grimsby. I contacted him and there and then he gave me the job of Lead Alto. Two weeks' notice was quickly given to Tony Evans and I booked my flight back to Derby.

I don't remember exactly how long I was in Belfast but I do remember it was still a cold and foggy day when I arrived back home. My mother came to pick me up at the airport. The Dakota had to circle around a few times before it could find an opening in the fog to see the ground. My mother was having kittens, thinking we were going to crash. It was a very bumpy landing to say the least. The runway (such as it was) was even worse than when we took off. It was wetter and bumpier than those weeks before. However we finally got down safe and sound, so all was well.

My grandmother had bought me a second-hand Ford Zodiac for my 21st birthday, earlier that year. It was in that car that I set off for Grimsby, feeling on top of the world.

12 - ART LESTER AND GRIMSBY

On the day of the first rehearsal in 1965, the new band in Grimsby was a bit ropey initially, until we all got to know one another, but Art knew how to get the best out of everyone, and before long, things started to sound like a good band in the making.

Art was also a good music arranger, who was able to arrange the music to suit the band's strengths and weaknesses. I couldn't have been working alongside a better person than my ex-saxophone teacher, to help me to reach that next level. It was all meant to be. My guardian angel was at work again.

I was playing Lead Alto with a bit of singing, in a band led by my saxophone teacher. The First Tenor player was George, who was an objectionable Scotsman, who didn't stay long, thank goodness. The Second Tenor, Frank White moved up to First Tenor and the Baritone Sax was Paul from Bradford. The Pianist was Tom. I don't remember the Bass player's name. On Drums was 19-years old Harold Fisher, who became my best pal in the band and we hung around together most of the time. First Trumpet was Bob, who left the band after only a short time, to be replaced by a Canadian called Gee. Finally, we had Barbara White (being Frank's wife) playing Second Trumpet. There were a few changes during the time in Grimsby but that was basically the band, apart from Anne, the girl singer.

Art was a big fan of the Stan Kenton band, and as most of us were in the same digs, Art would encourage us to listen to Stan Kenton's records. Stan Kenton's Lead Alto at that time was Gabe Baltazar. I loved listening to him playing his saxophone. Being with Art's band was a huge learning curve for me and Art encouraged me a lot. It was just like having my teacher five days a week and getting paid for it at the same time. He would write arrangements for us to play in the Kenton style that sounded great.

My playing came on, in leaps and bounds, during my time with Art's band. There was one thing that I did learn to do while I was in Art's band and that was how to play with aggression. It is very important when playing an instrument to be able to express all the emotions like sadness, joyfulness, aggression and dominance, when leading a saxophone section, so everyone in that section has something to follow. That's where the term Lead Alto applies in the music world. You will have read in Chapter 2 - 'Skeletons in the Cupboard' about my lack of feelings for my father. This may help in understanding what happened between Art and me next. With Art as my teacher and now bandleader, I had a great respect for him and put him on a pedestal, as some sort of father figure. However, after he started a relationship with the girl singer, my world collapsed again. I was so upset and angry, I felt as if I had been let down not only by my father but also by my role model, who I had placed on a pedestal. When I put the saxophone in my mouth that night, I played with so much anger and aggression that the Tenor Sax player next to me said,

"Your playing was so dominant and angry; I couldn't play anything wrong; you just dragged me along with you regardless."

The next pay day, I gave Art a fortnight's notice. He said,

"Well, I'm not going to accept it."

I didn't know quite what to do then, so I stayed and learned to get over myself. Learning to be dominant and to play with aggression when leading a saxophone section was something I was able to express in future years ahead and although I didn't realize it at the time, it was a lesson well learned.

With no offence intended to all the wonderful people who live there, I felt that Grimsby was as grim as its name suggests. It is situated on the south bank, close to the mouth of the river Humber. On the opposite bank is Hull. Both are major fishing ports, where the deep sea trawlers unload their catch. The Humber Bridge now spans the river, making it easier to get from one side to the other, if you wanted to go from Grimsby to Hull. However, during the time I was in Grimsby, you would have had to go the long way round, via Goole to get to Hull.

Just a mile or so from Grimsby is the seaside town of Cleethorpes, where we had our digs. Our landlady was Lil. She was a great sport and she needed to be, with a house full of musicians.

Harold Fisher and I would pal around together; he and I were only two and a half years apart in our ages. He was a great drummer, even at that age and was destined to go to the very top in the business. There was also a very young drummer from Grimsby who idolised Harold's playing; he would come to listen to the band in order to pick up musical tips from him. His name was Graham Jarvis. Our paths were to cross again in London some years later, when we played together in the same band. Graham went on to play in Cliff Richard's band after Cliff parted company with The Shadows. I personally loved Graham's drumming and to this day consider him to be the best drummer I have ever played with including later in life when I played with Eric Delaney.

Harold and I would often go to a café on the sea front, mid-morning for a toasted tea cake. They were the best tea cakes I have ever tasted.

They were happy days. During the time I was in Grimsby, Art took Harold and me to London, in order to look for a better clarinet for me. We went to Bill Lewington's, where there were many second-hand models. I tried lots of different clarinets but finally narrowed it down to two. Art wanted me to buy a Boosey & Hawkes 1010 but I liked the French make of Buffet better. That was the one I bought. I played that clarinet all through my career and am still playing it to this day. While we were in London, Art also took us to the Hammersmith Palais, to see the Joe Loss band. Art had been in Joe's band during the time he was working in London himself. Years later in my career, I also did some work with the Joe Loss band.

Back in Grimsby, during one of our nights off, I fancied a curry, so went into town, found an Indian restaurant and went in. It was a bit seedy to say the least. I was the only one in there and I sat down to order a meal. As I was waiting, I could hear them in the kitchen preparing my curry, all of a sudden I heard the chef snort up his nose, clear his throat and spit it out. I thought, "O.M.G., I hope that's not gone in my curry". However, I took a chance and ate it. Needless to say, I never went back there again.

During my time at the Mecca Hall in Liverpool, we had The Beatles playing there. At the Mecca Hall in Nottingham, we had the Rolling Stones. In Grimsby, it was the turn of The Who. Their first hit record was, "I Can't Explain". We had never seen anything like it before. They would ram their guitars into the amplifiers making the most hideous sound. The drummer kicked his drums over; they didn't seem to have any respect for their instruments at all. In the end, they finished their act by smashing a guitar on the floor. My pal Harold was horrified at the way Keith Moon treated his drums.

Personally speaking, I thought Keith Moon was a good drummer, underneath all that showmanship. He was the one who gave the group all the energy and drive. I think I've been around drummers long enough to have an opinion.

Keith Moon's other claim to fame was when he drove his Rolls-Royce into his swimming pool. I saw the pictures in the paper after it happened. Unfortunately, he killed himself in the prime of his life; what a loss. I expect The Who were making so much money in those days that they would possibly be able to buy new guitars and cars by the dozen.

The leader of The Who was Pete Townsend; coincidentally Pete's father, Cliff Townsend was a much respected alto sax player in London. He is reputed to have said to his pals,

"My son Pete is making more money in a week than I've ever made in my whole life."

At the end of that night in Grimsby, the group's road manager or 'roadie' as we call them had left a cymbal behind from Keith's drum kit. Harold picked it up and played it for a good number of years afterwards; he said it was a good one.

The baritone player found his future wife in Grimsby. She had a friend who was also looking for a husband, so we teamed up and in Grimsby, at the age of twenty-one, I had my first sex. Again, it wasn't to be, as after less than a year, Mecca suddenly decided to close the ballroom and turn it into a Bingo Hall. Sadly it was the first of many Mecca halls to close. Now, there aren't any Mecca dance halls left in England.

Once again, we all had to pack our bags and to go our separate ways. I went back home to Kimberley. I hadn't been home long before I got a phone call from Tony Evans, the   bandleader I had previously left in Belfast. During the time I had been in Grimsby, he had been moved from Belfast to the Empire in Leicester Square where I had sat on the balcony with my parents, watching the Johnny Howard Band, five years earlier. He said,

"Would you like to come and play Lead Alto with my band in London?"

I couldn't believe what I was hearing. Just nine months earlier, he considered me incapable of leading a saxophone section in Belfast. Now he was asking me to lead one in the West End of London. It didn't make sense. He explained that he was sick of session players putting deputies in the band when they had a recording session or something better to do. He wanted somebody who would be there all the time and not put deputies in.

Down to London I went, to do an audition. I got the job and started with the band the following week. I thought I'd now arrived in the big time but very soon, things were going to get even better still.

13 - FIRST JOB IN LONDON - 1966

I found a bedsit in Notting Hill Gate, which was handy for the tube into Leicester Square and on the opposite side of the road lived Gee, the Canadian trumpet player from the band in Grimsby. The bedsit was a bit tired and scruffy with just a two-ring gas appliance to cook on. I learned how to put one saucepan on top of another to save space and also steam things at the same time. Looking back I think I managed quite well under the circumstances, considering I was cooking for myself for the first time. I had to share the bathroom, of course. In the bathroom was a huge old gas boiler to heat the water. One day, the boiler had gone out. I fetched a match from my room to re-light it. When the match got close to the boiler, it lit with an almighty bang. The shockwave threw me right across the bathroom. I could have been killed.

On my first Monday afternoon, I arrived at the Empire Ballroom, to start my first session with the band, only to find that the man who had been playing Lead Alto when I did my audition had been moved to First Tenor sax and was sitting next to me. I remember his name was Jimmy Wallace. Jimmy was not happy about me being there as the new Lead Alto. In his eyes, I was the enemy, a young man of twenty-two who had just come down from the provinces and pushed him out of the First Alto chair. He was very unpleasant towards me and gave me a really hard time. I wasn't a happy bunny, but there was no way he was going to beat me into submission. This went on some time before he finally issued Tony Evans with an ultimatum,
"Either he goes or I do!"
I'm glad Tony made the right decision, and I stayed.

One thing I will remember Jimmy by was once when he was giving me a ride up the Strand on the pillion of his motorbike. As we rode, he turned and said,
"This is Biking up the Strand" which is a play on the lyrics of a well known tune called "Strike Up The Band" from the 1927 musical with the same title. I thought that was very apt at the time. Jimmy was replaced by John Powell from Birmingham, who I already knew from the band in Belfast.

My dad used to say, "Even a bad experience is an experience." This had been a bad experience, but it helped to shape my future life never the less.

I bumped into Jimmy again, many years later, after I had retired and moved to Bournemouth. It's a small world.

The job was hard work, as we were doing five afternoons at the Empire, Leicester Square and four nights at the Lyceum on the Strand. The

Lyceum was originally built as a theatre but during the time I was there, it was being used as a Mecca ballroom. It wasn't really suited for that purpose and since then it has been turned back into a theatre again. At the end of the afternoon sessions at the Empire, the band gear had to be moved from the Empire to the Lyceum. Likewise, every time we played at the Lyceum it had to be moved back again to the Empire for the afternoon session.

I was lucky; I only had my sax to worry about. However, it was not only a lot of playing but at the same time, a lot of valuable experience, just what I needed.

It was great to be in London. Every Monday lunch time/early afternoon, there was a gathering of musicians on a back street called Archer Street, just off Piccadilly Circus. It's hard to imagine it now. It would be packed with musicians. It wasn't just musicians from the dance halls but from the West End theatres, mingling with both traditional and modern jazz players, along with musicians from the classical orchestras. There was an orchestral club in the street as well. The street was totally blocked by human bodies on Mondays. Cars could not get through at all.

These musicians would gather there, looking for work or to get paid for work they had done the week before. There were agents and bandleaders looking for musicians and guys just meeting up, to see old work mates. You name it: it was all happening on Archer Street but only on Mondays.

Needless to say, there was a pub on the corner doing a roaring trade. I didn't really know anybody myself, but I had heard about Archer Street before. It was so exciting for a young musician, just up from the country. I was there just to soak up the atmosphere and believe me it was buzzing.

We have to remember this was 50 years ago and not everyone had landline telephones, yet alone mobile phones and computers. Archer Street was the best way for the guys to get engagements and to meet old colleagues. This all ended some years ago and nobody goes to Archer Street anymore, except for the cars. I'm so glad I was able to experience it in all its glory.

Some weeks after I was settled in the job, my parents came down to London to see me and my accommodation. My mother told me afterwards that she almost wept when she saw the bedsit and how I was living. Personally, I was untroubled about the state of the bedsit. I was a young man; I was OK and I was living my dream.

In the meantime, after leaving Grimsby, my pal Harold Fisher had found a job in Sunderland with the Gene Mayo Band. (I mention Gene Mayo in Chapter 7.)

Harold met his future wife, Joan in Sunderland. She was the girl vocalist with the band at the time, a lovely lady and I am still in touch with her today.

Sunday was our night off. One Sunday, I was invited over the road to Gee's flat for a party with other musicians. After a few drinks, the marijuana was produced and was passed around the circle. Although I didn't smoke, I had tried it a couple of times in Grimsby but it hadn't really had much effect, except to make me sleepy. So just to be sociable, I joined in the circle. However this stuff must have been a lot stronger than I had had in Grimsby. Instead of making me high it had the opposite effect and I went into what they call a 'downer'. For me, I felt the atmosphere and attitude in the room suddenly changed and I began to think someone was going to kill me with a knife. I got up and ran down the stairs, but in my imagination, he was following me. I ran outside into the street thinking I wouldn't be safe, a dog was barking at my heels, as I crossed the road to my bedsit but in my mind, the man was still following me. I thought,

"If I can get through the front door and into my bedsit, I'll be safe."

I got into my room and locked the door but he was still there in my mind. I got into bed and after a while I managed to get some sleep. It was a lesson well learned and I've never touched the stuff since. Never the less it was an experience, and it means that if ever I am involved in a conversation about the subject, I can include my experience, which helps me to be part of that conversation as well. Every little helps, as the expression goes.

About a month or so after I joined Tony's band, the drummer was leaving, so I got in touch with Harold Fisher, my pal in Sunderland and told him there was a job going at the Empire. He got the job and came down to join us. He stayed with me in the bedsit for a few nights, sleeping on the floor. I wasn't supposed to have anyone else staying in the room with me, so when the landlord found out he asked us to leave. So now, Harold and I needed to set out to find a flat for rent. We managed to find a newly-renovated basement flat in Vauxhall, so we moved in. Parking outside the flat was free, which was a good job, as Harold had his Morris Eight van, which he needed to carry his drum kit backwards and forwards, to and fro, between the two venues. Parking in the West End of London was also easier in those days.

During the afternoon sessions, we could drop off the drums at the back door of the Empire and park free of charge all afternoon in Long Acre, which is only a short walk from Leicester Square. Then he had to pack all his drums away at the end of the session, walk to get the van, load his drums and drive to the Lyceum, play, and do it all over again. It was hard going. That was one reason my dad wanted me to play the sax and not the drums, there was far too much kit to cart about, playing drums.

After finishing playing at the Lyceum, Harold and I would sometimes walk up to Covent Garden, where they were busy setting up the stalls for the early morning fruit and veg market the next day. It was buzzing with people rushing around, and lorries with produce to unload, parked everywhere. Best of all, there was a pub which had a special licence to stay open all night for the men from the market and a hot dog stall, selling various snacks. We would probably have a hot dog before going back to the flat.

Also, just off Trafalgar Square there was a post office that stayed open all night. We went in one night to buy a stamp and post a letter. What a good time I was having! It was great to be alive and playing in a band in the West End of London. After a while, I began to realise that, although I was playing in a Mecca Hall in London, I could just as well have been in a Mecca hall anywhere in the country as far as making new contacts were concerned and I was beginning to get itchy feet.

Harold was looking through the *Melody Maker* one day and spotted an advert for a sax and trumpet player, to join the Eric Delaney band. There was an address to write to. It was in Sudbrook Road, London SW12. I was more than interested, because Eric was a big name in those days and it would definitely be a huge career jump forward for me if I could get that job. Harold and I drove to the address expecting to find Eric there, but it turned out to be his agent, who told me he couldn't help; I had to write a letter addressed to Eric himself. So it was; I wrote a letter the next day and waited.

The next thing to worry about was the *Come Dancing* heat at the Lyceum. The programme, *Come Dancing* was not the same formula as it is today. Each week there would be two teams, competing for a place in the final and whoever won that heat would go to the next round, and the losing team was out altogether. The heats were broadcast from Mecca Dance Halls up and down the country. For instance, a team from Manchester may be competing with a team from Bristol. One would go through to the next round and the other team would not, and so on, until there were only two teams left. The other big difference was, in those days, it was televised live, so if anything went wrong it couldn't be stopped, to go over it again. This put a lot of extra stress on the bandleaders.

As Tony Evans normally only had three saxophones, he decided to add another tenor sax just for the TV programme. The sax player's name was Pete Warner, a session man and first class musician. During the course of the rehearsals, we were chatting and I told him I had written to Eric Delaney but hadn't had a reply. He said,
"Write to him again and mention my name."

I did that and hey presto, I was called to an audition and got the job. If that wasn't being in the right place at the right time, I don't know what is. It turned out that Pete Warner had been in Eric's band years before, when Eric had his big band.

Once again my guardian angel was looking out for me when I just happened to be in the right place at the right time, sitting next to Pete Warner on that television broadcast.

75

14 - THE ERIC DELANEY DAYS - 1967

I had already done an audition and been given a date to start with the band. Having served my notice with Tony Evans, it was back home to Kimberley, while waiting for a date to start with the Eric Delaney band. One day, before I was due to start with the band, I had a call from Eric, asking if I could do a one-night stand with the band, while his present sax player was still there, in order to give me more of an idea what would be required of me. I was so eager to get started and just couldn't wait. Eric was on the telephone, trying to speak clearly so I would understand where the job was. He told me it was at the Floral Hall, Harrow Gate. I wrote it all down exactly as he had pronounced it as two separate words, Harrow Gate. He told me what to wear and what time to be there etc.

As I'd been working in London, I knew exactly where Harrow was, so I set off from Nottingham for London and Harrow. When I got to Harrow, I began asking where Harrow Gate was. Nobody knew, and I thought, typical Londoners, they don't know anything. Eventually I found a police station and asked the same question - they hadn't heard of it either. I said,
"I've got it written down" and I got out the piece of paper to show him. The penny dropped. I had just driven well over a hundred miles in the wrong direction. Instead, I should have been in Harrogate, Yorkshire. Eric had pronounced it like Harrow Gate, and that's how I wrote it out. Can you imagine how stupid I felt? I had the phone number of the Floral Hall and had to ring him. He must have thought,
"What kind of an idiot have we got here?"
He said,
"Never mind, it's deep snow here. You probably wouldn't have got through anyway."

This was not the best of starts to my first big name band. In my defence, I was a very inexperienced young man, who still had a lot to learn and we didn't have post codes to put into our sat navs in those days.

When the date sheets came through after that, they always had the full address on them, just to be sure. Eric was born in 1924. He was a child prodigy and awarded best swing drummer at age 16. At the age of 17, one of his first jobs was with the Bert Ambrose Octet. The pianist at the time was the great George Shearing. I was once told this story about George Shearing. It may or not be true, but nevertheless, it's a great story. Allegedly, in the early days, long before he became famous, George was on tour with this band. In order to keep costs down, they had to share rooms. On one particular occasion, as the story goes, his room-mate wanted to read a book before going to sleep. Being blind, George couldn't tell the difference between light and dark. He kept saying to his room-mate,

"Is the light out yet?"

"No" was the reply, "I'm reading my book."

This question went to and fro for some time until his roommate got so fed up with this same question and finally said,

"Yes, George, the light is out" just to keep him quiet, whereupon George, believing the light was now out, immediately began to masturbate with gusto.

Eric was in the Geraldo Band between the years 1946-1954. He was just 22 when he joined. No doubt Geraldo's band would have been the platform for Eric's eventual fame. I have a feeling that Johnny Dankworth may also have been in Geraldo's band at the same time. Eventually, Eric started his own big band, touring the theatres and concert halls of Britain, carrying his own scenery around with him in two large furniture lorries, known as pantechnicons. One of the scenes was of a battle ship with the musicians placed at different levels to coincide with the decks of the ship. It must have looked spectacular.

Eric was a born showman and was one of, if not the first to use the two bass drum set-up in England, along with his trademark timpani. I don't know all the names of the musicians in that band except for Des Lumsdon, Lead Alto, Pete Warner, Tenor Sax and Kenny Ball, who was one of the trumpet players. It must have cost a fortune to operate at that level.

Around the same time, Rock and Roll was all the rage with the youngsters. Big bands were on their way out and along with other big bands of the era, eventually Eric went bankrupt. He had a hit record called "Oranges and Lemons" in the '50s. Johnny Dankworth also had a hit record around the same time with "Three Blind Mice". I remember hearing them both on the radio when I was a boy.

After winding up the big band, Eric carried on with a much smaller six-piece band, of which I was about to be part. My first official gig was in Penzance, Cornwall. This was the time to meet the rest of the band. I was surprised to see Ian Fenby there, as he had been the second trumpet with Tony Evans' band at the same time as me. I hadn't any idea he had also applied for the trumpet job till I arrived in Penzance. That was good; at least I knew one other person in the band. Steve Gray was on organ/keyboard, Maurice (Mo) Robinson on bass, Ian Fenby on trumpet, me on alto and Tony on guitar, with, as usual, Eric on drums.

I would have been around twenty-three when I joined Eric's band, still in the prime of life but old enough to appreciate how lucky I was. Everything was a new adventure, yet to come.

The first gig was a dance, but it soon became apparent that most of the work would be as a cabaret act, interspersed with continental tours, theatre tours and summer seasons. This was also the time when the big cabaret clubs were at their height in the north of England where we would usually do a 45 minute cabaret spot each night. We would usually do a week in each club.

Batley variety club was probably the biggest and best known of them all. We did the Batley club a few times while I was with Eric's band. Usually, we were top of the bill, but on one particular occasion we were on the same bill as Cilla Black. She was top of the bill and we were the supporting act. We didn't see anything of her during that week as she seemed to keep herself locked in her dressing room, which I found a bit strange, because on stage she always seemed to be so friendly, down to earth and approachable, but maybe she was tired of the adoration of fans and the only way she could get any peace was to keep herself to herself.

The Fiesta in Stockton was another one of the clubs we did regularly, along with Brighouse Variety Club, home of the famous Brighouse and Rastrick brass Band. There were clubs in Spennymoor, Barnsley and Greasbrough, to mention just a few. There were dozens of them, far too many to mention here. However, Greasbrough stands out in my mind.
(Yorkshire dialect and slang idiom is quoted in the next few paragraphs, like 't' for 'the' or 'to the' and 'as' for 'have' and also 'us' for 'me' or 'we')

When the doors opened in the evening, some of the men that had probably come straight from work would arrive for a night's drinking, still adorned in their cloth caps. Before the show, the evening would start with the obligatory bingo session.

Everyone had to be quiet while t bingo (the bingo) was on. It was more than your life was worth to make a noise while the bingo was being called. The club would book big names of the day for the cabaret.

I remember once when we shared the bill with Bob Monkhouse in Greasbrough. A committee man would usually introduce the act with an announcement something like,
"Can us as some quiet for t turn." (Can we have some quiet for the turn.)
However, it didn't matter who or what was on the stage, when someone shouted,

"t pies as cum" (The pies have arrived); folk just rushed for the pies in the middle of the performance, regardless. It was very much like the comedy sketches we see on the TV today, but for real.

As a matter of interest, I recently watched a documentary on the TV of Matt Munroe's life story. He also mentioned Greasborough and had a similar experience. The only difference was that he arrived in his Rolls-Royce and I arrived in my Austin 1100.

The band also did a lot of work on the American Air Force bases, both in England and in Germany. We enjoyed doing the bases and always looked forward to the T-bone steaks. I was surprised to find that most of the food on the bases had to be flown in from the States. This was the beginning of a whole new life for me and so far, I was loving it.

I hardly know where to begin. It was all so new, exciting and happening so fast. This was much better than being in a Mecca dance hall as far as I was concerned, as cabaret was the main bulk of the band's work, I must explain a little about how it worked. We would be standing during the performance, rather than sitting down behind a music desk as the big bands did. The set-up of the band was as follows: Eric was on a revolving rostrum at the back of the stage, with the organ and bass to his right and the trumpet, alto sax and tenor sax to his left. That would usually fill the whole front of the stage in a club.

The opening number was "Manhattan Spiritual", before introducing everyone in the band. When he came to our side he always said,
"On my right, we have Freeman Hardy and Willis (a chain of shoe retailers). On trumpet, we have a very fine musician, Mr Ian Fenby. In the middle we have the baby of the band, Jeff Mason."
And every time, without fail, Ian would say surreptitiously out of the corner of his mouth,
"Yeah, you're a baby alright."
(I couldn't retaliate on stage, with the spot light on me, so I just put up with it for years.) Eric continued,
"On tenor sax, we have Phil Chapman."
I found out in the course of time that, as a boy soldier, Ian had been bullied because he had sticky-out ears, so he decided to bully me and was using me as his whipping boy. He was also curious and couldn't understand why I didn't smoke, I didn't drink and I didn't go with women. I think I was a bit of a mystery to him. He must have thought I was a goody -goody. Little did he know what was lurking within me!

Because I was the youngest as well as small in stature plus the fact that I am an extrovert and a bit of a showman anyway, Eric chose me to do a few extra things in the band to help the show along; for example banging gongs, playing the tubular bells and playing the timps, while he played on his drum kit at the same time. One of the tunes in the act was Sandy Nelson's hit record, "Teen Beat".

Incidentally, some years after I had left the Eric Delaney band, I was called upon to make a record with Sandy Nelson and Duane Eddy. Eric taught me to play the timps while he played his drum kit. Playing this tune on the timps was very simple but effective. The rhythm I had to play was very repetitive:

X XX   X XX   X XX   X XX   X XX   X XX   X XX   X XX

Because it was a show, I had to look enthusiastic and every time I rushed passed Ian to get to the timps he would say,

"You love this don't you?"

I stuck this for nearly three years, before I eventually snapped. The band was playing at the theatre in Liverpool doing a variety show, where Frankie Vaughan was top of the bill. We were playing the music he gave us to play and during one song, I didn't have any music to play, so I just sat, listening. Frankie did a little dance routine, kicking his legs up as he did as part of his act. As he cavorted past me, he said,

"Clap or do something; don't just sit there." So I started clapping. Ian turned to me and said,

"There's a good boy, do as you're told."

That was the straw that broke the camel's back. As soon as the curtains came down, I squared up in front of him waving my finger in fury and told him in no uncertain words,

"One more word out of you and I'll ram that f***ing trumpet right down your throat."

He knew I meant it and after that he was as nice as pie. I learned a valuable lesson that day. I've come across three other trumpet players with similar attitudes during my career, but now I've learned how to deal with them and nip it in the bud right away.

Quoting that American phrase again: these days, "I don't take no shit from nobody."

So, back to the story: Besides playing the timps, I also played the tubular bells in "The Bells of St Mary's". Under normal circumstances they aren't very loud, so in order to be heard at the back of the room, Eric told me to bash them as hard as I could, with the mallets he gave me. Others before me had done just the same and they were more than dented but by bashing them hard, it looked much better visually for the show as well. Another piece I was involved with was "In a Persian Market" which required lots of running round and banging different sized gongs in the right places. Some of the other tunes we played were: "The Saint Louis Blues March" and, of course, "Skin Deep", which was Eric's big drum showpiece number with the revolving stage and the lights inside the two bass drums. I was also in charge of the revolving stage. All of the band would walk off stage leaving Eric in the spotlight. I would also be at the side of the stage, with the switch to turn the stage half-way round when he gave the nod. This left him with his back to the audience so they could see his feet on the two bass drums. Whilst his feet were banging away feverishly, he would wave his arms up in the air as much as to say, "Look, no hands", once again, being the showman that he was. When he gave me the nod I would turn it round one and a half turns while he was still thrashing away until he was back, facing the audience again. The band came back to finish it off.

Steve Gray, the organist wasn't with the band for long. He left in order to further his career in London as a music writer and arranger. He was replaced on organ by Dave Smith, who became my band buddy. Not long after Dave joined the band, we were issued with a schedule for a continental tour starting at a N.A.T.O. base in Naples. We were paid the equivalent of a return second class rail fare from London to Naples and given three days to make our own way there. It seems impossible to believe today but the cost of that return ticket was only £30. I have the evidence here in front of me right now. We all chose to drive ourselves and to share cars and expenses instead. This was my first continental tour with the band.

LICENSED ANNUALLY BY THE L.C.C.

Derek Boulton Management Ltd

DIRECTORS: DEREK BOULTON WINIFRED BOULTON WALTER BOULTON

37 SUDBROOKE ROAD, LONDON, S.W.12

TELEPHONE: KELVIN 2122/3

18th January, 1967

Dear Jeff,

Foreign Tour

I am enclosing a Schedule for the first two weeks of our Overseas Tour.

For Part I in Naples we agreed that you receive the equivalent of a Resident Weeks Wage for England.

For Part II in the Stuttgart Area we agreed you will receive 1⅔rd of a Resident British Weeks Wage, plus free B.O.Qs.

For Part III, which will be working from the Wiesbaden Area, I will discuss with you when I have the approximate Schedule. I will personally be in Wiesbaden to settle up with you at the end of the Tour.

A Second Class Return Rail Fare from London to Naples is £30. 12. 0d. and I enclose a cheque for this, plus £5. 0. 0d. travelling allowance, plus your first weeks salary £35. 0. 0d. (less stamp), making a total of £69. 18. 4d. I will deduct the stamps for the last two weeks at the end of the Tour.

If you have any queries please 'phone me immediately.

Kind regards,

82

Our outward journey took us from the UK, through France, Germany, Switzerland and through the Gotthard Tunnel into Italy and south to Naples. On our return, we went from Naples, back through the Gotthard Tunnel into Switzerland, crossing into Germany and to Stuttgart then Wiesbaden and home via France.

Dave and I travelled together in my car. I had a two litre Ford Corsair at the time, so we took that. It was the first time I had been on the Continent, never mind driving on the opposite side of the road as well. It was very strange at first but I seemed to get used to it quite quickly, and I had a good navigator in Dave. We drove through France into Germany, stopping at bed and breakfasts on the way.

Neither of us could speak the languages, but we seemed to get by. Then it was on to Bavaria and into Switzerland. It was getting towards spring but there was still snow and ice on the roads in the area. The Germans and Swiss are equipped for these conditions. Their cars have winter tyres with studs in to help them grip on the ice. I was totally unprepared for this and hadn't even brought any snow chains. As we got higher, the roads were just packed ice and we had to be very careful. Fortunately my father had taught me well; to stay in the highest gear possible, not to rev the engine and to try to keep moving. I had to put this into practice pretty quickly. I think we managed very well under the circumstances.

I remember we were close to Altdorf in Switzerland. That's the town famed for the William Tell story, so we stopped to look at his statue. We were looking for somewhere to stay for the night, but everywhere was full, so we moved on. We continued to not find anywhere, so we carried on further into the night. We were pretty high up in the Alps by now but carried on until we eventually reached the Gotthard road tunnel into Italy. We were both pretty dead beat by now.

As we were driving through the tunnel, I noticed there was a gap between the road and the side of the tunnel walls, so we pulled into the gap, got into our sleeping bags and grabbed some sleep. Lorries were thundering through all night but we were both dead to the world and didn't hear much at all. When we woke, there was ice on the inside of the windows, where our breath had condensed and frozen. I'm sure some of you won't believe it but Dave and I know it wasn't a dream.

Forty years later, I travelled through the Gotthard Tunnel again, but this time I was with my partner Harold and we were on vacation. On the way to the tunnel, Harold and I stopped to admire the statue of William Tell in Altdorf once again, but this time it was a lovely sunny day, during the summer months. The tunnel is so different now, with barriers all along the side of the road, there's no way anyone could do what we did, when I saw the differences between then and now, I found it hard to believe myself, what Dave and I had done, sleeping in the car that night, 40 years earlier.

Continuing the story about that trip, 40 years ago, we all arrived at the given hotel in Naples, where we were staying, within a couple of hours of one another. It was amazing. The first thing was to go to the base and to get something to eat and to set up. That base in Naples was where I had my first taste of Chilli Con Carne. After that I used to go up to the base most mornings and have it for late breakfast.

There were two different clubs on the base. One was for the enlisted men and one for the officers. We alternated between the two. Eric was a good man to work for and he was very fair. The only time he ever lost his temper with the band was while we were in Naples. During a band rehearsal that same day, we couldn't get something quite right to his satisfaction. Suddenly he yelled,
"Call yourselves musicians? I've shit 'em."

After the rehearsal, we all went to the bar and he bought us a round of drinks. I've never forgot that gesture.

A lot of the enlisted men had been conscripted from rural towns in the States and some of them even resembled Hillbillys; most of them hadn't any concept of anything outside of the United States of America.

I have had questions like,

"Hey man, you English?" and

"What language do you speak in England?" or

"Hey man. You speak good English."

I felt like saying, "That's because I am English, you pillock."

Eric had two bass drums. One had E on it, for Eric, and the other a D, for Delaney. The Americans thought his name was Ed. Classic!

I don't remember whether we were in Naples for one week or two but we certainly packed in as many of the sights as possible. One day we went across on a hydrofoil to Capri, to see where Gracie Fields had lived. Another day, four of us managed to find a back way up to Mount Vesuvius in the car, so we didn't have to pay car parking fees. There were some American service men up there as well. One shouted to his mate in American drawl,

"Hey Buddy, there's a man down here selling Haat Raacks." (That's supposed to be 'hot rocks' in English!)

I should have had a pee before we left Vesuvius but instead, got back in the car with the rest of the guys and set off back to the hotel. Fortunately, I wasn't driving that day, because after a while I began to get desperate, but drivers in Naples are maniacs There wasn't anywhere to pull in and nobody would let us through the heavy traffic. Fortunately one of the guys in the car knew that if you have a casualty in your car, you constantly hold your hands on the horn and wave a white flag out of a window at the same time, as if you're taking someone to hospital. Then the other drivers would let you through. So that's what we did, except ours was a white handkerchief. It was the most hair-raising car journey I've ever had, weaving in and out of the traffic but we got back in time before I peed myself. Phew, what a relief!

Another day, a few of us went to Pompeii. It was hard to believe what happened all those years ago and how it had survived in such a good state for all of that time. I've been back again more recently and they had uncovered a lot more since I was there the first time.

At the other end of the scale it was so sad to see the little children sent out on the streets of the slum areas to beg. I don't know how true this is, but we were told that some parents deliberately broke their children's legs or arms before sending them out on the streets. I had to keep pinching myself. Everything was new. I was having the time of my life and getting paid for it as well.

Eric had a blue Ford long-wheelbase transit van with a special parcel body on it, and a road manager, or, roadie, to do all the humping and driving. He was also responsible for Eric's drums and equipment. Apart from the drum kit there were a set of timpani and various other things to bang like gongs and tubular bells and along with all that was an electrically operated turntable which was originally designed for displaying cars in a showroom. This provided a rostrum for Eric's kit to sit on. It turned round occasionally while he was playing. You can understand how big and cumbersome it was to manhandle. The actual top came off but the base was cast iron and very heavy. When all the heavy stuff had been loaded on the van, the last thing to go on top of it all was the double bass.

It was time to head north again through the Gotthard Tunnel, into Switzerland, towards Germany and our next stop was Stuttgart. This time, on the way back, we arrived at the Gotthard Tunnel in the early morning. When we came out of the dark of the Tunnel on the Swiss side, the sun was just coming up over the horizon. The low rays of the sun were glistening on the crisp sparkling snow in all the colours of the rainbow; it was so spectacular; we had never seen anything like it before or since. I had to stop the car and get out for a few minutes. You could never capture that scene on camera or screen. It was a glorious moment I will never forget.

We had all set out in our cars, to meet up when we got to Stuttgart. Again, everyone seemed to arrive pretty much at the same time. We were staying in old German barracks this time. It was only twenty years since the end of the war and they were still being used by the American forces.

We waited and we waited for the van to turn up, but there was no sign of it for a couple of days. Eventually, the roadie arrived in a smaller, hired van. It turned out he had fallen asleep at the wheel, gone up the embankment of the Autostrada and the van had toppled over onto its roof, crushing the double bass under all its weight before opening up like a cardboard box and strewing its contents all over the embankment. Naturally, it was a write-off.

My readers will have to use their imagination to try to visualise the scene that happened next. We've all seen the cartoons where the 'baddy' runs off grinning, with a bag of gold or swag. Try to keep the image of that bag of swag in your mind and you're halfway there.

After finally meeting up with us, the first thing the roadie pulled out of the back of the rented van was a white bed-sheet with all the edges pulled together like a bag. The white bag was full of broken bits from the double bass body. All that was visible sticking out of the bag was the neck of the bass. It was tragic for the bass player, of course, but it was just the way he held the bag up like a trophy, with just the neck and broken strings dangling down, that appealed to my warped sense of humour, and I couldn't stop myself laughing. There were also a few minor breaks in Eric's timpani but we drilled a few holes and braced the legs with metal strips either side of the legs and we were ready to go.

There were quite a few American bases to cover in the Stuttgart area. Stuttgart as opposed to Wiesbaden is an industrial town and home to the Mercedes car factory. While we were in the area, Dave and I took the opportunity to visit the Mercedes Museum, which is out of town from the factory. There didn't seem to be many other people there that day, so we almost had the place to ourselves. It was wonderful to see all those gleaming cars in one place. The car that caught my eye was a two-door coupé.   I fell in love with that car and promised myself I would have one someday. It was twenty years later when I found one I liked. It needed some restoration but it was my new baby and I brought it back to life pretty much by myself. It was one of the older style models with a large radiator and the three-pointed star on the top. There was a period around that time when people were stealing hub caps from Volkswagens etc. and every time I took it to London I had to remove the three-pointed star from the radiator, in order to stop it being stolen. There was another car like mine in Bournemouth, where I live. The owner had bought it new and it was still in showroom condition. His personal number plate was UPU 2.

I once saw the number-plate SAX 1, which I thought that would be a great number for a sax player to have. I managed to flag the driver down and ask if he might be interested in selling me the number-plate, He said, "Sorry I'm a retired director of the Saxone shoe company and the plate belongs to the company." They were thinking of it as SAX ONE instead of SAX 1. Never mind, it was probably for the best; it would have been a bit too ostentatious for me, anyway.

Then there was the change to unleaded petrol, so I sold it. Thereby hangs another tale but I don't wish to bore you too much with that.

While we had been looking round the Museum, one of the guides had come and asked if we would like to see a film about Mercedes cars. We were the only ones in the cinema and they put the film on in English, especially for us. I was so impressed. That was a great experience and day out. Can you imagine a couple of German guys going to the Jaguar museum and being asked if they would like to see the film in German? I doubt it.

The band stayed in the area for about six days, before moving on to Wiesbaden. We did pretty much the same thing again, performing the cabaret show twice nightly in the various American bases in the Wiesbaden area. I liked Wiesbaden. It's a spa town and has a feel of calm and tranquility about it. The name, Wiesbaden translates to meadow baths. At one time it had 26 hot springs. Wiesbaden has spa baths like we have in English towns such as Matlock Bath and Buxton in Derbyshire and, of course, Bath.

We did a different base each night. The cabaret show lasted about three quarters of an hour, so we could do one show in the enlisted men's club and another one in the officers' club.

From Wiesbaden, it was back to England and a recording session in London. The journey back from Wiesbaden was pretty uneventful. I went back to Kimberley and Dave went back to Bolton, his home town.

Kimberley was a good place to be based for this job as it's only minutes away from the M1 and right in the centre of England so one can get almost anywhere within a few hours. There were several other continental tours. I remember one occasion in particular, when Eric had to stay behind in London to do some business and would be flying out later, while the rest of us would be driving through Germany to Northern Italy.

He asked Dave and me if we could take Pat (his wife) with us in the car. He gave us the address of a small hotel in Germany where we could stay en route, one that he had stayed at before on some previous trip. We eventually found this place in a back street. It was a bar on the ground floor with rooms above. We booked two rooms, one for Pat and one for Dave and me. We took our things up to the rooms and came down again to get something to eat in the bar. As we sat there I noticed that most of the other clientele were girls and the penny began to drop that we had booked into a brothel. What the management thought was going on between the three of us I can't imagine. I'm sure Eric could not have come to the same conclusion as us otherwise he wouldn't have sent us there.

We were en route to an American Base in Livorno, northern Italy as part of another tour of the American bases in Europe. We met up with Eric in Livorno. Later on, all four of us were sitting in a café in Livorno. It was around the time when mini-skirts were all the rage in Britain. Pat who was quite voluptuous was sitting near the window. We all know what young Italian men are like and before very long, there was a crowd standing outside trying to get a glimpse of Pat's thighs, because mini-skirts had not yet reached Italy! When we left the café it was a bit scary; I thought we were going to be mobbed at one stage.

Livorno is quite close to Pisa, so Dave and I took the opportunity to visit the Leaning Tower of Pisa, one of the wonders of the world. I like to make the most of any trips like this.

After the tour, I headed back to Nottingham for a few days, to recover before heading back to London to do a recording session with Eric and the famous American drummer Louie Bellson. Louie Bellson was deemed by Duke Ellington to be "the world's greatest musician". (Louie is his own preferred spelling but he is often listed as Louis.) The album is called *Repercussion* and it was made in 1967 at the Abbey Road Studios, later to become famous for the zebra crossing and all the Beatles records, not forgetting their genius producer, George Martin. This was the first time I had been in a recording studio, never mind being in the company of the great Louie Bellson. I was more than overwhelmed but put on a brave face, followed what the others did and tried to make out it was an everyday occurrence. I seem to remember it took two days to complete the record.

By this time, Tony, the guitar player was long gone. Instead, just for the recording, we were joined on tenor sax by Alan Skidmore, son of Jimmy Skidmore, a well-known jazz tenor player, of his time. I bought the album at the time and lent it to someone but never got it back so I can't remember all the titles of the tracks. One was "Skin Deep" which was Eric's feature, that we played every night in the cabaret, others were the theme from *633 Squadron* which was my favourite track on the whole album, the theme from *Lawrence of Arabia* and the "St Louis Blues March". Louie Bellson also favoured the double bass drum set up, as did Eric.

I do remember a duet between the two drummers, but for all the wrong reasons. This was one of Louie's arrangements and it meant the two drummers playing exactly the same. In fairness, they both had entirely different styles and it was hard for them both to adapt to one another's styles. While they battled away to get it right, the rest of us were sent to the canteen for a coffee. We came back and put the track down, finished the album and that was it.

After writing this piece about the album last night, I decided to search on the internet for 'Tracks on Eric Delaney Louie Bellson Repercussion'. The whole album was found and I listened to it again, for the first time in years. I thought it was a bit scrappy but if you're interested, you could hear it on your computer.

I can't remember the exact chain of events following making the record, but we probably did some more cabaret in the clubs before doing a theatre tour sponsored by Ovaltine.

15 - THEATRE TOURS WITH ERIC DELANEY

I mentioned the theatre tours earlier. The tours usually happened about twice a year. They were basically variety shows that covered most of the big theatres in towns up and down the country, and were sponsored by Ovaltine.

The cast was basically the same each time, with the odd change occasionally. Tommy Trinder was usually the compere, along with the obligatory six dancing girls, a two-girl speciality magic act, featuring dogs and pigeons, a comedy group, which was sometimes the Dallas Boys and at other times it might have been the Three Monarchs, a comedy harmonica trio and last but not least, a satirist called Peter Hudson.

Of course, also billed were ourselves, the Eric Delaney Band, who not only opened and closed the show, but had our own spot, to open the second half of the show, after the interval.

One of my earlier bandleaders nicknamed me 'The Evil One'. I do have a devilish streak in me and have played a few dastardly tricks during my life, especially on some of the acts we played for.

On one of these tours, the Three Monarchs were subjected to two of these tricks of mine. They all played harmonicas of different shapes and sizes. At the end of one of their renditions, the clown of the trio, whose name was Cedric pressed a button on the end of his harmonica and a bird popped up. I put a condom over the bird's head one day, so when he pressed the button the next time, the bird popped up with a condom on its head. The look on his face was priceless.

They also did another comedy number, involving drinking water. They had three glasses of water on a table behind them, trying not to let the audience see. The second and third person with their backs to the audience would secretly take a drink of water and hold it in their mouth.

The first one in the row would then blatantly take a drink of water for all to see. The one in the middle, who is already holding some water in his mouth, gargled and Cedric, at the other end, spits his out. On one occasion, we put a strong solution of salt in Cedric's water because he had to hold it in his mouth for the longest time before spitting it out. Fortunately, they took it all in good part, but they knew that it was the band who were responsible.

The two-girl magic act, featuring my friends was billed as 'Anna-Lou and Maria' where 'Anna-Lou' was the stage name of Anna Lou Daybell, an actress then professional magician. 'Maria' was the stage name for the other girl. Over the years, there were a number of 'Maria's, but this one's real name was Marion Way, and she retained the name Marion off-stage. They kept their magic props at the side of the stage. I was pretty curious to see how the illusion worked. I was looking at the props one day, in the wings of the stage, when Maria caught me and gave me a slap. I'm sure you will be aware how magicians like to protect their illusions. I watched them from the back many times but still never managed to solve the mystery.. This is how the sequence went: Maria would place a small white Chihuahua in one end of a tube, and a black Chihuahua would come out the other end. They would then put the small black dog in a washing machine. Not only did it come out white, but it had turned into a white German Shepherd dog. The Shepherd dog would then be put into a spin dryer and it came out as a big fluffy Standard Poodle. It was a good act and the public loved it.

The finale to the act was to black out the theatre except for two spotlights on the girls standing at the front of the stage, with their arms stretched out at their sides. A flock of coloured pigeons was released from the back of the upper circle. It's well-known that birds always fly to the light, and the spot lights were on the two girls with outstretched arms. As soon as the birds landed on their arms, the band would strike up with their playoff music. The girls would take a bow, and leave the stage, with the birds still on their outstretched arms. It was a very colourful and different act.

We worked with the girls quite a lot over the years and I got to know them very well. All three of us had the same love for animals. Roughly eighteen months later, we joined forces and bought a smallholding together and that turned out to be a saga in itself.

I don't quite remember the exact chain of events after the theatre tour finished. We probably did some more clubs. We usually started at a new club on a Sunday evening and would do a three-quarters of an hour spot every night. That was all the playing we did until the next evening. We did that every night for a week, finishing on Saturday night, then on to the next club, to start again somewhere else on the Sunday. It was a cushy job in some ways but when you're on the road, staying in digs in a strange bed in a place in the middle of winter there's not much to do and it can be a long day. Never the less, it was a great job to have. I would think to myself, "How lucky is that little boy from a village in Nottinghamshire, doing the kind of job he'd been working for all those years, slogging at his practice."

On a brighter note, we had a summer season to look forward to, with Morecambe and Wise in my favourite town of Bournemouth. Eric Delaney had rented a big house for the season, not far from where I live now. We all had our own rooms and lived together during that summer. We took it in turns to take Eric and his wife tea in bed each morning, but we always had to knock and wait for Eric to put on his wig before we opened the door. He was very self-conscious of his bald head, so you can imagine how he would have felt to have made an exhibition of himself in front of us all.

The whole of the cast had one week's rehearsal before we opened the show. The band was all togged up in their new white suits, all ready to go.

Also on the bill were the New Seekers and Semprini, the pianist, who had his own programme on the radio, *Semprini Serenade*. His trade mark opening introduction was 'old ones, new ones, loved ones, neglected ones'. (His first name was Alberto, which I found a bit incongruous against the name Semprini.) He was a lovely down-to-earth kind of man, who was very friendly. He owned a boat that he usually kept on the Thames and he had sailed it round to Pocle and moored it there for the summer. The compere was Michael Bentine, from *The Goon Show*. Finally, we had the obligatory girl dancers and, to top the bill, it was Eric and Ernie - Eric Morecambe and Ernie Wise (Wiseman.)

We were on stage all night, on a raised platform and apart from doing our own spot we were mostly behind a gauze curtain. We opened the second half of the show with "Manhattan Spiritual", followed by a Herb Alpert tune called "Lonely Bull", a haunting piece of music, that I particularly liked playing. Eric and Ernie did the whole of the second half of the show and made us all laugh every night. Looking back, it seems incredible now to think that there were three theatres in Bournemouth. There was the Pavilion Theatre starring Matt Munro, the Pier Theatre and the Winter Gardens, starring Morecambe & Wise. All played to packed audiences, twice nightly.

The Winter Gardens has since been pulled down. The Pier Theatre is now an adventure place for kids and even the Pavilion doesn't have a summer show any more; it only has one-night attractions. How the entertainment business has changed over the years!

Eric Delaney had brought his speedboat with him to Bournemouth for the summer. He liked water-skiing, and would also take the band with him, taking us out and teaching us to water-ski. We learned to drive the boat as well. That was great fun, and having the privilege to do it in the first place was another skill I was able to learn. Two people would have to be in the boat; one to drive the boat and the other to watch, in case the skier fell off. Sometimes, Eric and one other would be in the boat, which Eric would drive, while we took it in turns to ski. How lucky we all were. We were all novices, but Eric was much more accomplished, being able to just use one ski, whereas we had to use them both.

One day, while my parents were down on holiday, we were skiing from the beach and it was a fairly rough sea, when Eric decided he wanted to try to use just the one ski. After a few failed attempts he managed to get off on the one ski but didn't get very far out before he came off. Eric disappeared under the water which left just his wig floating on the top. Ian Fenby, who was looking out of the boat dived in and grabbed hold of the floating wig, holding it up high, exclaiming,

"Here it is, Eric!" and the very first thing Eric did was to plonk his wet soaking wig on his bald head which made him look like a drowned rat. He seemed very self-conscious about anyone seeing him without his wig yet we all knew he had one anyway. My parents were sitting on the beach watching all of this and my mother was in hysterics at the scene she had just witnessed.

Half way through the summer season, my cousin, Peter came down for his annual fortnight's holiday from Rolls-Royce. He stayed in my room on a blow-up mattress and whilst he was in Bournemouth, he would help out back stage with scenery etc. He thought it was very glamorous, so much so, that he stupidly abandoned his apprenticeship with Rolls-Royce to become Eric's roadie. When the summer season came to an end, he drove Eric's van and humped the equipment around for the rest of band. Dave Smith, the organist nicknamed him 'Peter the plastic humper'. It wasn't very kind, but there was nothing I could do about it. His mother was less than pleased, to say the least. Not only had he thrown away his apprenticeship with Rolls-Royce but he was running round after me and all the rest of the band; she didn't like that at all.

When the summer season came to an end, it was back on the road again, cabaret clubs, American bases, back to Germany, another theatre tour with the Ovaltine show. That's how it went on until the next summer season with Morecambe and Wise in Great Yarmouth. The rest of the cast were all different supporting artists for this show except for Anna-Lou & Maria, the two girl illusionists with the dogs, and a ventriloquist called Saveen, with a talking dog.

I can't for the life of me remember any of the other artist's names but there was Ivor Emmanuel, a Welsh tenor, with a very good voice, also a husband and wife folk-singing duo, and finally the usual girl dancers.

During the first week's rehearsal, Saveen, the ventriloquist used a live dog instead of the usual dummy. While rehearsing, he would go through his act, making a point of saying to the band,

"When the dog's on stage, I don't want any noise from the band."

That was like a red rag to a bull for me, and my devilish horns came out. As soon as we had finished rehearsals for the day, I went out and bought one of those dog whistles, that has such a high pitched sound which humans can't hear but dogs can. When Saveen came on stage to do his act for the first time after rehearsals and the show had started with an audience, I sat in the pit, blowing my head off on the whistle as hard as I could. Much to my surprise and disappointment, the dog didn't even bat an eyelid. Soon after he had finished his act, Saveen appeared at the pit door and said,

"Alright, who's the clever dick with the whistle?"

I couldn't believe it; he'd heard it but the dog hadn't.

Towards the end of the season, Saveen and I became quite friendly and one day he told me he would like to learn to play the sax and asked if I would give him some lessons. I agreed and we set off in his large 1960s frog-eyed Citroën with the air suspension; you may remember the model, the Citroën DS.

We found him a suitable saxophone and I began to give him lessons in his dressing room, before the show. After the lessons, we would probably have a beer, while he got changed in front of me, but before he prepared the dog I had to leave, as he didn't want me to find out the secret of his act.

It's only supposition on my part but I think he must have given the dog some kind of tranquiliser to keep it doped, because it always sat perfectly still on a pedestal during the act and never moved a muscle. The dog was a wire-haired terrier. The breed in general, had long hair from their jaws which, I presumed, he would use to cover up the mechanical apparatus below the real jaw. I can only assume that he had some kind of wire connection between himself and the dog so he could make the mechanism open and close, to make it look as if the dog was talking back to him. I'll never know the answer to that. I couldn't see whether or not it was operated by a switch under his foot, because we were in the pit below the stage, unable to see anything.

We opened the second half of the show on stage. Then, during the time we were scuttling back into the pit, the compere would entertain the audience for a few minutes, before introducing Eric & Ernie, to do the rest of the show. We were doing the show twice nightly and by the time we were about half-way through the season, we had a competition to see who could be the first to memorise the whole of the show without reading any of the music, keeping our music folders closed. The keyboard player was the first to achieve the goal. One night he brought his portable television in the pit with him so he could watch it while still playing his music.

Most of you will have been in a theatre sometime or another, so try to picture this: The audience sits facing the stage. The orchestra pit has a wall between the front row of the audience and the stage. Hidden behind that wall is the orchestra, but the audience can't see them. The keyboard player had placed his TV with its back to the pit wall, on our side, so the audience couldn't see it. But the screen was facing the stage. When Eric and Ernie came on to do their act, they could see the TV as well. As soon as the curtain came down, Eric Morecambe popped his head through the pit door and said, "Do you mind not watching the TV while we're on. I wouldn't mind, but the TV programme was more interesting than what we were doing on stage." Needless to say, the TV wasn't seen again.

This was also the summer when we all bought our own touring caravans to alleviate the need for digs, when we were on the road. Dave Smith, the keyboard player was the first to buy one, followed by me, then everyone else in the band realised what a good idea it was and gradually we all had our own little homes to take with us, wherever we went. I can't remember the make of Dave's caravan but I had a Safari, Ian Fenby and Phil Chapman had Sprite Majors and Eric and his wife, Pat had a Carlite Cruiser, which was top of the range at the time.

It was a brilliant idea of Dave's to get a caravan in the first place. They had so many advantages when constantly on the road and, during the summer, it was great to be able to open the door in the morning and to just step outside. The early caravans had only Calor Gas for heating and lights. The lights used the old gas mantles which are obsolete now, but Dave and I had ours professionally wired for electricity, which was much better. At the front there were single beds down each side. Towards the back was a wardrobe on one side where we could hang all our clothes up instead of having to live out of a suitcase, when we had been on the road before. On the opposite side to the wardrobe was a unit with cupboards and drawers. Across the back were a separate chemical toilet and a so-called kitchen, which consisted of two gas rings with a grill underneath and a sink with just one cold water tap. The water was in a container outside and I had to pump the water into the tap with a foot pump. It was pretty basic compared to today's modern caravans. If I needed hot water, I had to boil a kettle on the stove. I would wash my clothes and boil my whites in a galvanised bucket, but that was caravanning 50 years ago. It was just as well that I'd learned to cook on a two-ring stove a few years earlier, in the bedsit, during my time in London; it gave me a head start. I was still only 24 or 25 years old. None of this mattered, as I was having much more fun and life experience that most people of my age ever did and probably the same still applies to the youngsters of today.

Before the end of the season, my cousin Peter had realised the big mistake he'd made and he returned home. He couldn't get his job back at

Rolls-Royce, but managed to get a job with JCB, the heavy machinery company.   He re-joined the rock group he had been in before, on guitar, so he was set up. I did see him again once or twice, when we had a few days off whilst back home with my parents.

A year or so later, he broke up with his girlfriend and was so heart-broken by the break-up that he put his car in the garage, with a hose from the exhaust into the car and turned the engine on.   His mother found him before he became completely asphyxiated.   He didn't die, but his brain was so badly damaged that he never walked or talked again.   He had to be fed, washed and changed, living in a home until he was around fifty years old.   In the meantime, his mother had died and the only living relatives he had were my mother and me. I only saw him once during those years. He knew who I was, but couldn't communicate. He cried and I was so upset that I couldn't bear to see him again.

Since my mother died, I'm the last of the line, without any living relatives anywhere to my knowledge; no wife, no kids, just me.   However, I've had a most wonderful and fulfilling life, with no regrets or complaints; I'd do it all again.

As that summer season in Great Yarmouth began to draw to an end, two of the dancing girls approached Eric Delaney to ask if we would play through some music for them, as they were trying to form a singing duo. They were to be called Pat and Olivia and we played their arrangements for them, for which they were grateful and then we went our separate ways.

Some months later, the band was on the same theatre bill as The Shadows. Who could it be, hanging out with The Shadows but Olivia? We had a few words with her and that was the last I heard of her, until she starred with John Travolta in *Grease*. So I can say I knew Olivia Newton-John when she was just one of the dancers on a summer season in Great Yarmouth. All her early experience of dancing and singing paid dividends in the end; it is strange where life will lead.

Sadly, the summer season came to an end. The cast went their individual ways and the band set off for a new adventure in their caravans, back to the variety club circuit. Each time we arrived at a new club, the first thing to do would be to find a socket to plug into the club electricity. We became like a band of traveling gypsy minstrels.

I can't remember the strict order of the clubs or in fact where we went next but the one club which sticks out in my memory was the club at Brighouse. Many of you will have heard of the Brighouse and Rastrick brass band. Their headquarters where they practised were in Brighouse. While our band was at the club, I went to one of their rehearsals. I'm not really into brass bands but the sound they made in that room was beautiful. We've all heard the phrase it made my hair stand on end but that day the hairs on the back of my head stood up and I had shivers down my back. Neither before nor since, have had I had that same feeling when listening to music. The Brighouse club was a small converted cinema. We'd been there before, but this was the first time I'd had a caravan with me. What was very useful, both in Brighouse and also in other clubs was to be able go into the club during the mornings when the cleaners were there and to have a good wash in hot water.

We also did a theatre tour with Max Bygraves. Max had his own musical director, who was with him all the time. His name was Bob Dixon. During rehearsals, Bob was the one who would run us through the act. If there were any queries, they had to be directed through Bob, and if Max wanted to say something to the band, instead of telling us directly he would instruct Bob to tell us. It was a strange way to go about things. I've never come across that before or since. Despite all the smarm when he was on stage, coming across as 'Mr nice guy' he wasn't really a friendly man with the band at all. If we passed him in a corridor, back stage, he would put his head down and look at the floor as he passed. Musicians don't expect to be big buddies with the stars but usually they would give you the time of day; it's only polite. It's also usually the custom for the star of the show to give the band a crate of beer or a bottle of whisky at the end of a tour. But Max was too mean to even buy a bottle of beer and six straws. I used to live about four minutes' walk away from Max in a place called Westbourne which is west of Bournemouth, between Bournemouth and Poole. It's as close as you can get to a village in this area.

I would often see Max in his Rolls-Royce with the number plate MB1. I believe that Mercedes Benz offered him a huge amount of money for that number plate but he wouldn't sell. Max also had another car with the number plate MAX1. The road from Westbourne to where Max lived is called Alumhurst Road. On that road was a guesthouse called Linger Longa. Max would have to pass this guesthouse every time he went out, and my thought is that is where he got the idea for his series called Singa Longa Max.

There were also the autumn tour Ovaltine shows, around about the same time, during which Anna-Lou found a two-and-a-half acre smallholding advertised in the *Exchange and Mart* for only £3,000. We went to see it, but it was in a pretty rundown state. The house was uninhabitable, as the previous owner had kept sheep upstairs, chickens in the lounge and a pig in the kitchen. The smallholding was called Cherry Holt. The word 'holt' means a small wood or copse. As well as the house itself, it also came with a barn and two stables. It was situated in a small village called Clarborough, just outside Retford in Nottinghamshire. The property was accessed via a gated railway crossing to which only the owner of the property had keys and each time we wanted to take a vehicle across the track we had to ring the signal box for permission. There wasn't any electricity or mains water. That could have been a big problem, but we were able to cope with that for the time being, as we all had our own caravans to live in. There is farming in my genes somewhere and I was as keen as the two girls, so we went through the usual channels and bought it. The girls hadn't enough money. I had some savings, so offered to buy the place and they would pay me back. We all had our names on the deeds but Anna-Lou (Anna-Lou Daybell) and Maria (Marion Way) were the first two names on the deeds and I was placed at the bottom. How green was I? I always suspected that Anna-Lou could be gay, as she was definitely very much the dominant one, although I never saw any evidence of that side of her. I know Maria wasn't, as we had sex a few times but it wasn't ever anything serious. We all carried on with our respective careers until the spring. I continued doing the cabaret clubs with the band.

If we were doing clubs in and around Manchester, we would sometimes do two different clubs in one night, which meant breaking everything down after the first performance and trekking over town somewhere, only to carry it all in, set up and do it all over again. By this time we weren't reading any new music; it was the same few tunes over and over again. We would stand behind our music desks with our folders closed, on automatic pilot.

I was in a job I enjoyed but I began to realise that musically I wasn't actually making any progress. I felt that I needed a new challenge. By sheer coincidence, Eric told me that Ronnie Asprey, his former alto player had expressed an interest in returning to the band, which suited me fine, so by mutual consent I left the band, but not before telling Eric that I would be happy to re-join the band again if Ronnie left. That was exactly what happened. A year or so later Ronnie left and I went back.

16 - TAKING A BREAK - 1969

After the Delaney tour, I was now freelance for the time being and available for any work I could get. The musical director of Belle Vue, Manchester heard that I was no longer with Eric Delaney and he contacted me to see if I was available to do some work for him. His name was Derek Butterworth. Derek and I knew one another from the past and he was now responsible for providing musicians for the Circus and Theatre in Belle Vue, Manchester. He also had a band in a club in Manchester itself, called the Golden Garter. Between all of those venues he was able to give me quite a lot of casual work. One of the first things I did for Derek was in the Belle Vue theatre, playing for the popular star of the 1940s / 1950s, Donald Peers. His signature tune was called "In a Shady Nook, by a Babbling Brook".

I remember listening to him, singing that song on the radio, when I was still a little boy at home. I liked the song and it felt quite nostalgic sitting on the same stage, playing that song for him. He was still popular and his final hit record was called "Please Don't Go" in 1969.

I also did a few weeks at the Golden Garter Club. One particular week, the star was Eartha Kitt. Her act was very sultry. Before I actually met her, I hadn't been particularly keen on her, when I had watched her on the TV, but she was really nice in person and I talked to her a lot during that week. Her famous song was "I'm just an old fashioned girl, with an old fashioned mind … and an old fashioned millionaire". I have good memories of that week. Incidentally, I didn't know until I was researching Belle Vue, that it was closed in 1982 and has since been demolished to make way for a housing estate.

Spring was turning towards summer and I heard of a summer season in Brixham, Devon. I only had to mention to the bandleader that I had been working in the Eric Delaney band and the job was mine. Eric's name was also able to open other doors for me in the years to come. Everything stemmed from being in the right place at the right time, playing on that TV *Come Dancing* programme from the Lyceum, with the Tony Evans band. In Brixham, the band was made up of mainly young musicians making their way through life the same as I was. The bandleader's name was Keith Monk. He was a very good pianist and I was later able to recommend Keith and the trumpet player Tony Wally for the Eric Delaney band and we worked together again for a while with Eric, a couple of years later. The name of the drummer in Keith's band was Alan Boynton, with whom I also worked, some years later, in a West End society band in London, so Keith's band had some pretty good musicians even then.

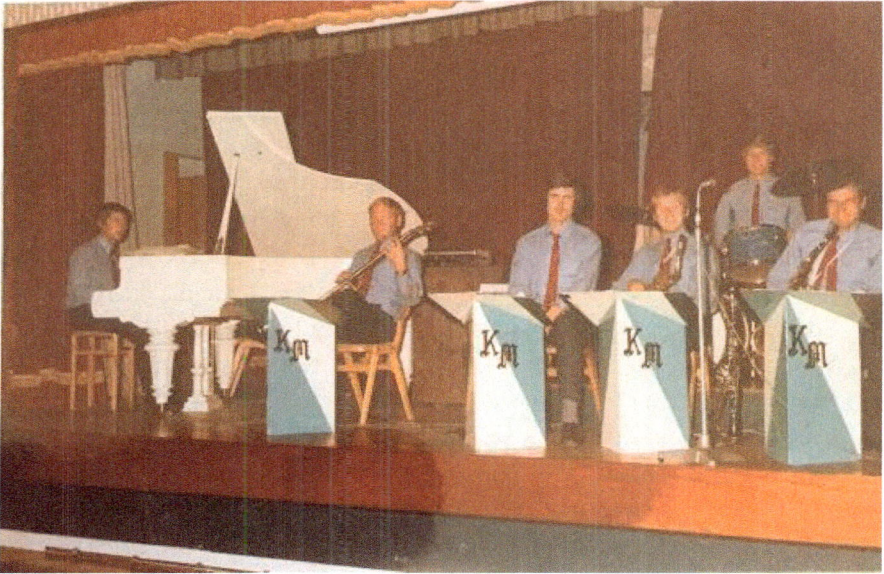

I enjoyed my time in Brixham. I had my caravan in a small site, in a farmer's field. The summer is great for a caravan. Just open the door and you have summer on your doorstep. As well as lazing by the holiday camp swimming pool during the day, I enjoyed exploring parts of Devon and Dartmoor. Brixham is on the south bank of the river Dart. On the north side of the river is the naval town of Dartmouth, which can be accessed by a ferry across the river Dart from Brixham. Overlooking the river Dart, the author, Agatha Christie had a house, now open to the public, which I have visited.

Somewhere in between these engagements, I would try to spend some time at the small-holding, trying to clean the place up a bit and helping the builder to fix the roof on the barn and outbuildings, in order to make them watertight while Anna-Lou and Maria were in Blackpool, at the Queen's Theatre, doing the 1968 summer season with Englebert Humperdinck, earning some money, to pay me back for my loan, or so I thought. No such luck; they had spent the money already and came back with a horse instead. Not only that, but they wanted to put the deeds of the property up as security on a loan to build loose boxes for horses. I flatly refused and that was the beginning of a break-up of the trio. I got my money back eventually, at the end of a pantomime that we did together in Nottingham. That was another lesson I learned; as my father would say, "It's all part of life's rich pattern."

At the end of the season in Brixham, I was invited as part of a band to play for a short tour, promoting the then new Vauxhall Astra car. Touring wasn't a problem for me, as I had my caravan. Keith and I kept in touch and the following summer, I did another Pontins holiday camp in Weymouth, Dorset.

I knew Anna-Lou and Maria were doing the pantomime in Nottingham the following Christmas (1969), so I wrote to Eric Tan, the agent for the theatres and got a place in the theatre orchestra for the Christmas period, so I could keep close to the two girls and make sure I got my money back at the end of the panto. During the panto, I was also able to stay at home with my parents in Kimberley, which was a bonus.

There were a lot of political issues in that pit orchestra. The local musicians didn't like any outsiders coming in to poach their jobs and I received a hostile reception from the start. One of the trombone players was the local Musicians' Union official and he pulled me up right away for being a month in arrears with my stamps. I was made to feel so uncomfortable, that I didn't go into the band room again for the whole pantomime. I just used to sit in the pit all the time during the intervals and silently practise my flute. As you might imagine, there was a lot of flute work in the pantomime, as it was the *Pied Piper*. The other trombone player was the conductor of the Nottingham City Police Band, in which I had played as a teenager, yet he disowned me as well. The other sax players tried to give me a hard time, so in the end I just kept my head down and did the job. Their attitude was just petty provincial jealousy.

However, I did have one buddy in the orchestra. He was a young guitar player from London. His name was Dave McQuater. His father was Tommy McQuater, a well-known trumpet player, who had played with the Ted Heath band and was now a top session musician along with the very well-known Kenny Baker, one of the best trumpet players this country has ever produced.

Our day off from the pantomime was Sunday, and one such weekend, Dave asked me if I would like to go to London and stay for a couple of nights with his parents. We drove down after the show on Saturday night and I was shown to my room when we got to his house. The next morning my breakfast was brought to my room by none-other than Tommy McQuater himself, a man who I had known of by name for years and here he was serving me breakfast in bed. It was surreal.

On Sunday, the band was recording the Tom Jones TV show, from the studios at Elstree. Dave and I went along to watch. This was at the time when Tom Jones was at the height of his popularity. As the show was also being televised for America, it had to be recorded twice. This was because the American TV system (NTSC) was different to ours in the UK (PAL), much to do with the number of scan lines that make up the TV image (525 for NTSC and 625 for PAL) but also the different number of frames per second, related to the old analogue cathode-ray tube TVs operating on either the electric mains frequency of 60Hz (USA) or 50Hz (UK).This meant the band members were getting extra money for recording the shows twice, plus, every time they were repeated, they would get repeat fees as well. You imagine how many times the show would be repeated in all the states in America. Elstree studios were known at the time by other musicians as 'Fort Knox' as it was a licence to print money and it was the best paid musician's job in the country.

Dave had been brought up with most of these guys and they were almost like uncles to him. He introduced me to the great trumpet player Kenny Baker and left me to make conversation, while he shot off to chat to someone else. I was speechless. What can you say to a music legend, who has done it all? It was embarrassing for me, to say the least.

On Monday morning, it was back to Nottingham, for the matinee performance of the pantomime. As the end of the pantomime run was approaching, I began my request for the money owed to me by the two girls. Anna-Lou was most nasty and said,

"You'll have to take us to court to get your money."

She could be a real bitch at times. After some to-ing and fro-ing, I got my £3,000 back but with neither interest nor covering any of the money I had spent paying the builder. Anna-Lou took me for the mug that I was.

In 1970, shortly after the pantomime had finished, I got a call from Eric Delaney's agent in Wiesbaden, Germany, asking if I could take a small band to Germany and Turkey, to accompany Nat King Cole's brother, Ike. He wanted a trio that included me as group leader but I needed drums and an organ.

I knew a man who had a modern electric accordion with the entire electronic organ sounds built in. It sounded just like an organ and he was also able to play the bass line with his right hand at the same time, just as any accordion player would do. It sounded good but looked wrong and very old-fashioned. I don't think Ike was too impressed with the image of the trio but it sounded good and that was all that mattered to me.

The three of us flew into Wiesbaden and made our way to the German office to collect a Ford Transit people carrier. I was given some money upfront, to cover expenses, like fuel and any problems relating to the Transit and general expenses. The other two guys were paid half their fee, the rest to be paid on our return to Wiesbaden.

We did one or two bases on the way towards the border. On our way to Turkey, we had to drive through Yugoslavia, which was still behind the 'iron curtain' then. I was told that whatever happened, I had to bring the van back, because if we left it there, the office would never be able to retrieve it.

So, we set off for our first meeting with Ike Cole. He didn't travel with us, as he had a private car at his disposal while we were in Germany. He flew to Turkey - lucky chap; for us the drive seemed endless. Ike sounded just like his brother, Nat King Cole, and played the piano as well. If you closed your eyes, you couldn't tell the difference between the two brothers. Needles to say, the American servicemen loved him.

When we got to the Turkish border, we were met by a local Turkish driver who knew the roads and how to drive on them. I'm sure they are much improved in the last 45 years since we were there and believe me they needed to be. The ruts were crossways to the road and it was like driving over a road of railway sleepers. If you drove too slowly, it would have been like riding the waves in a small boat, up and down, up and down. The best way to do it was to drive so fast that you could just skip across the top of the ruts. The driver knew exactly what he was doing but it was a bit hairy to say the least.

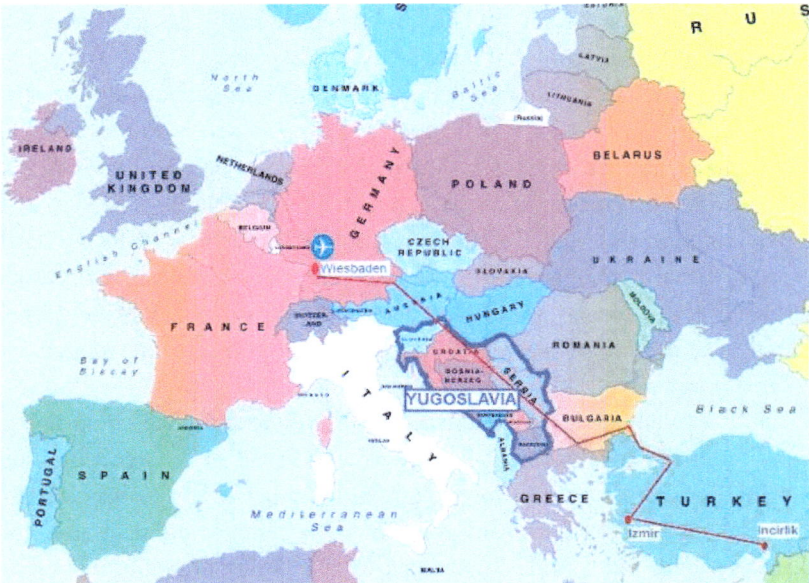

He stayed with us until we got back to the border, after the shows in Turkey. We did two bases in Turkey (Incirlik & Izmir) with two performances in each base. I had a scary moment in one of the enlisted men's clubs. We opened the show with the classic saxophone solo, "Yakaty Sax". What I hadn't realised was that "Yakaty Sax" is a country and western white man's kind of music and the enlisted men wanted more of a rhythm and blues/rock type of music.

I was out in the front, trying to make a show of the solo and this 6ft black guy stood right in front of me giving me the most evil stare I've ever seen, as much as to say, how dare you play country and western music in here. He scared the living daylights out of me, but the show had to go on, as they say.

When the shows in Turkey were over, it was the long trek home. The local driver took us back to the Yugoslavian border, and from there on, we were on our own.

We were trying to get as far as we could before finding somewhere to stay. It was just turning dusk when we put the van lights on. No sooner had we switched them on and a police car pulled us over to tell us we had a headlight out and we must stay in a car-park till the next morning. We couldn't understand one another's language but that's what it amounted to, so we stayed there all night and the police car kept driving by, checking on us through the night, to make sure we were still there. It was so cold in the van that we had the heater on, but only occasionally, so as not to flatten the battery. It was so cold that none of us had any sleep.

As soon as dawn broke, we set off. I was supposed to be in charge of the van and driving but I was much too tired to drive, so the young drummer said he would drive instead. We had the heater on and I soon fell asleep. I was awakened by a loud crash, as we had hit a bollard at the side of the road. The radiator was staved in and the van wouldn't make it to the border. The police were there again in a flash and were accusing us of falling asleep at the wheel. The drummer said he'd swerved to miss a deer but they'd heard it all before and weren't having any of that! We couldn't understand what each other was saying but we got the gist.

Eventually, they led us to a hotel where someone could speak English and interpret for us. I kept insisting that we had hit a deer. This kept going backwards and forwards for so long and neither side was backing down until the girl behind the desk said you would be better to admit it and end this. So that's what I did. I think I had to pay a fine which probably went straight into their pockets and away they went.

Now, the problem was the van, bearing in mind what I had been told about getting the van back to the border at any cost. It would have been late morning / midday by this time. There was a garage just across the road from the hotel and the girl spoke to the manager and they said they could get us on the road. They took the front off of the van and proceeded to solder all the holes up in the radiator. Bearing in mind that we were in a communist-run country, there were no spare Ford Transit radiators on the shelf. They worked all through the afternoon and when it got to about six o'clock in the evening, it still wasn't finished but the men worked on into the early night until it was finished. They supplied us with the equivalent of Radweld and off we went. I had phoned the office in Wiesbaden and arranged that someone would meet us at the border with a fresh van. Of course, I had to pay the garage out of the money I'd been given. We made it back to the border, changed vans and went off to finish the tour without any more problems. When we eventually got back to the office in Wiesbaden and the money was sorted out, there wasn't any for me; it had all been spent on the van. I couldn't believe how I was being treated after I'd got their van back. I said, "You'll never see me back here again and they didn't". Thus it ended, with me doing all of that for nothing.

17 - BACK HOME FROM TURKEY

I was completely exhausted when I got back from the Ike Cole tour, so I took some time off to recover but it wasn't long before the phone was ringing again. This time it was from an English agent, asking me if I could put a band together for a short tour of England, promoting the American Chrysler cars. The request was for a six-piece band, the same size as Eric Delaney's band. The combination was two saxes; one trumpet, piano, bass and drums.

I borrowed some music from my dad and off we all went. Everything went well and was totally uneventful and it kept the wolf from the door.

That Easter, I travelled down to Dorset, to start a summer season with Keith Monk at the Osmington Bay holiday camp just outside Weymouth. Apart from Keith and me, the rest of the members of the band were all new faces to me. The Tenor sax player was Jim Roberts, with Baz on Trumpet and Mike Grigg playing the Drums. Most members of the band were staying on the camp, but I had my caravan on a site in a small village called Warmwell, just outside Weymouth.

It was a pretty uneventful season as far as I can remember, except for the fact that Keith, Mike Grigg and I were to work together again in the future. Keith Monk was quite friendly with the entertainment executive for the Fred Pontin organisation and she offered us a free two-week holiday, at a Pontins hotel at Torremolinos in Spain. Only Mike Grigg and I were able to go on the holiday, so the two of us flew out to Spain, for what we thought was going to be a relaxing two-week holiday. Since he was a drummer himself, Mike and I were talking about Eric Delaney on the plane. A couple sitting in the seats in front of us heard us talking about Eric. The wife turned round to us saying they loved to see Eric Delaney when his band came to Club Ba-Ba in Barnsley, which was where they lived. We had played in that club a few times with the band, so she must have seen me working. Club Ba-Ba was more of a variety club, just a bit more up-market than a working men's club. When Mike and I got to the hotel, we found that the couple from Barnsley was also staying at the same hotel, so we would sometimes have drinks with them in the evenings. Before we went to Spain, I had been asked to take my sax with me but I thought the management just wanted me to play with the resident band.

However, no sooner had we got there that we were told we had to cover for the resident band on their night off. There isn't much one can do with just drums and sax but fortunately Mike could play a bit of guitar, so he borrowed one and we cobbled something together. Mike and I were sharing a room together. It wasn't long before he found himself a young lady. One day he said to me, "I don't mind the fact that you're gay but I would like to bring my girl up to the room". The problem was she was also with someone else and it was difficult to split them up. He asked me if I would take the other one off his hands for an hour while he had his wicked way. I wasn't too keen, but sometimes a man has to do what a man has to do! I didn't fancy mine but I helped him out, while he was busy.

Mine turned out to be married with three kids, but she was quick to let me know that she had had a hysterectomy. I got down to the job I was there for and afterwards she had the cheek to say,
"You're not bad for a gay bloke".

I was also spending some time talking with the couple from Barnsley. One evening, I was having a drink by myself in the quiet bar when the wife appeared. It was soon apparent that she was after my body. I wasn't interested in her, so, in order to put her straight, I told her that I was more interested in Dennis her husband. Even that didn't do the trick, and undeterred, she proceeded to tell me that when they were at home, both her and Dennis had one night a week that they each went out on their own with no questions asked. I seem to remember that we both joined Dennis for drinks, to finish off the rest of the evening.

A few nights later, I was invited to go out to a restaurant in the town for a meal with them. When the taxi came, Dennis sat in the passenger seat and I sat in the back with June. As soon as we set off, she put her hand out to hold mine, I thought, "O.M.G. what's she up to?" With Dennis sitting in the front seat, I was trapped so I had to go along with the evening. When we got back to the hotel after the meal, I was invited up to their room for a nightcap. While Dennis was preparing the drinks, June took me out on the balcony, to watch the sunset. I must say, it was a romantic sight, to watch the sun going down over the horizon. We both stood there with our hands on the balcony looking out to sea when she put her hand on mine. Fortunately for me, Dennis called us in for the drinks.

They both lay on the bed and invited me to join them, so I sat on the edge of the bed and I suddenly realised what might be going to happen next. Bearing in mind what June had told me at the bar a couple of nights before, I realised they were expecting a threesome. I'd never had a threesome before and didn't know what to expect. I was so scared; I was out of that room before you could say, "Jack Robinson". Looking back, if something like that happened now, I would jump at the chance! We kept in touch by post for a while but the mail just fizzled out in the end.

While I was back in Kimberley, after my return from Spain, I received a surprise phone call one day from Eric Delaney, to say that Ronnie Aspery was leaving the band and Eric asked if I would like my old job back, and could I start the next Monday, to do the last week of a summer season in Bournemouth with Ken Dodd. I was free and so it was that I returned to Eric's band. He had kept his word and I was able to keep mine.

18 - BACK WITH ERIC
~ After a short break ~

I felt refreshed after my short break and had packed in a lot of experience during my time away. There was just one change to the line-up and that was the bass player. Ian Fenby and Phil Chapman were the same and Dave Smith was still on the organ. It felt like coming home, but the personnel were soon to change. Dave Smith left to take up a post as a Hammond organ demonstrator in America and Ian Fenby was offered a good job on the continent, with a well-known bandleader, whose name escapes me.

I mentioned Keith Monk to Eric. He was the bandleader I'd recently worked with in Weymouth. I also recommended Tony Wally, the trumpet player from Manchester, who I'd worked with in Brixham, a couple of summers before. They both joined the band, so we were good to go.

The band continued as before, with the clubs, up and down the country. One week, we were playing at a club in a Yorkshire town called Spennymoor. I remembered Diane Peters, a dancer in the first summer season that I had done with Eric's band in Bournemouth, of which I reminded her.

On the same bill was a then unknown singing duo called Peters and Lee. A couple of years later, they had their big hit record with "Welcome Home". During the time that "Welcome Home" was at the top of the record charts, I was working in London with the Johnny Howard Band. This was the band I had listened to, with my parents in the Empire Ballroom, Leicester Square, a few years earlier, and was when I had made up my mind that I would be in that band one day.

We were doing an engagement in Holloway Prison for women. Myra Hindley stood right at the back, flanked by two prison officers. (Myra was an English serial killer, who, in partnership with her abusive lover, Ian Brady, had committed the 'Moors murders' – the rapes and murders of five small children.) So, what did John play? It was "Welcome Home" - not exactly the most tactful choice of songs to play for someone in prison!

Eric's band continued with some more clubs, until we were scheduled to do the American bases in England. Most of them were in and around East Anglia, which included Mildenhall, Bentwater and Alconbury along with other bases in the area.

I was listening to a heavy rock group in an enlisted men's club, on one of the bases. They had long hair down to their shoulders and called themselves The Moving Finger. (They had formerly been called The Anglians and sometimes were just Moving Finger.) They sounded really good, with a tight sound. I called Eric over to come to have a listen and he seemed more than interested in them himself.   Having forgotten who wrote *The Moving Finger*, I did an internet search and this is what came up:

The Moving Finger is taken from a quotation from the *Rubáiyát of Omar Khayyám* which is the title that Edward FitzGerald gave to his 1859 translation from Persian to English of a selection of quatrains (rubā'iyāt) attributed to Omar Khayyam (1048-1131). The relevant verse is:

The Moving Finger writes; and, having writ, Moves on:
nor all thy Piety nor Wit Shall lure it back to cancel half a Line,
Nor all thy Tears wash out a Word of it.

The 'moving finger writes, and having written, moves on' expresses the notion that whatever one does in one's life is one's own responsibility and cannot be changed. How profound is that? That saying is still around today in modern English as: 'You made your own bed, now lie in it'. Believe me; I've done that a few times in my life!

I have to admit to being a bit vague as to the chain of events that took place over the next couple of months, because things changed so quickly. However, this is how I remember things:

Keith Monk didn't take to the nomadic lifestyle and took a permanent job in a night club somewhere. After about three years on the road with Eric, Phil Chapman decided he wanted to settle down in Manchester, with his wife and young son. It meant that I was the only one left from the band that I had worked with before. I can only assume that Eric had been thinking about changing the image of the band after hearing Moving Finger on that American Base, some months before. The next thing I knew, he had booked the whole of Moving Finger, including the drummer, as his new band. I was the only one left from the previous band. The big problem was that they didn't read music; they played solely by ear. Moving Finger was based in Norwich. Eric asked me if I could go to Norwich for a week, to try to teach them the cabaret show, parrot fashion. I took my caravan to a site in Norwich and I tried my best to teach them but I didn't feel that I was getting very far. When Eric arrived later in the week, he was soon able to finish what I'd started; perhaps I'd done better that I thought. Every little helps, as they say. The names of the guys are Roy Bell, lead guitar, Ally Thorn, bass guitar, Brian Tatum, organ and Hilson Hatley, drums.

MOVING FINGER

Personal Management: Keith David
Banner Productions Ltd.,
13 Manvers Street,
Nottingham
Tel: Nottm. 50793/4

The cabaret show needed to be perfected and polished. The best way to do that was to take the new band on a tour of the American bases in Germany before presenting it to the British public. It was a really good group in its own way and although very different to anything I'd done before, it was still very pleasant to play with them. So, now we had two drummers and I wasn't needed to play the timps and to run around the stage, banging gongs any more; that was the new drummer's job. It also gave Eric the chance to play the two drum solo that he had done on the record with Louie Bellson. It was slightly amusing for me to watch Eric trying to teach Hilson (the other drummer) to play the solo without the written music to be able to follow. He was giving Hilson just as much grief as Louie Bellson had given him in the studio, some years before.

What was different on this tour to the previous ones I'd been on before was that Eric only came on the stage to do the cabaret show, while the rest of us had to play both before and after the show, for dancing, with Eric just sitting in the dressing room.

Although the group was very good in its own right, with harmony vocals and good material, a lot the repertoire consisted of twelve-bar blues. I will try to explain. The very basic twelve-bar blues is made up of only three chords: the tonic, the sub-dominant and the dominant.
As an example, in the key of C the twelve bars would be
C C C C
F F C C
G G C C

This sequence is then repeated over and over again.

Most early American pop songs were based on twelve-bar blues - that's why we called pop groups in England 'three chord wonders' in a derogatory way, because they didn't need to know much about music to make a hit record. That's all changed for the better now.

I became so exasperated, playing twelve-bar blues all night, while Eric was sitting in the dressing room that I stormed off of the stage, complained to Eric and sat down in the dressing room. He didn't say a word. The silence was deafening. I soon became more bored, sitting there doing nothing, so I went back on the stage with the boys. Eric definitely knew how to handle me. If he had told me to get back on that stage, I would have been going home on the next flight out.

We gradually started to do more complicated things, incorporating the sax. It took a while to improve the repertoire that included a sax but we got there in the end. We returned to England for a short break, in order to prepare for three months in Switzerland. Eric didn't have a roadie at the time. As we wouldn't be moving around so much, he asked me if I would be prepared to drive the van with all the equipment. I agreed, but only on the condition that I would not have to hump any of the equipment around. It was agreed that Moving Finger would take care of their equipment and would also deal with Eric's equipment at the same time, so I didn't have to do anything except drive the van and look after my saxophone.

By this time, I'd been on the continent a few times in my car or a small van but never with a large van full of musical instruments, which were classed as freight and therefore needed a customs carnet, describing exactly what was in the vehicle. I was told that if I encountered a particularly difficult customs officer, he could make me unload the lot to check it and then have to put it all back on my own. I duly picked up the van and set off with all the relative documents for Dover and over to France.

The van I was driving was the replacement for the original blue one which had been written off on the Autostrada in Italy, as mentioned in Chapter 14. It was a red, long-wheelbase Ford Transit van with a larger parcel body for the equipment. I arrived at the customs office at the port of Calais and proceeded to the office with all the papers, feeling more than a little nervous at the possibility of having to go through a search but I tried to look as if this was an everyday occurrence for me. I showed him the papers which he read carefully and then said in broken English "Are you in transit?"
I said "Yes, it's over there in the car park", turning and pointing to the Transit van, pictured here:

Ford Transit van

116

He looked at me, rather puzzled and asked the same question again. My first thought was that he was now going to make me unload the whole lot. Then it dawned on me what he meant. My final destination was Switzerland. I was only transiting through France. I felt such an idiot, but not having gone through all that when driving a car, I didn't know what to expect. It's all part of the 'University of Life'.

During the three months, we would be playing in night clubs called Hazyland, which was a chain of clubs run by the same person, who was apparently quite famous in Switzerland.

The first month was in Zurich. I seem to remember that the hours we worked were 10pm until 2am in the morning. We would play 4 three-quarters of an hour sets, with just 15 minutes break in-between each set. By the time we got to the dressing room, we just had time for a quick drink and it was back on the stage. Compared with the work we did in England this was slave labour. The band played each and every set, with Eric sitting in the dressing room, except for his three-quarter hour cabaret set, somewhere in the middle of the evening. It was still pleasantly warm in Switzerland during the summer months, even at 2 o'clock in the morning when we finished. My accommodation was about 15 minutes from the club and I could walk back each night in comfort.

As well as playing our own cabaret with Eric, we also had to play for a young black American girl vocalist called Ethel Ennis, known affectionately as 'The First Lady of Jazz'. I would often walk with her for part of the way to her accommodation, before continuing on to my own. One evening she said to me,
"It's wonderful to be able to walk home at this time of the night. I could never do this, back home in America."

In the summer, Zurich is a lovely place to be. It has an atmosphere all of its own. I had an American book with me called 'See Europe on $10 a Day'. Before you say, "Impossible", don't forget that this was 45 years ago. This book told you about the cheapest places to eat, where to find cheap accommodation and other numerous things to do in each major city in Europe.

In Zurich, I would eat at a restaurant opposite the main Post Office where the post office workers ate at lunchtime. It was very good, with a different 'special' on the menu each day. Occasionally, I would eat somewhere else but mostly opposite the Post Office. I also found a great naked sunbathing place, with separate areas for the men and one for the women and another one which was mixed. I went there a lot during that first month.

I recall one evening, on the walk to my accommodation, 15 minutes away from the venue. After Ethel Ennis had reached her accommodation, I carried on as usual towards mine. I was in need of a pee and as there wasn't anybody around, I turned to a hedge and had one. Just as I had finished, I heard someone coming and in my panic, I hurriedly zipped up and in doing so, I caught some skin in the zip. The logical thing to do was to try to unzip again, in the hope to free it, so when the coast was clear, I undid the top of my trousers and pulled them open, while at the same time trying to free myself but all to no avail. I struggled on to my accommodation and put the light on, to see what I could do about it. Eventually the only option left was to cut the zip away from the trousers and pull each side of the teeth out very slowly from the clasp separately.

Surprisingly, there wasn't any blood, just a weeping sore. The next morning it was just the same, more like a weeping rope burn. The problem was how to cure it. I couldn't leave it in the air to dry. I tried talcum powder but that didn't work and it wouldn't be a good idea to put a sticking plaster on it, so I decided to seek out a chemist to see if he had a solution. Trying to explain my problem to the chemist, in a shop-full of customers who didn't speak English was something to witness. I was trying to demonstrate the problem by pointing and making gestures by pulling my zip up and down. Everyone in the shop was in stitches. Eventually he gave me some ointment to put on, which did the trick but I had a diamond scar on the skin of my penis for years afterwards.

Swiftly moving on: The band made friends with a couple who came to watch the cabaret show quite often and somehow they found out it was my birthday while we were in Zurich and they invited us all round to their house for tea on the afternoon of my Birthday. They had a basement that had been turned into a 'man cave' and we all piled in.

The wife had made a bikini-clad torso birthday cake for me, shown in the picture of me with Eric.

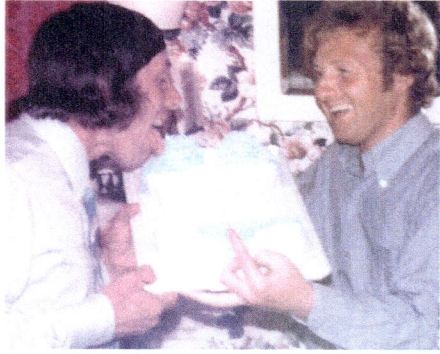

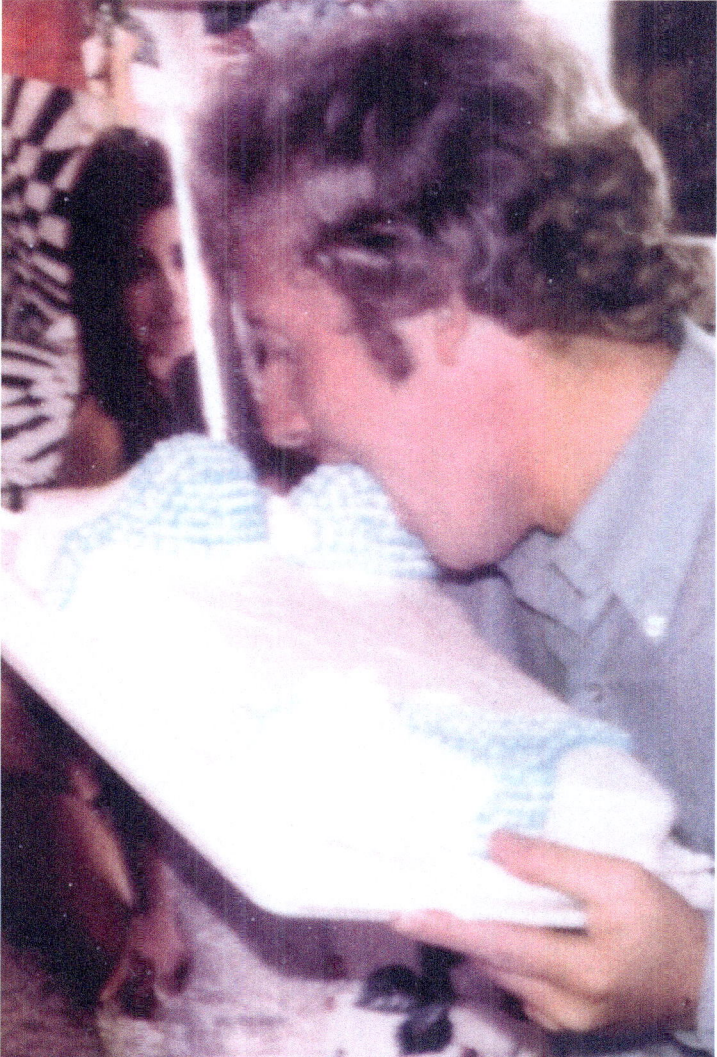

This same couple still came to see the band after we moved to our second venue, another Hazyland club in Basle for the next month of the tour. Basle is more of a commercial centre than Zurich but has the Rhine running through it and I used to like to watch the river barges, plying their trade, backwards and forwards. While in Basle, I also liked to walk round the shops, noticing that some things were cheaper there than in England. It was there that I bought a nice Swiss watch.

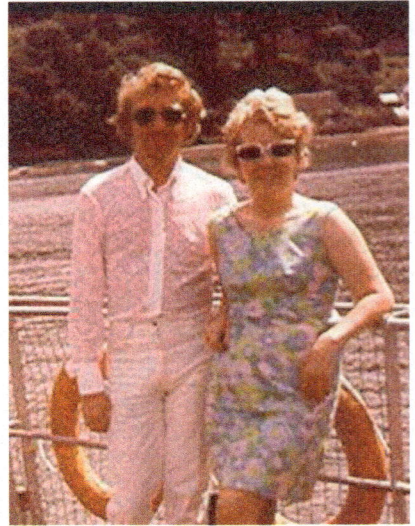

This was during the swinging '60s and the 'beatniks' with long hair and fancy clothes.

It was summer time and I bought a black and white voile shirt, along with a white lace shirt for men. They were all the rage for about two years. This picture is of me, wearing it, standing next to my mother on a ferry across the river Dart, near Brixham, Devon. During the last two weeks in Basle, my friend Harold, the school teacher came over to spend his six weeks of school holidays with me.

Apart from exploring the city, doing some window-shopping and enjoying the beautiful weather, we were also able to go out of town to do some sightseeing, because I had the band van at my disposal. We went to Altdorf, to show Harold the William Tell statue. It was also nice for me to see it again in the summer time and to be able to stop and have a look around, as previously, it had always been in the winter and deep in snow, when Dave and I passed through there.

Another day, we took the cable car up to the summit of Mount Titlis. The next day we visited Mount Pilatus. Pilatus still has the steepest rack and pinion railway (also known as rack railway or cog railway) in the world.

I enjoyed seeing these places myself but it's always twice as enjoyable to share your experiences with somebody else. There were also lots of nice restaurants in Basle and, of course, we had to have a fondue. Another thing I like to eat in Switzerland is the Bircher-Benner muesli, invented by the nutritionist Maximilian Bircher-Benner. I had the recipe and used to make it for myself for a while, after I got back to England, but it has to be made the day before and allowed to soak overnight. It was a bit of a chore, so I soon gave up on it.

Jeff, eating Bircher-Benner Muesli

Time was up for Basle, so it was then on to Lucerne for our last Hazyland club in Switzerland. I managed to get some low-priced accommodation from the American book I had. They were all very basic but my philosophy is, so long as I have a clean bed to sleep in, it's OK and you can't have anything more basic than living in a caravan, so for me this was a luxury.

**View from the window
of
the accommodation**

Harold only stayed for two weeks in Lucerne, because he wanted to have time to go back to Nottingham, to see his mother, before returning to school for the autumn term. Lucerne wasn't my favourite of the three locations but it had the lake and a nice holiday feel to it. From my book, I found a restaurant in Lucerne that did reasonably-priced meals and I would go in most days and order the 'special' from the menu.

One day, they brought me a plate full of different cheeses and nothing else; just cheeses. I felt sure that I could see the staff, stifling smirks but I ate it anyway. It was time to say goodbye to that lovely summer in Switzerland and to head back to 'Dear Old Blighty', in the big red van.

When I arrived at the border between Switzerland and Germany, I parked the van and proceeded as usual to the customs office, to show the papers. Unfortunately, I encountered an officious young German customs officer, who looked at the papers and proceeded to speak in his mother tongue, none of which I understood, so I said,

"Sprechen Sie Englisch, bitte?"

He replied in perfect English,

"Yes, but if you don't speak German, then I don't speak English."

That was it; I wasn't getting anywhere. I didn't know what to do and I began to think I was going to be sitting there for ever. Once again, my guardian angel came to the rescue and Eric turned up in his car and sorted things out. It appeared that there was some mistake in the carnet and Eric had to wire some money through before they would let me through into Germany with the van and equipment. The rest of the journey went without a hitch but I was glad to get back to England and to hand the responsibility of the van and its contents to someone else.

After getting back to England, we had a few days off, before starting the autumn round of the variety clubs and Ovaltine shows. One day, totally out of the blue, Eric presented me with a set of bagpipes. He had an idea for the cabaret, with the band marching from the back of the auditorium towards the stage, with me at the front, playing the bagpipes.

I'd never handled a set of bagpipes before, never mind played them, so I went out and bought a tutor book and a chanter to practise on. The chanter is a separate instrument which looks similar to the pipe that a snake charmer might use. Alternatively, perhaps you could relate to it more as a recorder that many of you may have learned to play at school. I learned how to play 'Scotland the Brave' on the chanter without much difficulty. The next challenge was to play it on the bagpipes. I'm sure most of you will agree that bagpipes are a bit like Marmite, you either love them or you hate them. It's better to hear them far away in the distance; the further the better, in my opinion. It must have been excruciating for the other members of the band, having to listen to me practising. The hard part was getting the drones to work. The drones are the three pipes that stick up in the air. They produce a chord as you would on a piano. They're called drones because they drone on and on. This reminds me of a tale the pianist from the Joe Loss Orchestra once told me. He said,

"I call my wife the dragon because she drags on and on."

So, eventually, we incorporated it into the cabaret show. I was able to get hold of a McEwan's tartan jacket that the waiters used to wear in the clubs and a cardboard 'tammyshanter' (tam o'shanter) for my head. Eric would be playing a drum solo on the stage, while the rest of the band would rush round to the front of the club and line up at the back of the auditorium, with me at the front, playing "Scotland the Brave" on the bagpipes and the rest of the guys behind playing various drums, with Roy, the guitarist right at the back, playing the big bass drum. We would march in, making as much noise as we could. It was something different and we didn't take it too seriously but the audience loved it. I kept those bagpipes for years and occasionally had some fun with them.

Spring came around and one day, Eric announced that he was going to the Bahamas for the summer and would be forming a new band out there. I was the only one he asked to go with him. He would get the rest of the band when he got there. That sounded like a fantastic opportunity for me. What more could this young man from a small village ask. Well, he did ask but he didn't get. The Bahamas was still a British dependency with British troops stationed there and I was told that things were so much more expensive than in Britain, and that even the troops were given more money when they were posted out there, than in anywhere else in the world. Eric was only offering me the same weekly wage as I was getting in England and I knew it wouldn't be enough, so I asked for more money. Eric told me he was working through an entertainment agent called Michael Black and I would have to write to him if I needed more money, which I did, of course, but the answer was, "No". I wasn't sure what to do next. If I accepted the offer and went to the Bahamas for the same wages I was receiving in England and on the continent, my bargaining power would be greatly reduced in other possible negotiations in the future, but on the other hand, how could I turn down an opportunity of a lifetime to spend the summer in the Bahamas? In the end, I decided not to go.

I was to see a lot more of Michael Black, a couple of years later, while I was in Johnny Howard's band in London. Incidentally, Michael has a brother called Don, who is a lyricist, and who has written countless songs, including lyrics for five James Bond films, *Born Free* and the Michael Jackson song "Ben".

After Eric got back from the Bahamas, he was doing a Sunday show at the Winter Gardens at Bournemouth. It was just a pick-up band, for a one night stand and he phoned to ask if I was free and whether I would do it for him. Of course I said, "Yes", and when he saw me, he said,
"It's a good job you didn't go to the Bahamas, Jeff; you would have hated it."
So, maybe I had made the right decision, after all.

In the meantime, while Eric was in the Bahamas, Moving Finger carried on as a group, doing and using some of Eric's cabaret numbers plus extra material from the American group, Chicago and pop songs like Rod Stewart's "Maggie May" and "A Horse With No Name", by a group called America. We performed under the name Moving Finger, Ex-Eric Delaney Band.

We also managed to get a booking for a month at the famous Top Ten club in Hamburg, where the Beatles honed their early performances, after their first recording success. Readers who have been on the continent will know that it is customary to have an attendant at the door of the toilets, collecting money as you went in. I'd heard about this lady who was down the stairs to collect the money in the Top Ten club. It was alleged that she also sold 'purple hearts' or 'blues' as they were sometimes called, which gave you extra energy.

To my surprise she was still there, but no drugs for me, thank you very much. Then there was also the well-known 'red light' district of the Reeperbahn for me to investigate.

The Reeperbahn is where the ladies of the night would sit on chairs in small shop windows, advertising what they had on offer, so prospective clients could walk up and down and select the one they wanted.

John Lennon is quoted as saying, "I was born in Liverpool but I grew up in Hamburg." I know what he meant! I believe there is now a square in Hamburg dedicated to the Beatles, called Beatles-Platz. Shortly after we returned from Hamburg, we signed up with an entertainment agency in Nottingham called Keith David, Banner Productions. They had produced a successful hit record with a group called Paper Lace. The name was a reference to the lace trade in Nottingham, which in previous times had been famous for its machine-made lace manufacture. There is still an area of the city which is called the Lace Market.

Despite being asked to do a short season in a night club in Doncaster, the work began to fizzle out and I had to make the decision to leave and move down to Bournemouth, and try to make a living down there with Harold, which I did for a couple of years, before going back to London.

My attire of the sixties

125

Open-air gig, August 1971

19 - MOVE TO BOURNEMOUTH

From the day I made the decision to move to Bournemouth, it became my home town and a base from which to work. That was in 1973. I moved in with Harold and we began living together as a couple. This was the beginning of a new life for both of us.

However, once I had moved to Bournemouth, one of the first priorities was to find some sort of work, to earn enough money to pay my way. There weren't any professional bands in the area, so I put the word about with the few local musicians I knew in Bournemouth and managed to get the odd job here and there, deputising in local semi-professional bands, including the then resident band in the Pavilion Ballroom, where I had spent the summer season and my 21st first birthday, a few years before.

Word soon began to spread and I started to find work but it was mainly at the weekends, Friday and Saturday and very occasionally a Jewish wedding on a Sunday, as there is a large Jewish community in Bournemouth, but that wasn't enough to make a living.

As I have already mentioned, Harold was a music teacher in the schools and was also able to help in my quest to earn some money. He knew the Music Adviser for the schools in Dorset. Fortunately, the Music Adviser was looking for peripatetic woodwind teachers in the area, mainly to teach the clarinet and flute.

I have to point out that there weren't any teaching qualifications required at that time. Peripatetic teachers were paid hourly by the Dorset

County Council. A few members of the Bournemouth Symphony Orchestra were also doing the same thing as me, in order to make a little extra money. If pupils didn't turn up for their lessons, it wouldn't really matter, as we were still getting paid to be there. On such occasions, I would do some practice myself and get paid for it.

Things are much different now, the councils don't pay for individual music lessons any more; the teachers have to invoice the parents direct, to receive payment. It's much more complicated and difficult to earn a living as a peripatetic now. Also, the teachers have to have qualifications - that piece of paper to say they have reached the required standard as instrumentalists, which doesn't necessarily make them good teachers.

Sometimes, I would be at one school in the morning and on to another school in the afternoon. I realised I had added an extra string to my bow, by teaching woodwind, so I visited all the music shops in the area to give them my business card, in order to let them know I was in the area and available to teach clarinet, flute and saxophone. Soon things were ticking along quite nicely and I started to get private pupils in the evening as well.

Although I never had formal training, I'm sure I was, and still am a good teacher. The art of being able to pass on your knowledge is a natural gift that I seem to have, especially with children; I seem to be able to come down to their level, while not being too technical. If they didn't understand anything I was saying, I could always manage to get around it and come from a different angle. For instance, when the kids came to their first clarinet lesson, I would tell them about the reeds necessary to play the clarinet and equate it to the reeds that grow by the riverbank. I would explain that's where the name comes from, and how it vibrates to make the sound by demonstrating with a piece of grass held between the two thumbs, which by blowing through, produces a sound. I don't know if any of my readers did that as a child but we used to do it when I was a boy.

To demonstrate the basic way to get a sound on the flute I would blow over the top of a bottle. This is a way of getting down to their level and I would always try to simplify things in any way that I could. I only ever had one pupil who failed an exam the first time, but there were reasons why; however she got it the second time. I had a great compliment from a woodwind teacher at the comprehensive school. She said,
"When the kids come up from the various junior schools in the area, I always try to grab yours first, because they know what they're doing."

After finding the report a few weeks ago on the aptitude test I took as a teenager, I remembered reading about some of the occupations to avoid and some that I would do well at. I'll write word for word what it said in the report on one aspect of the positive side: "You are above average in medicine and welfare, that is, any profession involving the teaching, guidance or welfare of other people."

I've always been ready to help others in the past, just as my dad was; that seemed a natural thing for me to do.

To re-read the aptitude test results in black and white made me realise that I must also be a born teacher and was able to produce the results to prove it. That aptitude test was so accurate in both positive and negative occupations; what to do and what not to do - that was the question.

I had quite a few private pupils in the evenings, during the week, but as Harold was living in a flat at the time, I couldn't teach at home, I had to go to the pupil's houses to give them lessons in their own homes, which wasn't exactly the most efficient way to do things, but needs must.

I had one brilliant private pupil called Sarah Quilter. I began teaching her from the age of nine. She passed her grade 5 Associated Board exam in double-quick time, which earned her a special certificate from the Royal School of Music. She went on to pass her grade 8 before she left school at 16. Sarah was, and still is a real hard worker, I have to admit to giving her special attention but she has since rewarded me in many, many ways.

129

I also taught woodwind in the same school where Sarah was a pupil. One day, while I was teaching, the head of music at the school asked me if I would form a jazz band with some of the other pupils in the school, so I formed a traditional jazz band with a marvellous young pianist, a drummer and a trumpet player and, of course, Sarah, playing the clarinet. They learned two or three tunes and were able to perform in the school concert at the end of the summer term.

I was also teaching a boy at the same school to play the clarinet. His name was Lionel Lowe. His father asked if I could give Lionel private tuition on the saxophone. I went to their house a few times, before his father announced that they were emigrating to Tasmania. That was the last I saw of him until the year 2020, nearly forty years later. I am now retired and playing clarinet in a local community band, just to keep my hand in, so to speak. One evening, a new man turned up with an alto sax case and asked who he needed to see. I pointed him in the right direction and we sat down to play. During the break, he came up to me and asked if I was Jeff Mason.
"Yes", I replied, to which he announced,
"I'm Lionel Lowe; you used to teach me at Ferndown Upper School."
I couldn't believe it. It's very strange to see a grown man you used to teach, when you remember him as a boy.

It's slightly different with Sarah, as we have kept in touch, while she was growing into a woman and gradually developing as a musician. Each summer, Bournemouth had a Music Festival with various classes, where anyone can show off their abilities and where each individual class is judged on its merit. I entered a clarinet Quartet made up of Sarah and another girl, who lived on the same road as her, and who I was also teaching. Then, from one of the schools where I was teaching, there was another girl whose name I can't remember, plus, there was a boy named Jolyon Moore, whose father had bought him a bass clarinet.

We won the class with the piece I chose for them, much to the disappointment of another teacher, who usually won everything for which he entered his pupils. He even had the audacity to go and ask one of the girls how old she was, in the hope that one of the members of the quartet was over age and he could get us eliminated.

Sarah wasn't content with just playing the clarinet; she wanted to play the saxophone as well. This meant double the lessons and double the practice, although, as I mentioned in Chapter 3 – 'My First Instrument', my then teacher, Wink said, "If you learn the clarinet first, the saxophone will come more easily."

Not content with that, she wanted to play the flute as well but she had lessons at school for the flute. I said she was a hard worker and how she managed to study for her GCE 'O' levels and GCSE, along with studying for her grade 8 clarinet at the same time, I'll never know. Even better still, she passed them all. I felt that the next goal for Sarah would be to study for her L.R.A.M. at the Royal Academy of Music.

My philosophy is; when a teacher begins giving lessons to a complete beginner, the pupil's knowledge of the instrument is usually nil or on the bottom rung of a ladder, with the teacher being at the top of that ladder. As the pupil gradually climbs that ladder, step by step, they get closer and closer to the teacher, until they're getting near to the top. It's then time to find a longer ladder with a much better teacher at the top of that ladder. Sarah was getting close to the top of my ladder and in her best interest I thought it was time she had a better teacher than me, so I recommended her to the Principal Clarinetist of the Bournemouth Symphony Orchestra. Unfortunately she didn't get on with him at all. I think she thought I'd abandoned her. I think she may have still been a little too young to properly understand that what I was trying to do was in her best interest, or so I thought at the time.

After getting married to Pete Bolter, she had two children, one of each, but still found time to go to Southampton University, as a mature student, on a part-time basis, taking a jazz course there. One of my big regrets is that I was unable to be there when she received her Scholarship of a Bachelor of Music or 'Mus Bac' as it's also known. This piece of paper has enabled her to teach in Bournemouth's most prestigious girl's school. To me, Sarah is like the daughter I never had. I'm so proud of her achievements.

Sarah now has her own modern jazz band and frequently plays at the Pizza Express Jazz Club in Dean Street, London, along with Jazz After

Dark and Toulouse Lautrec clubs, also in Soho, plus other venues in London most weekends.

Check out all the instruments she had beside her and not only that, she's a great jazz singer too.

Sarah's own web site is: http://www.sarahbolter.co.uk/

During the first year that Harold and I started living together, my parents spent their annual holiday, staying with us in Harold's one-bedroom flat. They were given the bedroom while Harold and I made a bed up in the lounge using cushions from the three piece suite.

The very first evening, we were busy making up a bed while my father stood there watching us, nonchalantly leaning with his elbow on the grand piano while chatting away, as if it was a regular occurrence. From that day on, my parents seemed to accept the situation, which made things a lot easier for me.

Jeff's Mother   Jeff   Jeff's Father

Not long after the summer holidays, Harold's 93-year old mother passed away. As the only child, Harold had to deal with everything in Nottingham, where she lived. I hired a large van and began to clear the house. There was quite a lot of furniture that Harold wanted, including his mother's grandfather clock and a beautiful old walnut writing desk that his father had bought years before. We filled the van completely with anything of any value. Anything left in the house was bought by a house clearance firm. We drove back to Bournemouth and unloaded all the stuff into the one-bedroomed flat that was already full of antiques. It became so full of antiques, we couldn't move around in comfort. After the house in Nottingham had been sold, being the only beneficiary, Harold inherited everything.

Once all the legal documents had been signed, he was in a position to start thinking about moving out of his rented flat and buying his own property. I had previously put some money to one side myself, in order to buy

133

a property of my own, when the time came. Relatively speaking, property is much more expensive in Bournemouth than in a village in Nottinghamshire. Although I had put in enough money to buy a bungalow near my parents, it was only enough to pay for half a house in Bournemouth. After quite a long search, we eventually found a property we both liked but despite both our contributions, we still needed a small mortgage, which Harold was dead set against at first. He said,

"I've never owed any money in my life; I've always paid for everything, and if I can't afford it, I'll wait until I can."

I tried to explain that house prices were going up and if we didn't act now we'd never be able to afford it. He was so set in his ways, it was like banging my head against a brick wall. He must have asked other people's advice and he eventually caved in.

By comparing today's house prices, our four-bedroomed detached house plus garage in quite an exclusive area will sound ludicrously cheap at £14,750 but we were still £4,000 short. We saw our solicitor and secured a £4,000 mortgage, to be paid back within ten years. We paid it back in five, and it was the best thing we did.

The house had been lived in for years by an elderly couple and needed renovation throughout, so we set to, with completely re-decorating inside and out, over a period of time. It even had its own original bell system in the house, with a bell push button in each room, to summon the housemaid when required. I had great fun calling Harold to come and scrub my back whilst having a bath. The kitchen was a particular nightmare with what were probably the original sink and a wooden draining board that was rotten, as well as being a veritable health hazard. That's when I built the afore-mentioned famous MFI flat-pack kitchen units.

Harold wasn't really a very practical person, so most of the re-decorating was done by me, with some help with the painting from Harold. My parents were now able to come down for most of their summer holidays, because the house had four double bedrooms and they could have a nice room at the front of the house to themselves. My dad was very helpful while they were there, by painting both sides of all the doors, a job I hated doing.

That year, I bought my Mercedes Coupé, pictured on page 88.

Eventually, over the next couple of years, my father's health deteriorated. His Alzheimer's was progressing and he had run into a car on the way down and reversed into a Jaguar in a car park on his way home. On the day before they left for home, he told me that he'd be dead by the time he was 70, and, sure enough, he was. They never came down to Bournemouth together again.

So, now I was able to teach my private pupils at home instead of driving to all their individual houses and I had Harold to help by playing the piano when they were practising for their exams. This went on for about three years.

The following summer. I was asked by Keith Monk if I would like to do another summer season with him at a Pontins holiday camp in Weymouth, Dorset. Obviously, I jumped at the chance, as Weymouth is less than an hour away from Bournemouth and I would be able to come home every night. There was another sax player in the band, Jim Roberts, who also lived in Bournemouth, so we would ride down to Weymouth and back together and have a good chat at the same time.

After the summer season, it was back to doing gigs with local bands. I was driving back from a gig one night, with the car radio on, listening to a jazz programme. At the end of the programme, it mentioned the names of the players in the band.

135

Amongst the names was Harold Fisher, my old flat-mate from our days together in Grimsby and London. When I'd left London to join Eric Delaney's band, he had stayed in London with Tony Evans and later joined the Johnny Howard band, the band I had watched in the Empire Ballroom, Leicester Square, years before, telling myself I was going to be in that band one day.

Harold Fisher's first break was to get a tour with the then popular P. J. Proby, a part of whose act was to split his trousers on stage and now Harold was being mentioned on the radio. I thought, 'what the hell am I doing here?' and I then began to wonder if I'd made the right decision to play with Eric Delaney's band instead of sticking it out in London a bit longer. I pondered over it for some time and then decided to do something about getting back in the swim of things. I contacted a few people, including the baritone player, Paul Woodburn from Art Lester's band. He was already working in London with Ray Ellington's band, not to be confused with Duke Ellington, the American bandleader. Paul said,

"Huh! We're working at the Dorchester Hotel tonight; I hate that place."

I thought, "You should be so lucky; I'd love to be doing what you're doing".

At the same time, I also contacted my old flat-mate, Harold Fisher. Eventually, I got word on the grape-vine, that Johnny Howard was looking for an Alto, doubling Baritone Sax. I got his phone number and gave him a ring. He said,

"I'm sorry Jeff, but I just fixed a sax player from Tony Evans band but could you do a gig for me this Saturday at Oxford."

I looked at my diary and found I already had a job with a local band and said,

"Sorry John, I'm already working" and the call was terminated. I'm not always quick off the mark and after I put the phone down, I thought, "You idiot! Fix a deputy for your job down here, get your brain in gear and sort it out." I got back to Johnny Howard and told him I had fixed a deputy and would like to do the gig with him instead.

The gig was at the Pressed Steel Fisher social club, on the ring road in Oxford. Only expecting it to be a one-night stand, I swiftly got on the phone to Tony Evans saying,
"I hear you might be looking for an alto player, any chance?"
He said, "Great, Jeff, can you start next week?"

On Friday 16th November 1973, I arrived at the social club and introduced myself to John. I had heard that the Tenor sax player was John's right-hand man, so I set about finding him, bought him a drink at the bar, had a chat and gave him all the soft soap about how much I'd always wanted to be in the band etc. During the course of the evening, there were a few alto parts missing from the library, mainly the Glenn Miller tunes which I knew off by heart, "In The Mood", "Little Brown Jug" and "American Patrol". I played them all, without the music in front of me. I think that must have impressed John and at the end of the night he said,
"Look, Jeff, I've been thinking of having 4 saxes, instead of two. Would you like the job on Lead Alto and I'll put the other guy on Baritone."
I thought, "Wouldn't I just!"

This was another case, where the name Eric Delaney opened a door for me and a sign that my guardian angel was still looking out for me. I'd finally achieved my ambition that I had been aiming at for years and all the previous experience I'd packed in finally paid dividends. Needless to say, I couldn't sleep that night after I got home, but the next day I had the onerous task of phoning Tony Evens to tell him I couldn't start with his band on Monday. All he said was,
"Nice one, Jeff" and put the phone down.

20 - ACHIEVING MY GOAL – MID 1970s

Through a bit of luck, I had finally achieved the goal that had been in my mind since the afternoon when I sat on the balcony in the Empire Ballroom, Leicester Square, some ten or more years before.

Naturally, I talked things through with Harold. Because I'd put my cards on the table from the beginning of our relationship, explaining to him that my music career came first, he didn't seem to have any objections. After all, l would only be away for maybe three or four nights a week and we would still have time to be together in Bournemouth on my days off. I don't think he minded too much, because he'd been living alone for most of his life plus he was still teaching at school during the day, helping to keep his mind occupied.

My first thought was to find somewhere to stay in London or at least somewhere nearer than Bournemouth. I contacted my old drummer pal, Harold Fisher to see if he could put me up temporarily until I could find somewhere else to stay. By this time, he was married to Joan, the girl singer he had met in Sunderland and they had a young son, Damian.

As luck would have it, they had a spare bedroom at their house in Brentwood, Essex and they both agreed to let me stay for a while. Harold had played in John's band during the time I was on the road with Eric Delaney. I have already mentioned in Chapter 4 that Johnny Howard had a Sunday morning programme on the radio, called *Easy Beat*. Harold told me a story of what happened while he was with the band.

Easy Beat was broadcast live from the Playhouse Theatre, on the north side, near the river Thames. Apparently, the guys were in the pub before the broadcast one Sunday morning and either the clock was slow or they just weren't keeping an eye on the time. Suddenly, they heard the introduction music to *Easy Beat* on the radio in the pub and had to rush down to the studio, double-quick. I think John had to do the first number with what band he had left in the studio until the others arrived.

You may recall from Chapter 12 that I first met Harold in Grimsby, when he was only 19 years old. I had predicted that he was destined to get to the top, as he was an excellent drummer at that young age. Between me joining Eric Delaney's band and when we met up again at their house in Brentwood, we had hardly seen one another during that time. He had stayed in London and I had chosen a different path.

Harold was now the first call drummer, for recording sessions in London. He was doing three recording sessions a day, often in three different studios. He had three different drum kits and his own personal roadie, who would roughly set up his number one drum kit at the first recording studio. Harold would come into London from Brentwood on the train and all Harold would have to do would be to adjust the finer points of his drum kit, to how he liked it and do the recording session. In the meantime, the roadie would go to the next studio of the day and set up his second set of drums, while Harold was doing his first session. The roadie would then go to the third studio and do the same thing while Harold travelled on the tube. The roadie would then have to go and collect the drums from the first two studios and so on. All Harold had to do was travel in and out on the train every day. He really hit the top of his game and was also in demand in Germany, being flown out to do sessions there quite frequently.

It was certainly an eye opener for me. I didn't ever reach those dizzy heights. With my temperament I couldn't have stood the constant pressure. I was perfectly happy as I was, thank you very much. I stayed with Harold and Joan for roughly three years before Joan became pregnant with their second child. When the hormones kicked in, she felt she didn't want another man about the house which is quite understandable, plus the fact they would soon need my room anyway.

I found accommodation in Staines, Middlesex which made things easier for me. As it's on the west side of London, which meant there wasn't the need for me to trek all the way over to Essex every time.

In Johnny Howard's band there were no more sound checks, no more rehearsals. At this level you're expected to be able to read everything at sight, exactly, which, of course, is also what is required on recording sessions.

I was leading a four-piece sax section. The two Tenor sax's were Alan Dilly (John's right-hand man) and Johnny Francis, plus the Baritone player, whose name I can't remember, who was none too happy about not getting the job on Alto, as he had first been promised. I'm sure he felt just as I had done, when Tony Evans offered me the Lead Alto position in Belfast and then he gave it to someone else a few years before, but you win some and you lose some, and on this occasion, I was sticking to my position.

Not surprisingly, the Baritone player didn't stay long and I believe that he eventually emigrated to Australia. Not long after the baritone player had left the band, John reverted to his previous and favourite line-up of just two saxes, Alto doubling Baritone, and Tenor, who in this case was Alan Dilly. The line-up was piano, bass, drums, guitar, two saxes, one trumpet and one trombone plus four singers - two boys and two girls. One of the girls was

Sally. She started on the same day as me and we also left at the same time. Del and Linda were two of the others and Garry James made up the fourth.

From Wednesday 21st November 1973, the date of my first engagement with the Johnny Howard band, I remained with them for 17 years. It will be almost impossible to remember everything in detail and in the order that things happened, so I'll aim to talk about the highlights of those years, with hopefully a few amusing stories along the way. As Eric Morecambe used to say,

"He plays all the right notes but not necessarily in the right order."

I'll tell you all the true stories but not necessarily in the right order.

By this time, Mecca were utilising all the dance halls as bingo halls but they were still running an agency to provide bands for private functions. They had three bands on their books: Joe Loss, Ray McVay and Johnny Howard.

At first, most of John's work comprised one night stands, up and down the country, for which we had an old coach. The heating on the coach was less than adequate in the winter. It could be very cold, so we all took our sleeping bags to keep warm. The bass player had a particular sense of humour that appealed to me. One night it was so cold he wrote these words in the condensation on the inside of the window,

'Another Triumph for Eskimo Tours.'

On another occasion, we were on the way back to London after a gig when the accelerator throttle cable broke on the coach. We had to take a floor panel up, to get to the engine. I stood the rest of the way home with a broom handle on the throttle lever, keeping it wide open, in order to get back to London. It was even colder that night with the air rushing up through the open floor panel. Every time the driver needed to change gear, he would shout and I would release the broomstick for a moment while he changed gear and then re-apply it again. It seemed a very long way home that night.

One private party, during the warmer weather, there was a garden party, at the country home in Oxfordshire of a well-known newspaper publisher. It was a very exclusive affair for his friends and family. He was very particular as to what he wanted and as to the timing of various events during the evening having to be very precise. During the time when we were not required on the stage, we were assigned a room and told not to leave that room unless we were going to the stage or to the toilet. Food and drinks were provided for us in that room but it was bit claustrophobic to say the least. In order to pass the time, some of us played Scrabble.

Another similar party was a Bah Mitzvah, for the son of a retail tycoon, at his mansion on Highgate Hill. It was a stunning place. I'd never seen a private house like this before. I vividly remember it had its own oval ballroom with walnut panelling, which was covered in roses. The smell was a bit overpowering but it was certainly a sight to see. The cabaret was Kenny Ball and his Jazzmen. (I mentioned in Chapter 14 that Kenny Ball had been in Eric Delaney's big band, before forming his own jazz band.)

This was my first taste of a society party. I've never seen so many Rolls-Royces in one place at the same time either before or since. It was a side of life I wasn't ever expecting to experience; this kind of living was a world away from the working men's club in Greasborough.

During the years to follow, I'd often be sitting, eating a meal with the rest of the band at the Savoy, the Dorchester, Claridge's or other top hotels, being served by a waiter and thinking about the alternative of being in a working men's club in the north of England, eating pie and chips from a paper container on a Formica table.

If we were going to the North on the coach, we would meet up at St John's Wood, which was not very far from the studio where we recorded the LP with Louie Bellson.

Once, when the coach had returned to St John's Wood during the early hours of the morning, I was then on my way back to Brentwood on the Marylebone Road, past Madame Tussauds. There wasn't any traffic about at that time in the morning and I wanted to get back to Brentwood as soon as possible, to get some sleep. I pulled up at a set of traffic lights and a police car drew up beside me. The officer in the passenger seat put his window down and I did the same. He said to me,
"Is this a private racing track or can anybody join in? We've been trying to catch you from back there." Just then the lights changed and he just said,
"Go on, be careful."

Another similar scenario took place at a later date, also on my way back to Brentwood, but this time I was driving through the East End of London. I went over a railway bridge and just over the other side was a policeman with a hand-held speed gun. He stopped me and said,
"Do you realise you were doing 50 miles an hour in a 30 mile zone? Is 40 miles an hour too much to ask?" and then he let me go. I couldn't see that happening nowadays.

A similar encounter with the police took place a few years later, after there had been a petrol shortage. Drivers were asked to keep speed down to

50 miles per hour, to conserve petrol. In going backwards and forwards to London, I realised how much fuel and money I was saving by going at 50 mph. After the crisis was over, I continued travelling at 50 mph. One day, I was stopped on the motorway by the police. We both pulled over onto the hard shoulder and I was signalled to get out of the car. I was asked if I'd been drinking and then given a breathalyser test, which, of course, was negative. I asked why the breathalyser test? The officer told me that some people drive slowly when they have been drinking. They then asked me why I was only doing 50 mph.   When I explained the reason, they told me that it was dangerous to drive so slowly, since the crisis was now over, because the large lorries drive at 60 mph and they would be coming up behind me so fast, not expecting anyone to be going so slowly and I was in danger of being run into from behind by one of these juggernauts. We drivers all know what lorries are like on the motorway. I think I must be one of the few drivers who have been stopped for driving too slowly on a motorway.

If we were travelling west, we would meet the coach just past Hammersmith, near a factory that made shoe polish. It was known to us as Cherry Blossom Corner. There was a layby there for the coach to pull into, plus a few small roads in the area where we could park safely without charge. I think it was a known place for the bands to pick up as we would often meet the Ray McVay's coach there at the same time, also on its way west.

Once, we all met at Cherry Blossom Corner on our way west, along the M4 to Swansea, to do a live *Come Dancing* TV show from Swansea, which was organised by Mecca Dancing, the company that Johnny Howard was still working for at the time.   I have already mentioned the *Come Dancing* series in Chapter 13 – 'First Job in London'.

John had augmented the saxophone section to 5 saxes for the TV show and booked one of the top three session Lead Alto saxes in the country at the time. They were known as first call players, as the name suggests, as they were the first people to be called when anyone was required for a recording session in this country. The man who Johnny Howard called to do his TV show was Peter Hughes. His nickname was 'Peter Perfect', because he just didn't make mistakes in his music playing.

When Henry Mancini, the big American music writer and conductor came over to England to make a record, his first call Lead Alto was always Peter Hughes. Peter was also the person who played "Yakaty Sax" - the solo during the introduction music to the *Benny Hill Show*, where Benny Hill chased the girls round the bushes in fast motion. I was later to sit next to Peter

Hughes in a sax section for three or four years and it was true, he just didn't make any mistakes. I was sitting behind Peter on the coach, on the day we went to Swansea, when John came around the coach, giving out the music we were playing that day. It was the first time that anyone had seen the music to be played on the TV that night.

(Don't forget, it was a live performance, with no room for mistakes. Remember, as I also said earlier in this chapter, that there were no more rehearsals at this level; you were expected to be able to play everything on sight.) As I've already mentioned, I was sitting behind Peter when John gave him his music and I distinctly heard John say to him,
"You can give anything you want to Jeff - he can handle it" but Peter didn't even hand me the lead part to a simple waltz. I was a bit miffed to say the least and held a grudge for years but was later able to get my own back when I was playing Lead Alto on a recording session and I handed him a flute part to play, knowing full well that the flute was Peter's worst doubling instrument and he cocked it up, so we had to do it again. I said to myself, "Yesss! Got Yer!" but later, as I've already said, we became great friends.

Although we still continued doing the one night stands, using the coach, for quite a few years, Johnny Howard was beginning to get society engagements in the West End of London. I think he must have left the Mecca agency by this time and set up his own agency instead.

Although John didn't appear himself, he was responsible for supplying musicians for the Bruce Forsyth one-man theatre tours. I only played for Bruce twice, when the regular sax player was off. John also supplied the musicians for the *Mike Yarwood Show* tours during the time that he was very popular. Mike had his own musical director called Graham Lawrence. I was the Lead Alto in that band during the tours but returned to the main band after the tours ended.

Most of the work for the main band suddenly began to come from big hotels in London such as the Grosvenor House Hotel, the London Hilton on Park Lane, the Dorchester, and not forgetting the Savoy, on the embankment. During the period that I was in the band, we must have played in most of the major hotels in London except for The Ritz.

This is allegedly how it worked. Every hotel has a banqueting manager, and if someone wanted to hold a function - a dinner dance, an awards ceremony, a hunt ball, a wedding - you name it - the hotel would arrange everything for you. If a bandleader happened to grease the palms of a banqueting manager with silver, the banqueting manager would then recommend that band for the client.   At that time, Johnny Howard was quite friendly with a Jewish banqueting firm that operated underneath a Synagogue just behind the Carlton Hotel at Marble Arch. The banqueting suite was aptly named the King David Suite. We would play there most Sundays, because the Jewish Sabbath ends at dusk on Saturday evening. During the winter months, we sometimes played there on Saturdays as well.

We were playing at an engagement at the Intercontinental Hotel, which is situated right at the bottom of Park Lane, on the corner, overlooking Hyde Park Corner. Just before Hyde Park Corner, there used to be parking on single yellow lines after 7pm and I would always try to get a parking space round there, when I could, because it meant I didn't have far to walk with all the instruments I had to carry.   On one occasion, I was driving very slowly, looking to my left as I went, searching for a possible space but there wasn't one, so I carried on round the corner and took the next left which was a narrow parallel road to Park Lane. Occasionally, there could be an odd space there.

As I drove slowly up that road I became aware of the flashing blue light of a police car. I couldn't pull in to let him pass so carried on round the next corner. The next thing I knew was that they had pulled up behind me, a policeman yanked open my door and said in a vicious demanding voice,
"Get out of the car, give me your keys and get over by that wall."
I was being watched over by his fellow officer while he checked my number plate and other details on his phone. The scene was like something from the American cop dramas we now see on the TV. All my details were in order. He said,
"Why were you driving so slowly?"
I told him I was a musician, looking for a parking space and showed him my instruments in the boot of my car. However, I think because it was so close to Shepherd Market, the 'red light' area, he must have thought I was kerb-crawling, when in actual fact, I was just looking to my left all the time, searching for a parking space. The police must have thought I was searching for a lady of the night not a parking space.

I thought of how ironic it was, remembering the incident with my mother standing on the pavement, very close to the same spot all those years before, when someone in a car tried to pick her up.

Speaking of kerb-crawling: on a completely different occasion, I was burdened with instruments, on the way to my car in the back streets, around Piccadilly Circus, after an engagement at the Hotel Café Royal A car with

144

two young women in it pulled up beside the kerb. One of the women opened her window to ask if I would like a good time. I felt like saying, "No thanks, I've just had one." I thought, 'good grief, this is a whole new role reversal, if you like, the women are now doing the kerb-crawling in their cars, instead of the men.' In any case, they were certainly barking up the wrong tree, asking me that question!

However, I eventually found a space near the Intercontinental Hotel. It was imperative for me to try to get as close to the venue as possible, because by this time I had so many different instruments to carry about, plus their required stands to put them on. I needed the arms of an octopus. It was rather ironic that my dad didn't want me to be a drummer because drummers have so much kit to carry around; now I had a similar problem. I needed four basic instruments for the job for which I was being paid: Alto Sax doubling Baritone Sax, Clarinet and Flute.

Johnny Howard liked to keep up with all the new pop songs in the charts. At one point, there were hit records in the charts, all at the same time, and requiring me to play Soprano Sax and Piccolo as well as the basic four. John used a particular deputy piano player who would do odd jobs with the band when required. It got back to me that he had been saying to other musicians, "Have you seen Jeff Mason? When he comes on the stage with all those instruments round his neck he looks like a bloody Christmas tree". That was good publicity for me.

My reputation must have been growing because not long afterwards, Johnny Howard's band was playing opposite to the Joe Loss Orchestra at the Lancaster Gate Hotel for a very important wedding. Joe Loss was still alive then and during the evening, he sent his right-hand man over to ask if I would like to join the Joe Loss Orchestra, playing Tenor Sax. I had to say, "Thank you, but I can't" as I wasn't prepared to leave John at that point. There were two reasons why. The first and foremost reason was that I wasn't going to swap my alto job to play tenor sax, which wasn't the instrument I liked to play, and secondly I'd been told that Joe's band was more of a show band and not musically as good as John's band, so I chose to stay with the lesser known but musically better band. However that wasn't to be the last time I was offered a job with Joe Loss's band.

Some of the newer hotels don't have a permanent dance floor, as the rooms are meant to be multi-functional, in order to host conferences and such like. Instead, they have a dance floor that comes in sections which can be clipped together and laid directly onto the carpet to make the dance floor.

The problem is that there was a lip or very small step to get onto the dance floor.

The function for which we were playing was a high-class Jewish wedding. Just before it was time to cut the cake, the catering manager came from behind the stage, looking very pleased with himself, with a smug grin on his face, wheeling a three-tiered wedding cake on a trolley. When the front wheels of the trolley hit the edge of the dance floor it suddenly came to an abrupt stop but the cake kept going and fell in a heap on the dance floor in front of everyone. An even funnier part was seeing the manager on his hands and knees, trying to scoop it back onto the trolley.

The band was in hysterics. I was splitting my sides, while Johnny Howard was looking most annoyed, shouting, "Don't laugh, don't laugh." The bridegroom sniggered, the bride was in floods of tears and the bride's mother was white with rage. I can't begin to think how much that that big day must have cost the parents to give their special daughter the best day of her life, only to have it ruined by a stupid catering manager.

John had quite an extensive library of music, including popular Jewish tunes. The most well-known Jewish tune to English speaking people is "Hava Nagila". The vocalists had to learn the words in phonetic English but they also had devised their risqué parody, which even in those days would be more than their jobs were worth to sing out loud over the microphone. Sally would turn to the band and sing the alternative words to us for our amusement. But in this present world of political correctness, I think it's better not to include those words in this book.

In the meantime, back home in Bournemouth, Harold along with a friend of his who owned a car began selling some of Harold's mother's bits and bobs at local antique fairs in the area whilst sharing the stall together. They did quite well with the antiques. They soon caught the antique selling bug and began buying things to sell at the fairs which led to bigger and better things later on.

One of the last coach trips we did was in Sunderland. Just having driven from Bournemouth to meet the coach at St John's Wood, I needed to get some goodies to eat on the way to Sunderland. Amongst the things I bought was a warmed-up meat pie from a corner shop. For some reason John couldn't be on the coach and was flying up to meet us at the gig later. It was the bass player's birthday and he had some birthday drinks at the back of the coach and let it be known that the back of the coach is traditionally where the hooligans sit not only on our coach but it also applies to most bands I've been with. I was invited to join the hooligans for once.

Four of us polished off a bottle of Jack Daniels and started on the whisky. I'm not a drinker and I'm the first to admit to not being able hold my liquor so I went back to my seat to have a sleep. I don't remember anything else until I woke up in the band room in Sunderland, already changed into my band uniform. It turns out that I had tried to get up to use the on-board toilet in a drunken stupor, hit my head on the hard armrest on the seat trying to get up and given myself a mild concussion. I'd been sick down all the clothes I'd been wearing and a couple of the guys had to strip me and change me into my band uniform and carry me to the band room. The poor coach driver had to clean up the mess, threatening to leave me in Sunderland, as he didn't want me on his coach again. When John arrived he apparently made a beeline for the hooligans blaming them saying,
"What have you done to Jeff?"
I don't remember any of this at all. There was no way I could get my instrument out of the case never mind play it. I was, in essence, drunk in charge of an instrument, so I had to sit in the band room all night, with a bowl by my side, in case I needed to use it.

The band was playing on the stage immediately above my head and I didn't hear a thing all night. What made it even worse was we had a new saxophone player called Simon Currie, who had never played with the band before. It was his first gig with the band. In fact it was his very first job as a professional musician, after just having graduated from the National Youth Jazz Orchestra. We became great pals and he told me afterwards that he had thought to himself, "What have I got myself into here?" I woke up a bit when the guys came into the band room and I remember saying to John, "You've got to sack me, you must sack me." The boys put me on the coach, I promptly went back to sleep and woke up just before we got back to St John's Wood. John paid me for the job, while docking some of my wages to pay the coach driver for his inconvenience. I got in my car and drove home.

Afterwards, I tried to blame it all on a dodgy meat pie that I had bought in the corner shop before we left from St John's Wood that day. From then on, the episode was known as the night of the dodgy meat pie. John never said another word about it; I know he'd had worse over the years, from what I'd heard.

One year, the band did a week at the NEC (National Exhibition Centre) in Birmingham, backing variety acts at the bi-annual British

International Motor Show. The band did an opening spot, followed by an illusionist. There was a dare-devil trick motor cyclist, who was more suited to a circus than a variety show but I suppose it fitted in with the theme of the motor show. Finally, at the top of the bill were the Nolan Sisters. They were still very young and at the height of their popularity then.

Two of the highlights of my career up to that point were playing Lead Alto on two separate occasions. The first of those occasions was for Sammy Davis Jr and the second was for Dionne Warwick. The Johnny Howard band had been booked to accompany them on their short tours of England. Sammy Davis Jr brought his own Piano, Bass, Drums and Lead Trumpet with him from the States but the rest of the band was John's. The musical arrangements were so well-written, it made them easy to play, plus I had the added advantage of having Ronnie Chamberlain sitting next to me on Second Alto. Ronnie had been Ted Heath's Lead Alto and was now a top session man, I was to play in the same band as Ronnie, later on in my career; what a nice unassuming man he was. What an honour it was to have been able to know him and to work with him.

Back to doing the private functions in London: One Sunday evening at the King David Suite, a new trombone player arrived. His name was Bobby Byrne. He was a larger than life Irishman from Dublin, who didn't waste any time announcing that he was gay. I was still trying to keep my sexuality to myself and thought, "O.M.G. how is the rest of the band going to react to this news? I'd better stay well clear of him and keep out of his way as much as possible. I don't want anyone else to know I'm gay."

If Bob ever reads this, he would laugh his head off, because later we became good friends and he knows perfectly well what my first reactions were to his joining the band. Before joining John's band he had already been playing in the Joe Loss Orchestra and with Ray McVay. Both of those bandleaders and members must have accepted him, as did the members of John's band. I didn't hear any disparaging words spoken of him behind his back; everyone seemed to accept him for who he was and not what he was. I can honestly say that Bobby is the only other gay musician I have ever knowingly come across in my life.

However, while I was lying in bed, the day after writing that statement, I remembered being told of a well-known sax player of the day who lived in quite a good area of London and who never married but had a butler to look after him instead. I took that information on face value at the time thinking, "It's alright for some of these rich musicians" and didn't think any more about it, or even try to analyse it until now. But it's possible that he was gay and deep in the closet. The butler could have been the undercover story for his lover; one never knows.

As well as playing the trombone, Bobby also sang with the band quite a bit and was a great entertainer; the crowds adored him.

Standing next to Alan Dilly, the tenor player, he and I would chat a bit and soon we had become friends. He started asking me if I had a girlfriend. I said, "Yes" and the next question was,

"When are we going to see her?"

"She's in Bournemouth", I said, hoping he was going to drop the subject,

"I can't bring her to these private functions."

"Why not bring her to Grosvenor House; she could sit on the balcony and no one would say anything?"

"She doesn't like London", I said,

"and she is a classical musician; she doesn't like the kind of music we play; she would be bored to death."

That seemed to satisfy him, for the time being at least.

As fate had it, the following summer, John's band was doing every other alternate Thursdays with Ray McVay at the Pavilion Ballroom in Bournemouth.

"When are we going to see your girlfriend?" asked Alan.

"She's busy on Thursday nights", I said.

Alan was like a dog with a bone; he just wouldn't let it go. In the end he broke me down until the only way to stop him was to come clean and so it was; I'd been outed. Soon the rest of the band knew but never said anything and none of the guys treated me any different. Because we had so many changes of personnel and different deputies in and out of the band all the time, the word must have been spread far and wide in the small community of the band world. I had a couple of minor incidents but nothing I couldn't handle so I needn't have worried what other people thought, after all.

It certainly didn't stop me getting better work after leaving Johnny Howard's band. Thinking that I was now more established as being a good player by this time, I felt that so long as I did a good job, no one seemed to mind about another person's private life and that's how it should be.

Time passed. Alan Dilly retired from the music business and was replaced by a great young tenor player by the name of Brian Ling.

One really enjoyable trip was to Qatar in the Persian Gulf. We were playing for an English oil company out there. The band flew over to Qatar.

We arrived during the evening before the gig. We were met at the airport by members of the company we were working for and all taken to a house where food and drinks were waiting for us. When the car I was traveling in arrived at the house, the driver just got out of the car without bothering to lock it. My instruments were in the boot of his car. I asked,

"Aren't you going to lock your car?"

He said, "No, don't worry. Nobody steals anything here. If they do, the authorities chop their right hands off."

Everyone would then know that they had broken the law. I think it's a good deterrent; pity they don't do it in England. Apparently one of the reasons it's always the right hand is because after it's been chopped off, they can't wipe their backsides properly.

We were all staying with members of the club in their homes, two to each family. I was sharing with the guitar player, Kenny Wood. The next morning, he and I were taken out to see the area which consisted mainly of desert. I seem to remember we saw one wild camel.

The job we were there to do was the company's party for all their workers. They even had their own leisure club, with a beautiful swimming pool. It was a huge compound and although Qatar is what they call a dry country, meaning that no alcohol is allowed, the Brits could still drink in their own home and within the club compound. It was like a hot summer's day in England, when we arrived. Thank goodness we had been advised to take our swimming costumes, as the first thing we did was to get changed and get into the pool.

It was the winter period in Qatar, and as far as the Brits living out there were concerned, we were completely mad to go in the pool; it was too cold for them. I think their blood must thin over a period of time, to compensate for the extreme hot weather during their summer.

This new young tenor sax player was a bit of a maverick and he threw his sax into the pool, before diving in after it and playing a tune in the pool.

In this photo, I'm 4th from the left,   ⬇ middle row.

Looking at the group photo again reminded me of a story that Sam the trumpet player told me one day. He had been a trumpet player in the band of the Royal Horse Guards as a young man. When they had a big pageant like the *Queen's Coronation* for instance, they weren't allowed to drink anything the night before or the next morning either. The uniform with the silver breastplate was so heavy that they had to climb on the horse using the special steps. Once on the horse they had to sit there all through the pageant because if they got off the horse, they wouldn't be able to get on again, if they needed a pee they had to sit there and do it in their boots, even in the winter, Yuk!

The other photos show the men still building the stage in the swimming pool while we were there. It was just built of scaffolding poles on blocks of wood at the bottom of the pool and looked to me very unsafe considering we would also be having electricity on there for the amplifiers and sound system. I was more than disturbed to be on that stage and worried about it all the time we were playing.

Shortly after the trip to Qatar, poor old Sam fell out of his loft at home and damaged his right shoulder so badly that he couldn't ever play the trumpet again.

I had previously played with a brilliant young trumpet player from Bournemouth, whose name is Ian Spencer. I introduced him to Johnny Howard and he joined the band. I'd first met Ian some years before, when he was only 15, playing in a semi-professional band in Bournemouth. He was a good young player even at that age, and I do like to help young people just as I had help and good fortune myself when I set out on life's journey.

Fortunately, everything went well without any problems and the next morning we flew back to England. Here is a picture of the two girls, in a rather provocative pose, enjoying a drink during the flight home.

One day, I had a phone call from the entertainments manager for Pontins holiday camps, asking if I could form a small 5-piece band to play every Monday during the summer, as relief for the resident band's night off, at one of their camps in Weymouth. As the summer months were a quiet time for John's band, particularly as the job was every Monday, a day when it's usually quiet for the bands. Anyway, I gladly accepted, so booked a local trio that played together all the time, and added Ian Spencer (now with John's band) and myself to make up the five musicians, using some of the music from my dad's old library.

After digressing once again, it's back to the Qatar story. John's band was booked to do the same thing the following year. They still put the bandstand in the pool but because of previous concerns we had about water and electricity, it was a much sturdier affair.

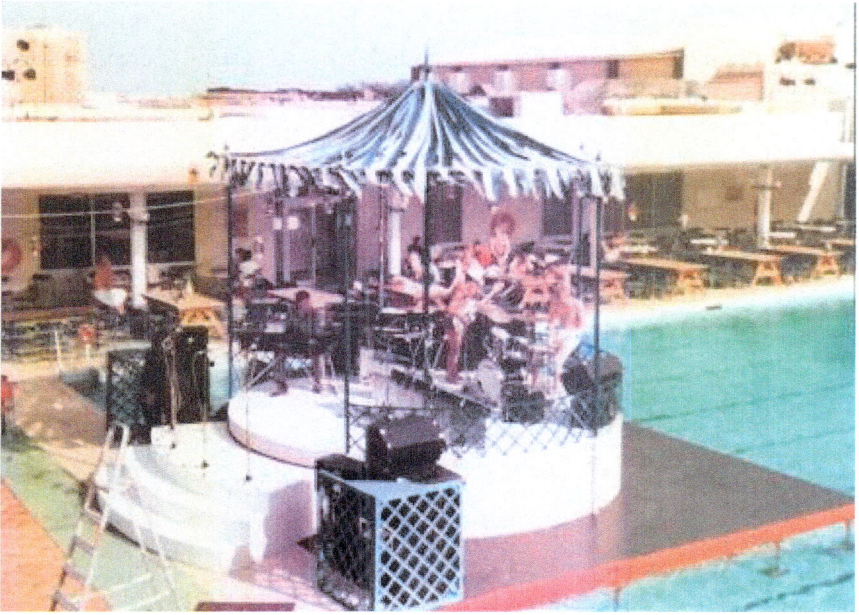

Johnny Howard somehow also managed to get a three-year contract to supply bands to play in the two casinos in Monte Carlo. The main one in the square is called the Winter Casino. It's smaller than the summer one. It's open in the winter with only a 4-piece band. The summer one is much newer and bigger and sports a large theatre stage to easily hold a 14/15 piece band and an auditorium with a roof that opens up to enable anyone who is interested to be able to look at the stars in the night skies.

One night each week, Monte Carlo holds a spectacular fireworks display. To be able to watch that through the open roof was a wonderful experience to behold. The casino is situated on a small peninsula, right on the sea.

I went out for the first season and really enjoyed going up to Monaco and seeing the famous Pink Palace where the Prince Rainier and Princess Grace Kelly of Monaco lived. Grace Kelly, the famous film star was still alive and living in the palace during the time I was there. The thing I did enjoy was to be able to walk back to my apartment late at night in my shirt sleeves and it was still warm. In the mornings I'd walk down to the harbour for breakfast, overlooking all those expensive privately owned motor yachts moored there. Prince Rainier even had a helipad on his yacht.

Because I had my own apartment, Harold was able to come over, for a short while. However, I couldn't live that lifestyle permanently; it's all very false, being what I like to call 'plastic'. In any case, they didn't have any Indian restaurants in Monte Carlo then! John leased an apartment himself for three years, right on the front, overlooking the man-made beach. It cost him one hundred thousand pounds a year. He bought all the furniture and even the wall paper in England and had it shipped out to Monte Carlo. I thought it was a waste of money, but money was no object for him in those days and he sometimes enjoyed letting us mere band boys know about it.

Having said that, I was flown out, given a one-bedroom rented apartment and it didn't cost me a penny. John wasn't in Monte Carlo all the time, as he had to keep running back and forth to England to do the occasional important function in London with a skeleton band. John was becoming more and more popular in society circles, so much so that if 'Mr and Mrs so and so' had the Johnny Howard Band to play at their wedding then others had to have him as well, in order to keep up with the Joneses, so to speak.

In fact, the main band was so much in demand that John had to start satellite bands in his name, in order to cope with the demand. He gave Bobby Byrne his own band called Johnny Howard's Singers and Swingers. Three of those members had a stammer, including Bob; we nicknamed them the Stutters and Stammers band. Del Bingley also had his own small band with his wife Linda and two of the main band singers. When Del and Linda's band wasn't busy, they would return to the main band.

On one occasion, when John was auditioning girl singers for one of his satellite bands, one particular girl singer came for an audition. She was called Silvia King apparently her business card read Silvia King - Born to Sing. The other sax player said to me, "It's a good job her name wasn't Freda Fluck".

I led one of John's satellite bands for four summers. This came about because I had worked at the Pontins holiday camp in Weymouth three times already, once on a season with Keith Monk, another season with someone, whose name I don't remember and finally with my own little five-piece band that did the Monday night relief for the main band. So, I was asked by Pontins' executive entertainments manager if I would like to do a season with my own bigger main band at the Osmington Bay holiday camp. I had to say, "No" because I wasn't prepared to leave Johnny Howard for a summer season, only to risk finding myself without a job at the end of it. The Pontins' executive got round it by asking Johnny Howard to put a band on the camp with me as the leader.

He agreed and no doubt was taking a fee for himself as well, as he was already acting as an agent himself, when sending Bobby Byrne and Del Bingley out with their own bands. The band I was to lead would be called the Johnny Howard Connection. I had this band at Osmington Bay for four consecutive summers. The best thing for me was that I still had a job to go back to in the winter. I've already explained that work for the main band in London was usually quieter during the summer months; John could easily find someone to cover for me while I was away.

For the first season, I used local musicians, which was something of a mistake. I hadn't taken into account the differing abilities between local Bournemouth musicians and the standards that were required in London. However this was a big learning curve for me and we muddled through somehow.

I am a bit of an extrovert by nature and had learned a lot from Johnny Howard on how to talk to the public and how to choose the right tunes at the right time. I think I managed quite well as a first time front man. I had to learn the correct tempos for each of the different dances including sequence dancing that I hadn't come across before. I must have done alright as I was re-booked for the following year. It was also nice to be at home every day.

The 2nd year band

For the second year, I was allowed to add an extra musician. Now I had a seven-piece band instead of the original six. Being a sax player, I chose to add another sax, because I was doing all the announcing, counting the band in at precisely the correct tempo for the dancers plus most of the singing. I needed someone to cover the First Alto music. This time John put an advert in the *Melody Maker* and we got some superb players, including a guitar player, whose surname was Blood. He purportedly was a descendant of Captain Blood, the Pirate. He had a good voice and was able to do the pop songs, while I did more of the standard tunes aimed at the middle aged crowd.

During the second year, the camp put on two separate weeks, each of which was called *Bless 'em All Week* where they asked the gentlemen to wear a service uniform and the ladies too, if they had been in the forces, otherwise to dress as land girls or in dresses of the1930s/1940s.

Most of them did their best to make it a great fortnight. I had to find as many WW2 tunes as I could and our pianist put together a medley of songs including "The White Cliffs of Dover", "We'll Meet Again", (also known to musicians as "Whale Meat Again"), "Show Me the Way To Go Home" etc.

Bless 'em All Week

The band was asked to re-create a *Worker's Playtime* type of musical theme in the canteen at lunchtime, while the guests had their lunch. The highlight of the week was to have artists of the era. The two main ones that stick in my mind were, firstly the ventriloquist, Peter Brough and Archie Andrews, his dummy. Some of my readers will hopefully remember the radio series *Educating Archie*. Think about this. Is there anything more stupid than having a ventriloquist act on the radio? Apparently, he was notorious for moving his lips. I've never seen anything as bad as him trying to do a live show in front of an audience! Secondly, the star of the week was Vera Lynn. It's an honour to have played for that lady.

At each of the Pontins camps around the country, they held ballroom dancing competitions for lots of different standards and lots of different types of ballroom dance. At the end of the season, all the winners of those heats would come to Osmington Bay for two weeks of competitions, leading to the finals of each dance. They chose Osmington Bay because it was known as the major ballroom dance camp of the whole of the Pontins camps. That's why it was so difficult for any bandleader to succeed there. In the history of the competition, Pontins had previously brought in a specialist strict tempo band for those last two weeks of competition but halfway through my second season, the resident band was asked to stay on for those extra two weeks, to play for the competitions. I must have been doing a good job; it was a feather in my cap.

Dancing Competition Finals

The third year had pretty much the same line-up of musicians, except I had a trombone player instead of a guitar.

The 3rd Year Band

For my fourth and final year, I was told by the manager that they were cutting out one of the cabaret performers and with the money saved, I could have as big a band as I wanted. I didn't want to be too greedy but I added another two saxes and a trombone. With the extra saxes, I could do all the Glenn Miller music and some big band arrangements that I'd had from my dad.

I had two very proud parents

The 4th Year Band

At the end of that fourth season, the manager of the camp was being moved to one of the other camps. The following year the band was to be cut back to its original size of six, which I decided I didn't want to do, so for the next two years, Johnny Howard sent Bobby Byrne there instead.

The main band began to do work for some of the Royal Family. Queen Elizabeth, the Queen Mother was guest of honour at one function we played for. We watched her dance with Douglas Bader, who was the famous World-War 2 ace fighter pilot, who lost both legs in a earlier crash but was later still allowed to fly again, winning many dog fights in the air and was a highly decorated and respected celebrity. That was a moment for me to remember.

Also, every summer, the band would play at the Berkeley Square Ball. The ball was in aid of charity and the tickets were so expensive that only the very rich could afford to attend. The Square would be surrounded by a temporary high barrier wall with an arena built inside containing a stage for the band. We would play for dancing and general entertainment, which was always attended by a different member of the Royal Family each year. One year it was Princess Margaret; another year it was Prince Philip. The only senior Royal Family member who didn't attend at that time was Her Majesty Queen Elizabeth II. We didn't ever play at Buckingham Palace either; that honour was reserved for The Joe Loss Orchestra.

One other Royal engagement for the Johnny Howard band was to play at Prince Philip's 70th birthday party, held at Windsor Castle. I had a special pass for that day which I kept for years but when I made my last house move I threw it away, thinking, what's the point of keeping this. Now I wish I had.

The band was getting so busy, which was a good thing for me, because I was earning lots of money but I seemed to be spending less and less time at home in Bournemouth. However, Harold didn't complain, because as a self-employed man, if I didn't work, I didn't earn.

It must have been around this time when I became 50. I began to feel restless and unsettled with the band and would be standing playing, while at the same time thinking that I didn't want to be here playing music anymore. But what could I do about it? I didn't have any qualifications to make a change of career. Nobody wants a fairy when she's 50.

Then I began to think how lucky I was to be able to be doing what I considered to be the best job in the country for me. Thinking of all the hundreds of other musicians, who had been playing in those Mecca dance halls up and down the country and what they would have had to go through when they suddenly found themselves without any work; what could they do when forced to make a career change? I kept telling myself, I'm the lucky one, because I'd survived.

I don't think I sometimes appreciated what a good player I had become but that wasn't enough to make me feel any the more content. I think I must have been going through the male menopause. I am aware that some people say there's no such thing as maybe the male menopause doesn't affect everybody. But it certainly unsettled me for a few years.

One particular year, we didn't have a single night off from the middle of October until Christmas Day. Not only were there engagements at night but we were also doing radio broadcasts during the day. The band was frequently featured on the *John Dunn Show* in the afternoons plus *Music While You Work*, which was revived for a while but soon dropped again. My dad made a point of recording every broadcast we did and would sit, playing them back. I know he was very proud of me, despite not being able to show it. I even got mentioned at the end of the *Music While You Work* broadcast for playing Acker Bilk's "Stranger On The Shore".

We were also the resident band for a new TV talent show for unknown new artists never been seen before on TV. One of those artists was Paul Daniels, assisted by with Debbie McGee. Of course, Paul Daniels was hardly off our TV screens during the peak of his career. Maybe some people will remember the mock talk show, *The Mrs Merton Show*, and the interview between Mrs Merton, played by Caroline Aherne, when she asked Debbie McGee,
"Tell me, Debbie, what was it that first attracted you to the millionaire, Paul Daniels?"
That was a classic interview, in my opinion.

I used to dread the build up to Christmas, as it got nearer. Two of the last jobs we did before we finished for Christmas were two consecutive days when we would play twice a day for large combined office parties at the Kensington Palace Hotel, one in the afternoon and one in the evening. The thing I hated most about those parties was that on every table there would be lots of fluffy cotton-wool snowballs. When the alcohol began to take over, they would dip them in their drinks and throw them at one another and also at the band. It was disrespectful to get a wet soggy mess thrown into your face, while you're trying to do your job. After working flat out for two and a half months, the stress was beginning to tell.

One particular evening at one of these parties the sax player next to me was blowing so hard I couldn't hear myself so I began to blow my head off to make myself heard. Johnny Howard walked over to the sound desk and turned my microphone down, so when his back was turned I turned it back up again. Then, he came back to the desk and turned me off altogether. I was so pissed off at this stage that I just picked up my saxophone and walked off. He sent someone after me to try to calm me down but I wasn't having any of it. I'd had enough and went home. As far as I was concerned, that was it. I'd left the band. I was no longer a professional musician. After all, I had achieved my goal in life, or so I thought.

21 - A NEW DIRECTION

I went home to Harold and Bournemouth, wondering what to do next. I didn't want to do any teaching again because, although it could be rewarding, it could also be disappointing when word would get back to me that certain previous pupils had given up playing their instruments, now that they were studying for school exams. I used to think, "What's the point of me putting in all my effort to teach them, for them just to give up?" But on a positive side, to be taken out of a class of students and asked to stand in front of a teacher on a one-to-one basis was good self-discipline and character-building for them, because they couldn't hide behind anyone else in the classroom; they had to stand in front of their teacher and produce music, with no hiding place.

For those who did carry on with their music, there were various local groups to join, like the community band, with which I am now playing for pleasure, since I retired. For those who were lucky enough to have gone to university, there are always various groups there to join. One route I began to consider was the antique trade, which Harold was still pursuing, with his friend Ken.

Harold had a couple of other friends who were already doing the big Sunday fairs in the West End of London. Harold was a bit of a connoisseur of Bohemian glass, having a collection himself, as shown in this picture of his display cabinet.

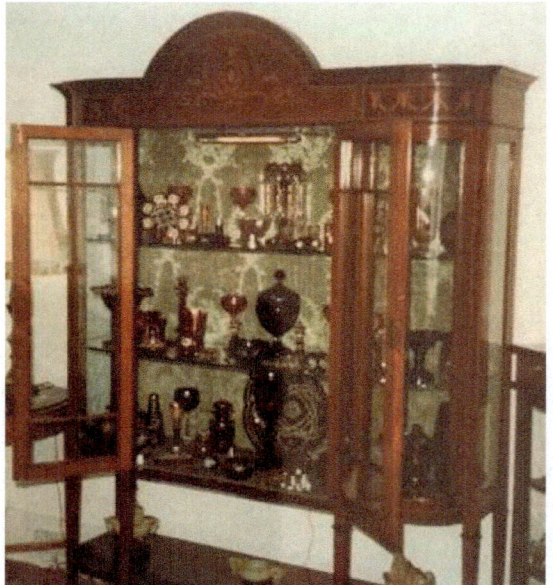

So, we set out to look for Bohemian and French glass and any other quality *objets d'art*, to buy in the provinces and eventually take to London to sell.

Bohemia was once part of the Austrian Empire and then part of Czechoslovakia and is now part of the Czech Republic.

There were quite a lot of antique shops in Boscombe, which is adjacent to Bournemouth, so we had a look there, as well as in a market in Wimbourne. We also knew of a Thursday market in Bath, so we tried that as well and found a few things that were reasonably priced. Gradually I learned what to look for and seemed to have had an eye for things; I'm a very observant person anyway. We did a few local fairs, to test the water and to give me a bit of experience. With a bit of guidance from Harold's two friends, who were already doing the London fairs, we gave the London fairs a try. Harold's two friends gave us the names and phone numbers of two different lady fair organisers, so we took our first steps into the big city. The first one we did was with Patricia in Shepherd's Bush.

As 'newbies', we were given an ante-room, off the main entrance which people seemed to pass on their way in, choosing to go into the main hall first and calling into our room on the way out, after having spent most of their money in the main room. After doing the fair a few times we were moved into the entrance hall where people could look at our stall both on the way in and also on their way out. That was a lot better. We tried another one of Patricia's fairs which was held on the first floor of the Hilton Hotel, Park Lane. That first day, we completely sold out of everything on the stall and I was beginning to think we were onto a really good thing, until I finally realised that our prices were far too low.

Taking into consideration our time, petrol and fees for the hire of a space at the fairs, we needed to bump up the prices to make it worthwhile. This was a whole new learning curve for both Harold and me, so we set out to buy new stock for the next fair with the money we had already made. It wasn't much, but we were learning fast.

We also learned that continental antique dealers would come over to England for the weekend. There was a market in Bermondsey in the East End of London, very early on Friday mornings, followed by the famous Portobello Road one on Saturday and the West End fairs on Sundays. The dealers would be there first thing, as soon as the doors opened for the Sunday fairs, looking for Bohemian glass, silver, porcelain or whatever it was they specialised in. Another useful thing we discovered was that Japanese people like to buy sets of an odd number of items such as five drinking glasses or a set of five cups and saucers which we could buy cheaply, as people in England only want sets of six. We would haggle a bit and buy sets of five items providing they were of good quality. We were then able to sell them to the Japanese at a good profit.

167

I think we were also helped by my natural ability when setting up the stall to be able to place things in such a way that it always seemed to look attractive. It may have been my artistic temperament kicking in but it all helped to draw people to our stall. Soon we discovered about the enormous fairs that were held twice a year. The biggest one then was situated on a disused airfield in Newark, Nottinghamshire.

That should give you an idea just how big these fairs are. It took almost the whole day to get round them. Another one was held at the racecourse at Shepton Mallet in Somerset. That was the nearest large antique fair for us, living in Dorset. Another one we would go to was Ardingly. They've added more venues since we did them, including Newbury Racecourse. These antique fares are where the dealers like to go, looking for bargains, but you had to be there when they opened the gates otherwise others may get them before you. The best thing to do was to book a table there yourself, then you could get a look round before the public were allowed in.

We tried that once but we didn't sell much, our prices were too high for a venue like that, but we did manage to buy a lot of things, which was why we were really there. We came away with bags and bags full of new items to take to the London fairs. As far as I'm concerned the best giant fair to buy from was the one held on the airfield at Newark. We were told that the dealers would line up, the night before to buy and sell from the back of their lorries, before even getting through the gates to the site.

As Newark isn't that far from Nottingham, I would combine it with a trip to see my parents at the same time. Having decided to pay for a dealer's spot at the fair without any intention of setting up my own stall, I stayed with my parents the night before, got up really early the next morning and joined the queue of traders selling from the backs of their lorries. That way, I got an equal chance of picking up the best bargains before the general public went onto the main field. When the gates had opened, I dashed around the field as they were unloading and setting up to try and find even more bargains before members of the public were allowed in. All transactions were done by cash only. I carried the cash required to buy my purchases in a body belt that was hidden under my shirt because at any one time I could probably have been carrying anything up to eight or nine hundred pounds around with me. Everything seemed to work out very well but on a day like that I was worn out with all that running around. I went back to my parents in Nottingham with bags full of goodies to show to my mother, then stayed another night to get over my very tiring but productive day.

We began to get a good reputation, so much so, that the London dealers began to make a bee line for our stall first, as soon as the doors opened. Some of them thought I knew more than I did and started to ask questions about this that and the other; it would seem that we must have been doing all the right things. We had already come a long way since those early days in the ante-room at Shepherd's Bush.

We had to be at the venues of the Sunday fairs by ten o'clock on the Sunday morning, so Harold and I would load up the car the night before and set off from Bournemouth quite early in the morning, in order to be there on time. One weekend, there were two fairs in Park Lane on the same Sunday. They were organised by two different people. The one at the Hilton was organised by Patricia and the other one was at the Dorchester, organised by Kate, another lady with whom we also worked. We had enough stock by now, so we decided to do them both. Harold would go to the Hilton and I would go to the Dorchester. We loaded the car with double the stock and drove to London. I dropped Harold off at the Hilton and carried all his boxes to his table and drove to the Dorchester, did the same and parked the car. That was an extraordinary day.

There had been a Middle Eastern lady, buying lots of things from my stall, followed around by a man she had with her who paid for everything. She wanted to pay by cheque. In general, the dealers didn't like taking cheques, in case they bounced. After asking the lady for her name and address on the back of the cheque, she signed it Princess somebody (I can't remember the surname.) I even felt a bit embarrassed for asking her.

She went round the fair doing the same thing. She left with her bodyguard man carrying all her purchases. Out of curiosity, I followed her out to her out to the door. Parked right outside by the curb were three stretch limousines one just for her and her driver, one for her kids and one for some flunkies who held the limo doors open for her. I had never seen anything like it.

Meanwhile, I was wondering how Harold was getting on at the Hilton. When things began to quieten down a bit, I asked the stall holder next to me to keep an eye on my stall and popped down to the Hilton. Harold had practically sold out, so I rushed back to the Dorchester to fetch some of my spare stock to fill his stall up a bit. What a day that was. Harold's two friends who had introduced us to the London fairs had moved up to the next level which was to have a small shop in the Portobello Road. This enabled them to catch the foreign traders a day before they came to the Sunday fairs. It may seem hard to believe in today's state of the antique trade but both Japanese and American dealers would come over to Britain in order to fill containers of antiques to ship back to their countries. Harold's friends knew such a dealer. They would save all the bits they thought he would like until he came over and then put them all out, for him to choose what he wanted. I still have a friend in America who used to come over twice a year with his wife and fill a container full of furniture and objets d'art, to replenish the stock in their shop in New Jersey.

During the following summer, I was asked to do a summer season at the same Pontins holiday camp at Weymouth, where I had worked before with Keith Monk but this time it was with a different bandleader. It fitted in OK with doing the fairs, it just meant that I had to put a deputy in with the band on Sunday nights and I knew just the man for the job. The summer season wasn't the only engagement that I managed to fit around the antiques. An old pal of mine contacted me to see if I might be interested in a two-day trip to Berlin, with his band playing at a conference for the Bernie Inn steak houses. It was more of a booze-up for the managers than a conference. The year was 1990, the year the Berlin Wall came down. It was amazing to see the difference between the two halves of East and West; the Eastern side looked almost derelict compared to the West. I picked up a small piece of the Berlin wall and brought it back home. I still have that piece; only a piece of concrete when all's said and done, except I know its origin.

Two of the guys standing with me, by what remained of the Berlin wall.

I'm glad I was able to be a witness of those new beginnings for Germany.

We continued doing the fairs for about another eighteen months when out of the blue came a phone call from Johnny Howard, explaining that he had sent his Lead Alto to Monte Carlo for the summer, so would I be prepared to cover for him until he got back, I said OK, on the condition that I would still be carrying on with the antique fairs on Sundays. I knew I could just about manage them both, at a pinch.

The antique fairs finished at 5pm which gave me 45 minutes to pack up, fetch the car, load up and drive to the venue, which was usually the King David Suite just behind Marble Arch at the top of Park Lane and if I was lucky, enough time to grab a KFC or a burger before getting changed into my band uniform to start at seven. I had a few close shaves time-wise and it was a very tiring day, but I usually managed to make it.

Towards the end of that last summer season in Monte Carlo, Shirley Bassey was appearing at the Summer Casino for one night. She had her personal musical director who would be conducting Johnny Howard's band. The music required her to have five saxophones and John only had four in Monte Carlo. He asked me if I would go out, to make up the five saxes. I was flown out and given a room in the Hermitage, the most expensive hotel in Casino Square, Monte Carlo. After I checked into my room, I made my way to the Summer Casino ready for a rehearsal.

The Lead Alto player was Scott Povey. He knew there was another Lead Alto player coming out but he didn't know it was me. Apparently he was preparing for a tussle for the Lead Alto chair but when he saw it was me he was only too pleased to offer it to me. But I had other ideas; I was more prepared to take an easy ride. I thought, "Give him the hot seat; let him play Lead while I play Second Alto." I wasn't about to challenge him for his position in the band, particularly as he was also a Nottingham boy, who had lived about two miles from me during his youth.

There was one musical arrangement in Shirley's cabaret act that required two piccolos. The conductor said,
"Only one piccolo, nobody's ever been able to play two piccolos in tune yet."
We were determined to prove him wrong, so during the performance we defied him and played the two piccolos.

After the show, Scott and I went to the staff canteen for a bite to eat and a drink. I re-iterate at this point, that I am not a big drinker. Usually at home I will only have half a pint of beer or two at the most. I wasn't used to the French beer either. I admit to having more than I should have had that night and have no idea at all how I managed to get back to the Hermitage.

The next morning when I awoke, I broke wind in the bed, but it turned out to be a lot more than just wind. I made a terrible mess on the sheets of this prestigious hotel and was in a panic as to what to do. I was still slightly inebriated and crawled into the bathroom on hands and knees. With my head

171

down the toilet bowl, stuff was coming out both ends. I cleaned the floor in the bathroom and tried to wash the sheet, to no avail.

So I packed my bag, checked out and beat a hasty retreat to the airport. I was so embarrassed over this incident, but my musician friends loved to hear that tale because believe it or not, it was so out of character for me. I think that's what makes it all the more amusing to them.

Towards the end of that final year of John's contract in Monte Carlo, Scott somehow managed to blot his copy book big time. John didn't want him back in the main band in London so it ended up, with me staying on in the main band, as if I'd never been away. I was to remain with the Johnny Howard band for another five years.

22 - JOHNNY HOWARD PART TWO

I received a list of engagements from John, I turned up for the first gig and it almost seemed as If I'd never been away, except for a couple of changes of personnel, it was just back to the old routine. I was still able to do the Sunday antique fairs but I had to do them on my own, because Harold was in Bournemouth. However, he and I were still able to hunt around the weekly markets together for new stock on my days off at home in Bournemouth.

I would occasionally have a stall at Kempton Racecourse at Sunbury-on-Thames, held on Tuesday mornings. I had to do this on my own, of course, because Harold was teaching on weekdays. Once, I spotted an item on a silver dealer's stall that would be perfect for Harold's private collection at home. It was quite expensive, and unfortunately I didn't have enough cash for the purchase, so I paid by cheque, which is something I don't usually do. I was asked to put my name and address on the back of the cheque, which I think in retrospect was a big mistake.

A few months went by and one day we came home to find a window at the back of the house had been broken. Nobody had been in the house because I'd screwed all the downstairs windows closed. On further inspection, we found drops of blood in the drive; the burglar must have cut his hand badly. We called the police and they checked for finger prints but were unable to get any results. One thing they did say was to stay alert because they may come back again later when things had quietened down. My first reaction was to get a burglar alarm fitted but Harold was dead set against it so I was over-ruled.

Some months later, I was doing a job one Friday night with one of John's satellite bands at the Wessex Hotel in Bournemouth. It was very unusual for me to be at home on Saturdays, so we decided to go to Boscombe, to look at a Worcester porcelain figure I'd previously spotted in one of the antique shops. We must only have been away for less than two hours. When we returned and went into the kitchen, the back door was open. The lock on that door was one of the old-fashioned ones that had a big metal key, too big to carry around so we had just left it in the door.

Once the burglars were in the house, all they had to do was unlock the door and away they went. We had two big coal bins by the back door. One of the burglars must have stood on the top of a bin. From there he would have been able to climb onto the upstairs toilet soil pipe, which was at a slight angle, so all he would have had to done was to pull himself through a small window into the separate toilet which I had left slightly open. I had noticed

173

that it was open before we left as I'd gone to the garage to get the car, but thought I can't be bothered to go in again to close the window.

They must have been watching us go out from round the corner because they stripped the house of all Harold's silver. They were professional thieves, as they only took the solid silver and left the silver plate; they knew the difference between the two, and knew exactly what they were doing. They even used our own suitcases to carry our things away. That broke Harold's heart, as some of the silver had been handed down as family heirlooms and some had been left to him by a friend who had lived in the flat above Harold before we bought the house. Amongst the silver they took was a twelve-piece silver cutlery set, knives with solid silver handles, forks and spoons all in a fitted box, they took the silver but left the box and closed the sideboard doors behind them.

Similarly, with a display cabinet containing a collection of scent bottles that Harold had. They took all the ones with silver mounts, put the ones they didn't want back in the cabinet and closed the door. There was a five-branch solid silver Candelabra, with two matching three-branch Candelabra each side that stood on the sideboard in the dining room alongside a silver teapot, sugar basin and milk jug which was also stolen. I rushed round all the local antique shops to warn them that if anyone tried to sell them a large quantity of silver to let the police know but when the police came round to look for fingerprints they said this was a professional job and the silver would already have been sent abroad or melted down. I'll never know how the thieves knew we had all that silver but my main suspect was the silver dealer from whom I had bought that decorative glass egg at the Kempton race course, and who had asked me to put my address on the back of that cheque.

My thinking was justified to some extent, when, some months after the burglary, the two friends who had the shop in Portobello Road saw that

174

same egg on the stall of a lady dealer who we also knew. She allowed them to bring it to our house. It sat there on our breakfast room table, but we couldn't claim it back because the lady had bought it in good faith, not knowing it was stolen property. Because she had paid a good price for it, we couldn't by law claim it back. Another reason we couldn't claim was that the insurance company had already included it and paid out on our claim. We just had to take it on the chin and hand it back to Harold's friends.

We would see the silver dealer from Kempton Park at some of the same fairs we were doing in the West End but I couldn't challenge him face to face because there was no proof he was involved. However, I did wonder if he had been. This took place around 25-30 years ago; the estimated loss was around £50,000 even then, so it would be a lot more than that at today's prices. The insurance company was very good, they didn't quibble too much but even so, Harold didn't get the full value of the loss. It was that experience that made me realise that friends are much more important than possessions.

There were still engagements in London for me to attend, so Harold had to be left in Bournemouth, to deal with the loss by himself for the time being. Soon after that Harold started to have problems with his eyesight and was diagnosed with glaucoma, which is caused by pressure behind the eye. He was given drops to put in twice a day but things didn't seem to improve very much. He couldn't settle alone in that house any more, so suggested we sell up and move nearer to London, so I could come home every night.

It became my job to start looking for a property near to London during the daytime, while still working in the band at night. My starting point to start looking for a new home was around the Osterley Park area on the A4, between London and Heathrow. Osterley Park is an extremely nice area with a tube station that would have been very useful for getting into London. I had used the station before, to park my car, when going into London on the tube, if we had a job during the daytime.

The big problem was to find a house that we could afford with a big enough room to accommodate Harold's grand piano. You can fit a big piano in practically any room in an average house but you can't get much furniture in at the same time.

I looked at one or two 1930s semi-detached properties, where the two rooms had been knocked into one but they were long and narrow. I knew they couldn't be made to look nice and Harold wouldn't go for them. I soon began to realise that the type of property we were looking for was well out of our price range. The nearest property I found was in Richmond. It was something that looked like a converted meeting room which had been turned into a dwelling. It was basically one huge room with a kitchen and downstairs toilet at one end and a mezzanine floor directly above it, consisting of two bedrooms and a bathroom. We could have fitted all of the furniture in the one main room plus the grand piano. With the right décor plus beautiful curtains, the place could have been made to look sumptuous. We hummed and hawed about it, but it was on a steep hill and there wasn't a space for the car, so we had to walk away.

Our £14,750 house was now on the market for £180,000. I was prepared to take out a £20,000 mortgage, because the repayments would be about the same as the cost of travelling between Bournemouth and London plus my accommodation costs. This would give us a £200,000 budget, with which to find a decent house.

Since moving from Harold and Joan Fisher's house in Brentwood, I had been living with a middle-aged couple in Staines, Middlesex. The husband was about to retire from his job as head teacher in a school for children with learning difficulties. They were planning to move back to Stoke-on-Trent, in the potteries, which was their home town. Their house was a four-bedroomed detached house which they were planning to put on the market, but which they were prepared to let us buy at the price we could afford, so we went ahead and bought it.

It wasn't perfect by any means, but we managed to fit the furniture in, and at least we were able to go out buying new stock as well as spending more time at home together during the day, plus knowing I would be back every night, sleeping in my own bed. One of the first things we did was to have a burglar alarm fitted.

You can't even begin to compare Staines with Bournemouth but it does have the River Thames. We only had to cross the road and go down a small passageway to be able to walk or cycle along the towpath. We often used to walk along by the river into Staines to do the shopping. It could have been worse. One day, we took a boat trip down the river to Hampton Court Palace. That was a nice day out.

Meanwhile, Harold's glaucoma was getting progressively worse, so we went to the doctor in Staines who sent him to the local eye hospital, where he saw an oriental eye specialist, who soon discovered that that the eye drops he'd been given in Bournemouth weren't the right ones for him, as he was allergic to the preservatives. He therefore needed some different drops without the preservative and that made all the difference.

Getting back to my work, which is the main point of the book:

Along with the King David Suite, a large majority of other engagements were at the Grosvenor House Hotel, either in the smaller function room or in the Great Room, with its four magnificent chandeliers. It is oval-shaped with a balcony that runs all the way round the room. For one function held in the Great Room, the client had festoons of flowers intertwined through the iron railings all the way round the huge balcony. They must have cost more than hiring the 16-piece band that Johnny Howard was now standing in front of. Not only that, but the client had also flown Sacha Distel from France for the cabaret, along with his own backing band. The money that some of the rich society people must have is almost beyond belief; situations like that certainly opened my eyes.

On another occasion the band was doing a booking somewhere out of London and during the course of the evening I broke the reed on my Saxophone, I had to nip off to the band room to get a new reed. Apparently, as I ran off the stage, John turned to the bass player and said,
"Where's Jeff gone, it's not Christmas is it?"
(This was a reference to me once having walked out on him on Christmas Eve!)

During the time when Harold and I were living in Staines, I went to see the doctor because it was painful to hold my right arm in the position required to play the flute. I demonstrated the position I needed to hold my arm. He told me I had a frozen shoulder and the only way to cure it was to have a cortisone injection, while adding,
"But I don't want to give you one; you would have to live with it for the rest of your life."
That sort of comment was no good to me, as I needed to be able to play my flute, as part of my living.

I happened to be speaking about this to Melt Kingston, the bass player and he said,
"I'll cure it for you."
Unbeknown to me he had the natural gift of healing. As I had previously come across the psychic power of the old lady in the cafe all those years ago in Nottingham, who predicted that I would be a policeman. I was prepared to try anything once, so let him have a go. He didn't need to touch me at all. He just put his hand close to my shoulder. Soon I began feel the heat from his hands, as he started to perspire profusely, occasionally shaking his hands towards the floor as if he was shaking the pain away from my shoulder. It took a matter of minutes before he stopped. I went home after the gig and when I awoke the next morning, the pain had gone, never to return. I saw him

use those powers on other members of the band, after they'd seen how he'd helped me.

One summer, during my return to the main band, we were booked to do the relief night for the resident band at a Pontins holiday camp at Pakefield, Suffolk every Monday night for the whole summer. We used a coach for that journey, as it was quite a trek from London.

I think the gigs were on Mondays, but it really doesn't matter which day it was. Johnny Howard had been a semi-professional alto sax player in his youth, along with his brother, who had been a drummer. They had formed a small semi-pro band and John still owned an alto sax. (I choose my words when I say owned.) He would bring it along sometimes and pretend he was playing it, just to make a show.

He brought it to Pakefield one night and was strutting around miming very well. In Glenn Miller's "In the Mood" there is an exchange of sax solos. The alto plays four bars solo followed by the tenor sax for another four bars and then it's back to the alto again. I would play the alto solo while John mimed it, the tenor player played his four bars and I played the next and so on. One night at Pakefield, I just ran off during the four-bar exchanges and left John to it, much to the delight of the rest of the band, who saw the funny side. Needless to say, we never saw the sax again after that.

At Pakefield, there was also a girl Bluecoat, called Mitsi, who fancied herself as a bit of a singer. She thought she was going to be a pop star but she was really awful. She would stand right in the middle of the dance floor and murder ever song she tried to sing. I used to play a semitone out, to put her off but I don't think she ever noticed.

You may recall from Chapter 18, when I was with Eric Delaney's band, that he bought me a set of bagpipes, and I mentioned that I had fun with them later. This was one of those moments. This girl singer liked to sing "Amazing Grace", which had bagpipes on the record. One week, I decided I would take my bagpipes to Pakefield. No one in the band even knew I had a set of bagpipes at home, let alone that I could play them. I didn't tell anybody that I was going to do this. I left the stage, put on my tartan jacket and tam o'shanter and began to walk out onto the dance floor, playing "Amazing Grace". The bagpipes can only play in one key, and, unfortunately for her, she wasn't singing in the same key that the bagpipes play in.

When I came out from the side of the stage, the band couldn't play for laughing. Mitzi the Bluecoat thought it was wonderful and beckoned me to join her in the middle of the floor. As I got nearer she began to hear the clash of the different keys she turned to me and said out of the corner of her mouth,

"You're taking the piss out of me, aren't you?"

Without stopping, I nodded, "Yes" back to her, with which she threw the microphone on the floor and ran off crying. She wasn't the only one crying either. The band was crying with laughter. The drummer was falling off his stool with laughter. Needless to say, she never sang with the band again.

Sometime later, the Johnny Howard band was booked for a big conference in Zurich, Switzerland, one of my favourite cities. We flew over with all the equipment, early on the morning of the engagement, because the stage had to be set before the conference started. This then gave us all day in Zurich.

After some exploring, we all met for lunch, which entailed some rather heavy drinking. (You have already read about my experience on the coach to Sunderland.) I wasn't that drunk and I didn't disgrace myself but I did struggle to do my job that night. When we got back to the hotel after the gig, I went straight to bed while most of the other guys were having a party in a room down the corridor.

I hadn't been in bed very long when the hotel phone rang in my room. It was the boys down the corridor asking me to join them. I said, "No" at first but they insisted that I join them, so I said,

"OK, so long as I can come as I am."

What they didn't know was that I sleep in the nude. Don't forget, I'm still inebriated and being an extrovert exhibitionist, I was ready to do as they asked. I looked out of the door to make sure no one was around and hurried down the corridor to their room. Del the singer opened the door. They were pretty shocked when they first saw me but I was beyond caring. I laid on one of the beds in the room and Del took a photo; check out the eyes in the picture - they speak for themselves.

Later, they dressed me in just a bow tie and cummerbund, exposing just a tiny bit of my genitals, below the lower edge of the cummerbund.

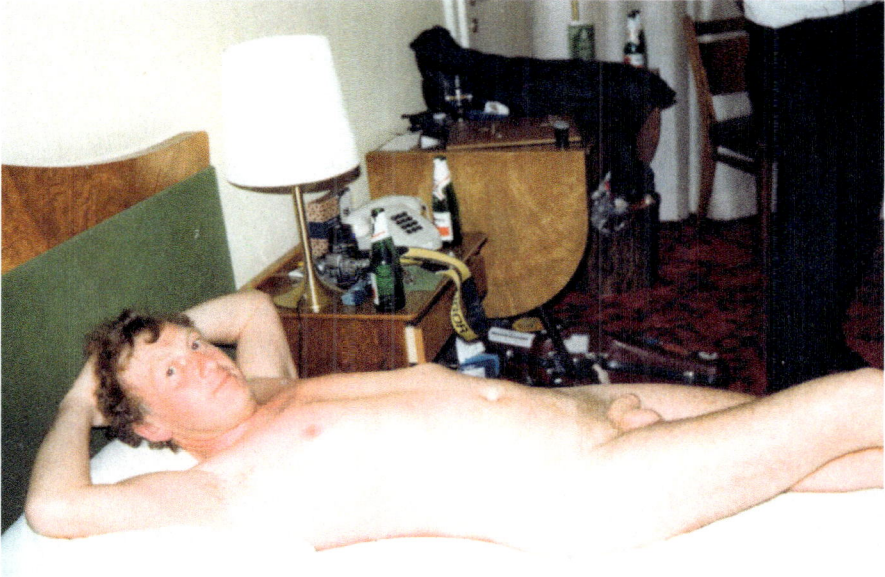

181

After the novelty wore off, it was time to return to my room. My roommate for the night was already in the room. I knocked and asked him to open the door for me, as I'd forgotten to take my key. He refused. I was standing in the corridor, stark naked, when I heard the lift coming up. Eventually, he opened the door at the last minute. Phew! The next morning we all flew back to Heathrow. Of all the things I got up to during my working life that was one of the most memorable.

On a separate occasion, the band was playing somewhere in the country. During the break, we were given a large platter of sandwiches. Everyone dived into them; there were hands grabbing sandwiches from all angles until there was just one left in the middle of the platter. John had missed out, as he'd been caught chatting to the client. Nobody wanted that poor little last sandwich. Aided and abetted by the tenor sax player, I picked up the sandwich, opened it, wiped my penis all over the ham inside, and put it together again. Along came John, who commented,
"I see the gannets have been at the sandwiches again", while proceeding to eat it. I don't know how we managed to keep straight faces. I swear that's the truth. Just in case any of my colleagues ever read this, my partner in crime on that day was Dave Bishop.

Through a contact I had, I was asked to make an album of Barry White songs. Instead of the vocals, I would play the tunes on the alto and tenor sax. I arrived at the recording studio just off Marble Arch. One or two of my musician pals were already in the studio. The rhythm section was just like the original Barry White records; all I had to do was play the tune. My parts were quite difficult, as they were written exactly like Barry White would have sung them; the phrasing I had to play was exactly the same and had to be precise. I also had to play a harmony part on top, which is called double tracking, so there was no room for errors. I must have done a reasonable job because I was asked to do another one at a later date. I got paid and thought no more about it.

Some time later, I went home to see my parents and my dad said,
"Have you made a record?"
I said, "Why?"
He told me there was a record they were playing while the BBC television test card was screened. For any of my younger readers who don't remember the test card, I'll try to explain.

It was used by TV engineers as well as by the public, to help to adjust the picture on the television screens, getting the colours just right, as well as straightening out alignment of the image.

Up to around forty years ago, the TV companies didn't start their programmes until around mid-day; they weren't broadcast 24/7 like they are now. Before programmes started, they would just have a test card on the screen but they played background music.

My parents liked to have the music on, while having their lunch, waiting for the One o'clock News. I know that all saxophone players have their own distinctive sound, just as every person has their own voice that's recognisable to their friends. My dad had listened to me practising for so long, he recognised my sound and apparently he said to mother,
"I reckon that's our Jeff."

One of the gigs we did was for a Hunt Ball in the Great Room at the Grosvenor House Hotel. There are many fox hunts all over the country. Among the most well-known are the Quorn Hunt, the Leicester and the Bicester. Some nearer to London are the Crawley & Horsham. Probably the closest to London is the Ashford. This function in the Great Room was a combined Dinner Dance for several of these hunts.

I used to like listening to a show on the radio called *Round the Horne* with Kenneth Horne and Kenneth Williams. It could be very funny but sometimes a bit close to the knuckle. One of the scenarios was about the Waddock Hunt. This gave me an idea for the Grosvenor House Hunt Ball. During the evening, I hatched a plot, of which the rest of the band was aware. At that time there was a song riding high in the charts by Stevie Wonder. It was called, 'I Just called to say I love you.' It was John's current favourite and he would call it out at any opportunity he had, so I knew it was a certainty to use for what was my plot.

183

I wrote on a piece of paper:

Could you please play
"I Just Called to Say I Love You"
for members of the Thurrock Hunt.

We passed the note to a waiter to give to John. We all watched him, pacing backwards and forwards, looking at this request while we were playing something else. When that tune came to an end, he moved towards the microphone and announced it to the whole room. He tried to count the band in, but nothing happened. Not one member of the band could play for laughing. I still laugh even now, when I tell the story to friends.

I have mentioned before about how my bronchitis affects me, particularly during the winter months and it has appeared to get worse as I've got older. I had long suspected that the worsening is connected to pollution, as when I had previously been driving backwards and forwards to Bournemouth, it always seemed to start when I was on the motorway, owing to the fumes from the exhausts. During one particular winter, while living in Staines, I was coming home during the night and passed Heathrow airport. I had to stop, get out of the car, and lean over the bonnet to cough my heart out, it was so bad.

There is a pollution monitor on the top of the Debenhams store in Staines. I discovered that Staines is one of the most polluted areas of London, because it's on the take-off side of the airport and it's also near one of the busiest parts of the M25 motorway. I went to see my doctor about my endless coughing. The doctor told me the cough wouldn't get any better unless I moved away from the Thames Valley. Talking everything through with Harold, we both recognised that neither of us had made any social friends in Staines, except for our immediate neighbours. At least I had my colleagues in the band but all Harold's friends were in Bournemouth. We made the decision to sell up and to move back to the seaside in dear old Bournemouth where the air is much cleaner.

We put the Staines house on the market and started to look around in Bournemouth. The housing market wasn't as buoyant at that time, we lost a bit of money on the Staines house but managed to find (with a little bit of help from one of Harold's friends) a much cheaper, bigger and better house than the one we had bought in Bournemouth some years earlier. It needed a lot doing to it but it was basically sound.

Harold was able to spend his last years back in Bournemouth with his friends. After we moved back to Bournemouth, it was back to the weekly commute for me. Until I retired, I lodged with one of our ex-neighbour's from Staines.

Before renovation

After renovation

Melt, the bass player brought his tarot cards with him to the gig one evening. I asked if he would give me a reading during the band interval. I don't know what all the cards mean but I do remember that one of the cards was the hangman. Together with other cards the combination pointed to the fact that I was on the edge of a cliff and if I didn't jump I would be pushed. That was the top and bottom of it. I didn't think much about it, and for the time being, things just carried on as usual.

Some months later, five of the band, including me had a letter from John saying, as from such and such date, I will be booking musicians as and when I need them. He didn't actually sack anybody but I thought it was rather an ingenious way of gradually phasing out the older members of the band. Those members to be phased-out were me, the tenor player, the trumpet player, the guitar player and Sally, the singer. In fairness, I was not only the oldest but Sally and I were the longest-serving members. In my case I had gone from a blond younger man to a white-haired old codger.

Johnny Howard did like his blond young men around him, his current favourite was the blond boy singer and I was replaced by a young blond Alto sax player. In fairness, times were changing; it was becoming more difficult to get work for the band.

The Drink-Drive ban had been introduced and there weren't so many of the kind of big dinner dance, where people would have wine and spirits with their meal, before driving home. They either had to come in taxis or not at all. That impacted on places like the Grosvenor House Hotel, along with the other big hotels we worked in. Later on came the congestion charge, which made things even worse. Except for Saturdays and Sundays, most of the weekday functions began to fizzle out. John wanted younger people in the band who could relate more to the young brides and the 13-year old bar mitzvah boys.

I must admit, I lost a lot of weight through worry, during the first week or so. It was back to the drawing board and freelance work for me and the others. So Melt and the tarot cards were right, I didn't jump off the cliff but in the end I was pushed. Things were to work out much better before long. My guardian angel was always behind me.

23 - A FREELANCE MUSICIAN - 1991

Over the years, I prided myself that I hadn't been out of work for more than just a few weeks at any one time. Latterly I'd had the antiques business to fall back on, if necessary. I'd been with Johnny Howard for seventeen years and told repeatedly by other musicians that loyalty was the quickest way out of the music business. On the surface, it appeared that could maybe be true, but it turned out that during the next few years, until I was forced by circumstances to retire at the age of 62, I had the most varied and interesting end to my career.

This time, I was in a happier place financially than I was when I had a break from Eric Delaney's band. I needn't have worried; because it wasn't long before word got around that I was available, and the phone began to ring. Howard McGill, the young alto player who took over from me in Johnny Howard's band had previously been booked to do a summer season at the conference centre in Bournemouth, with Russ Abbot and Bella Emberg, which he couldn't do now, so he gave it to me.

The engagement was perfect, as it meant I would be home for the summer, earning good money right from the start of my freelance career. It was a pretty uneventful summer season as far as I can remember. Not at all like the ones which I had previously done with Eric Delaney in the past. The Bournemouth conference hall doesn't lend itself to that kind of entertainment, as was proved by it being the first and last summer season to be held there.

After the summer season, one of the first people to call was the entertainments manager, who booked the musicians, cabaret acts and dancers for P&O cruise liners, asking if I could do a ten day cruise round the Mediterranean, as a deputy for the regular alto player, who had to have some shore leave.

This was the first opportunity I'd had to do a trip on the boats since those early days, when I auditioned for Geraldo. The cruise ship on which I would be travelling was the *Oriana*.

When I arrived, the person for whom I was deputizing was still on the ship. He was someone I had worked with in the past, in the Johnny

Howard band. The working conditions for musicians had changed over the past thirty-five years or so since I'd auditioned for Geraldo during the early 1960s. In those days musicians had more or less passenger status. Now they were treated more like seamen, just like part of the crew with lots of do's and don'ts, but more of the 'don'ts' than the 'do's.

First of all, I had to learn about how to operate the water-tight doors on the lower decks in case of an accident. Then I had to do lifeboat drill, to be able to help people into the life boats in an emergency. The man who was instructing us was a pompous jumped-up individual who got my back up straight away. I hadn't been in the armed forces or ever had to take orders from anybody before. I was too old now to start taking orders from him. He recognised my rebellious attitude straight away but I wasn't having any of his nonsense.

We couldn't drink at the bars, fraternise with the passengers or go around the swimming pool; we could only drink in the crew bar, which was called the Pig and Whistle and eat in the crew mess. Eating in the crew mess was probably the best of the restrictions. The quality and variety of food available was top-class, plus you could go back to have as much as you wanted. Finally, the biggest blow for me was when the ship was in port. All the passengers and majority of the crew were going off for shore time, or day trips of the area. The musicians had to stay on board ship for half of the day in order to perform what they call in-port manning duty. That meant being on duty at the top or bottom of a stairwell to direct any of the passengers left on board to safety in case of fire. I stayed on board in most of the ports; it wasn't worth getting off most of the time. The only time I did go off the ship was in Athens, because I wanted to see the Acropolis.

When the ship arrived back into Southampton, I couldn't get off quickly enough, telling myself I'd never do that again; I was too old to be ordered about by jumped-up little nobodies. As I was getting off the ship, I bumped into the entertainments executive who asked me if I'd enjoyed it, I said,
"No, don't ever ring me again to do another one", but they rang again twice before they finally got the message.

Howard McGill, the young alto player who took my place with Johnny Howard had left Ray McVay's band to join John. I got in touch with Ray, so we swapped jobs, which enabled me to join Ray's band instead. What a culture shock it was for me, John's band was musically excellent with what musicians call a tight or neat sound.

Ray's band on the other hand was loose-sounding, with more of an easy-going attitude, which was related to the different kinds of personality of the bandleader. John was always very smartly dressed and correct, whereas Ray was more laid back and easy going. Half of the sax parts were either missing altogether or not in their correct place in the library; I couldn't find anything. Most of the time I had to play from memory, or make something up, not at all what I'd been used to with John's band.

At that time, Ray didn't have that many jobs compared to Johnny Howard, allowing me to do other things in between Ray's gigs. I had known Ray McVay since he had his very first band at the Mecca dance hall in Derby called the Locarno. His real name is William McVey. His was one of the first dance bands to be more of a show band and changed the concept of a lot of bands who followed in his footsteps. My dad used to take me to the Locarno when I was a teenager to watch the band. At the time it was an entirely new way of approaching things.

Ray was very popular with the Mecca organisation. At one point he did all the *Come Dancing* TV programmes, becoming more well-known than Johnny Howard. I heard a funny story about Ray and *Come Dancing*. For any ballroom dancing competitions, the tempos must be exactly at the correct speed, hence the term Strict Tempo. In order to be able to get the timing precise, the band had to be correct with the speed during the *Come Dancing* programme. In order to be sure if the tempo was correct, Ray's brother (who was a trombone player) would lay out of sight under the piano with a metronome giving Ray the correct tempo. I recall that I had a metronome on my music stand, while playing at Osmington Bay holiday camp. It was the main Pontins camp for the ballroom dancing enthusiasts. They too could be quite pedantic about the correct tempos; I also had to be just as precise likewise.

In the past, Ray had always had a big band but the current gig band was just six musicians and three singers. Apart from his gig band, Ray had quite a few fingers in other pies. He had a request to supply a big band to accompany a Frenchman, who fancied himself as a singer. In his own mind, this Frenchman thought he sounded like Frank Sinatra. He was awful. Ray must have already heard him sing, because when the band was in the rehearsal room first, Ray told us how bad this man was but added,
"Don't laugh. He's got pots of money and he's paying the bill for all of this."

You've never heard anything like it; when he started to sing, it was difficult not to snigger. We nicknamed him French Frank. I don't remember exactly, but I have a feeling we rehearsed in London for about a week before the gig which was in the Palace of Versailles, in France.

On the morning of the gig, we all flew out with the equipment. After it was all set up, there was a lovely lunch laid on, including the obligatory French wine. After the meal I went for a nap but typical of the trumpet players, they carried on drinking. This Frenchman must have been really loaded, He'd invited all his friends to this lavish party, in the hope they would crowd round the stage with adoring faces. Instead, they just carried on talking and drinking with each other not taking a bit of notice; it could have been anybody as far as his friends cared. I think we only did one set before it was all over. Never mind, the job had given me the opportunity to see the Palace of Versailles, something I wouldn't have done ordinarily. We flew home the next day and that was the end of that.

It was a lucky day for me when I started working with Ray McVay. Whenever he had work that required a big band, I was on it, one way or another. Shortly afterwards we flew out to Saudi Arabia for one night to play for some kind of a beach party. The stage had been built on the beach, surrounded by beautiful white drapes that wafted in the warm sea breeze, reminiscent of the Arabian Nights. I'm not at all sure who or what the party was for but it was a great experience for me. Again, there was a fantastic meal provided before we started work. I remember the lobster above all else.

After the gig, we all went back to the hotel, where everyone was allocated rooms which had to be shared. I was sharing with the tenor player who refused point blank to share with me because of my sexual orientation. There wasn't any nastiness; he just said he wasn't prepared to share with me. The hotel receptionist repeatedly told Ray there weren't any other rooms available. Eventually, I said to Ray,
"Don't worry about it; I'll just sleep down here in reception on this couch".
It was very strange how a room suddenly became available for me. After that incident, Ray always made sure I had my own room. That was one of the very few times my sexuality caused a problem. Even then, I reiterate, there wasn't any actual nastiness; most people accepted me as a good musician, which is how it should be, as what goes on in my private life does not affect my ability to do the job.

Lots of work started to come my way, including a phone call from the Joe Loss Orchestra to do part of the world cruise on the *QE2*. I knew that Joe usually did the whole of the world cruise, but by now Joe was retired and no longer appeared with the band. This particular year they were only doing part of it. The reason I had been asked to do this cruise was because the regular Alto player was in hospital, undergoing a triple heart by-pass and would be off work for some time.

The band was now being run by Sam Watmough, the trombone player, who had been with Johnny Hilton, the bandleader, at the Grafton Rooms in Liverpool all those years ago, but he had just left Liverpool before I joined the band. As Joe Loss was not appearing with the band any more, they had only been offered the last leg of the cruise.

The whole band, including me, flew out to Israel to meet the *QE2* at the port of Haifa. Having previously said I wouldn't do another cruise, this time was different. The Joe Loss Band had full passenger status. We had our own table in the Dining Room; we could drink at the bar, fraternise with the passengers and have a swim in the pool. This was really living the highlife. Although Johnny Francis was correct when he told me this band was more of a show band than a musical one, I tried to enjoy the experience and ignore the musical side. The ship docked at a lot of ports in the Mediterranean on the way back. This time I was able to get off for the whole day and explore the various cities. Finally, we arrived back at Southampton. That wasn't the end of my engagement. I had been booked for at least another six weeks, as the Alto player was expected to be off work for at least that amount of time.

The band didn't have that much work, maybe two performances a week, most of which involved travelling on the band coach. Most of them seemed to be long trips. One was to York, to do a public dance, where I saw a couple of faces who had been regulars at the Pontins holiday camp in Weymouth, during the time I was the bandleader there. The best gig was a concert in Liverpool, where I was the Lead Alto of a full five saxophone team which was a bit of a rarity by then; most other bands only having four saxes.

By now, I was beginning to get lots of offers, mainly from other sax players I'd worked with over the years and I was beginning to wish I had gone freelance sooner. Those words of advice I'd been given before about loyalty being the quickest way out of the business were beginning to make sense, it would seem it was better to have lots of fingers in lots of pies. I was very friendly with a baritone sax player called Dave Willis, who used to do a lot of work with Johnny Howard. He also had lots of other connections and was able to pass things on to me that he couldn't do himself, while at the same time recommending me to other bandleaders for alto work; I suppose you could say he championed me. Dave and I became close friends, continuing long after we both retired. Sadly, Dave passed away earlier this year, 2020. I had visited Dave and his wife Isabel's home several times during the past few years and I will miss our phone calls.

In 1993, I had a call from Ray McVay. He was taking a Glenn Miller style band to Japan for a five week tour and asked if I would like to go along on Baritone sax. Many years before, my drummer friend and flat mate Harold Fisher had done a tour of Japan. Then, I had wished that I would get opportunities like that, so now it was my turn.

The Lead Alto was Ronnie Chamberlain, who had previously been the Lead Alto with the Ted Heath Band. Not only was he a great saxophone player, but also a lovely person too. I had the privilege to work with him a lot after that tour. Scott Povey was on second Alto. Scott is the Alto player from Nottingham, who was in Monte Carlo, when I flew out to play for Shirley Bassey, some years earlier.

Bobby Byrne, my gay trombone player friend was also on the tour, so at least I knew some of the guys. The Drummer was Bobby Orr. I remember going along with my drummer friend Harold Fisher to see Bobby, years before during my first job in London. Bobby Orr was playing at the original Ronnie Scott's club in Soho, London. Bobby was a big name then and was still a great drummer when I worked with him. I was now playing in the same band as him, along with the great Ronnie Chamberlain. This felt like another step up the ladder for me.

We rehearsed for four days, before leaving for Japan. This was the kind of thing I'd been missing out on before. Everything comes to those who wait, so they say. The tour was so well-organised, from the moment of stepping into Heathrow airport until returning five weeks later. Everything was taken care of, as may be seen on the first page of the itinerary. After the tour of 30 concerts, we flew home on 21st October.

RAY McVAY ORCHESTRA "1993"
JAPAN TOUR ITINERARY

MONDAY 13TH SEPTEMBER

15.30 Meet at the ALL NIPPON Check-In desk, Terminal 3, HEATHROW AIRPORT
       Flight NH 202; departing 17.55

TUESDAY 14TH

13.55 Arrive at New Tokyo International Airport and go to hotel by coach.

HOTEL : KORIYAMA VIEW HOTEL ANNEX : TEL. 010 81 249 39 1111; FAX. 39 1654
       10-10, NAKACHO, KORIYAMASHI 963, JAPAN

WEDNESDAY 15TH

OFF
HOTEL : KORIYAMA VIEW HOTEL ANNEX
23.00 Leave baggage outside room door for collection

THURSDAY 16TH

09.50   Leave hotel for concert hall by coach
13.00   Rehearsal
18.30   1st Concert (Yonezawa-shi Shimin Bunka Kaikan)
        Back to hotel on foot after the concert.
22.00   Leave baggage outside room door for collection

HOTEL : TOKYO DAIICHI HOTEL, YONEZAWA
        1-13-3, CHUO, YONEZAWASHI 992

FRIDAY 17TH

08.50   Leave hotel for Hotel Italia Ken by coach
16.20   Leave hotel for concert hall by taxi
18.30   2nd Concert (Niigata Kennin Kaikar)
        Back to hotel by taxi after concert
22.00   Leave baggage outside room door for collection

HOTEL : HOTEL ITALIA KEN TEL. 010 81 25-224-5111 FAX. 224-7679
        7 NISHIBORIDORI NIIGATASHI 951

SATURDAY 18TH

11.10   Leave hotel for Niigata Station by taxi
11.51   Depart from Niigate Station by Joetsu Shinkansen 'Asahi #310' (for Toyko)
13.52   Arrive at Tokyo Station and to hotel by coach
15.50   Leave hotel for concert hall by coach
18.30   3rd Concert (Kawasaki-shi Kyoiku Bunks Kaikan)
        Back to hotel by coach after concert
22.30   Leave baggage outside room door for collection

HOTEL : HOTEL TAKANAWA   TEL. 010 813 5488-1000 FAX 5488-1009
        2-1-17 TAKANAWA, MINATOKU, TOKYO 107, JAPAN

193

We flew with the Japanese airline ANA, which stands for All Nippon Airways. After arriving in Tokyo, we were driven by taxi to the Koriyama hotel. After unpacking in my room, I decided to go to the lobby, to see if any of the rest of the band was around; no one was around. I found out later that instead of unpacking first, it would have been a better idea to dump the suitcase in the room, leaving the unpacking until later. The rest of the band who had been there before had all gone out for a drink. I had no idea where to go for something to eat or what to order if I did find anywhere. I'm ashamed to say that my first meal in Japan was a McDonalds.

The band was joined by an American trumpet player by the name of Zeke Zarchy, who had once been the lead Trumpet with the original Glenn Miller Orchestra. As you might imagine, he was now getting on in years and was playing fourth Trumpet with Ray's Japanese band for most of the concert. Ray would introduce him as one of the original members of the Glenn Miller band. He would then come to the front of the stage to play a solo.

Dear People of Japan,

I am indeed honored to be invited again by the Ito Music Company to visit your most beautiful country of Japan. As always, I look forward to seeing my many friends, the lovely countryside and the majestic Mount Fuji.

The fine Ray McVay Orchestra is a treat for anyone who wishes to recapture the sounds and spirit of the great Glenn Miller orchestra. Our previous tours have met with the most enthusiastic receptions and I'm sure you will be enjoying an even greater show this year.

Sincerely,

Zeke Zarchy

Zeke Zarchy
Special Guest/Trumpet

194

Zeke Zarchy

In the mornings, there was always an American-style self-service breakfast, available in all the hotels we stayed in; all we had to do was to find our own evening meals. I wasn't too keen on the Japanese food but there were a lot of Chinese and Italian restaurants, so I ate in those most of the time. Sometimes you could find a restaurant with American-style food, with plates of imitation plastic meals in the window. When you decided which one you wanted, you just called the waiter to the window and pointed to the meal you would like and they cooked it for you. Where there's a will there's a way, as they say.

On the itinerary, you will see pictures of suitcases, planes and the Bullet Train. On the first train journey we were taken to the station by taxi but on other occasions it could be just a short walk away from the hotel, in which case the Japanese promoter whose name was Mr Ito would walk ahead of the band, carrying a white flag on a stick, so we could all see him. We would walk in pairs behind him. The naughty boys at the back would whistle Colonel Bogey as we marched along, mimicking scenes from the film 'Bridge over the River Kwai'.

My first impression of the Bullet Train was how everything about it was so organised. The platform had various numbers written on the edge, the tickets had corresponding numbers on them. We had to line up behind our matching number on our tickets. The train arrived dead on time, it stopped directly on the corresponding numbers, so when the doors opened we just had to walk straight onto the train, with no rushing around to find the nearest door, as we have to, here in England. Everything was so precise. No time was wasted in the station, before we were off again.

Incidentally, if you would like to see a Bullet Train, they have one in the National Railway Museum in York. They go so fast that your feet can swell up just as they do on an aircraft when flying. It was an absolutely amazing experience.

Ronnie Chamberlain & Bobby Byrne
asleep on the Bullet train

If we didn't use the train between the cities, we would fly. Most of the planes have cameras on the front landing wheel, which would be switched on when approaching the runway so you can watch the landing on your little screens on the seat in front. This can be a little disconcerting, to say the least, when you first see the plane getting closer to the ground. What appealed to my sense of humour was when the stewardess made her 'thank

196

you' address in broken English. Many Japanese have difficulty pronouncing the letter 'L', so when she said,

"Hope you had a pleasant f_ight" it came out as "Hope you had a present fright."

It certainly was a fright to see the runway looming up at such great speed through the camera, when landing for the first time.

One thing for which I wasn't prepared was the reception from the Japanese audiences. They absolutely loved the Glenn Miller sound, which really surprised me, considering the conflict between Japan and the USA during the Second World War. For the first time in my life, I experienced crowds of people waiting outside the stage doors of the concert halls, asking for autographs. Some would even come on board the band bus in order to get our autographs. I thought, "What do you want mine for? I'm not world famous." Most of them didn't realise we were all English, not American.

We did 30 concerts during that tour, with occasional days off, to explore the sights. Most of the cities I'd never heard of but some of the better known ones were: Tokyo (obviously), Osaka, Kyoto, Nagoya, Kobe, Takanawa.

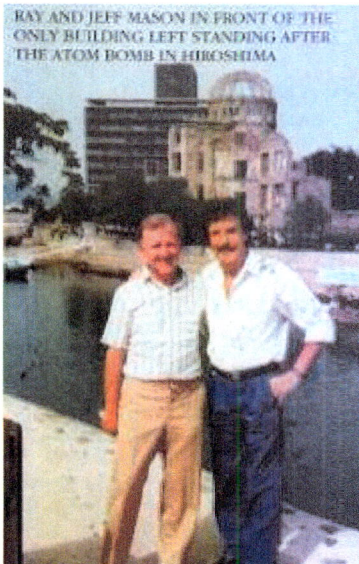
RAY AND JEFF MASON IN FRONT OF THE ONLY BUILDING LEFT STANDING AFTER THE ATOM BOMB IN HIROSHIMA

Last but definitely not the least was Hiroshima. What had been the epicentre of the bomb is now a peace park. It was somewhat of an eerie place, without any sound of birds and most people were also quiet, paying their respect. I had heard that birds don't sing at the sites of German concentration camps. I experienced that same eerie quietness in the peace park for myself.

In the park there's a museum which I visited. I was moved by seeing artefacts, including the famous step where a boy had sat and left an imprint of his bottom, still there for everyone to see.

It was interesting to see the situation from the Japanese prospective rather than the usual American view of the catastrophe.

197

As with many things, we have all experienced from time to time, it doesn't matter how many pictures you may see of a situation, they don't ever have the same impact as seeing them first-hand for yourself. I find it better to go out on my own to do the things I want to do, instead of aimlessly wandering around in a group, getting nowhere. I like to soak up the culture, and I think this was something that had rubbed off from my partner Harold.

Temple, Kyoto

Despite my Mother's pre-conceived dislike of the Japanese people, because of the husband one of her relatives coming back from a prisoner of war camp, looking like a skeleton. I found them very charming; I think the word genteel may sum up the situation very well. They would greet you with a bow and a smile. If we went into a department store, there would be two young ladies to bow and open the doors for you, I imagine it was more like Victorian England was years ago. They had more respect for their culture and traditional way of life than we do, especially in this present time in England.

It's now 27 years since I was there; it's quite possible that things have changed by now; I don't know. You weren't allowed to eat or drink anything in the street. There wasn't any litter or any Coke cans left lying around. I was once told off by a Japanese lady for eating an apple, while walking down a residential street. Speaking of apples, one of our concerts

198

was on a less tourist-visited island, where the locals didn't see many Europeans.

I wanted to buy some apples from a market stall, pointing to the apples I wanted, holding up four fingers to indicate how many I would like. He wrote down the price. After paying him, he tentatively held out his hand for me to shake. Japanese people don't shake hands; they bow to one another. His beaming smile said it all to me. If you could have seen the happiness in his face to have had the physical contact with another person's hand, it was truly heart-warming.

After the concert that night, we were taken to our hotel, which was more of a motel than the 4-Star type hotels we had been staying in. I can only describe the accommodation as a plastic pod; the whole thing was a compact moulded plastic pod. It did have hot and cold running water with washbasin, toilet and shower. The whole thing, including the wardrobe and bed were all one big mould. The bed was more like a bath with a mattress in it, which was also quite small, being designed to accommodate the Japanese stature. Ray McVay played merry hell with the promoter for the sub-standard accommodation, but it was in rather a remote part of Japan and I for one was pleased to see and have the experience.

I had seen pictures of a large indoor aquarium just on the outskirts of Tokyo. It had a tunnel you could walk through and look at sharks, stingrays or turtles from underneath the water. Bearing in mind that this was 37 years ago, it was the first such one I'd seen; I was keen to go to have a look it.

I went down to the underground railway, in order to find out how to get there. I was completely confused because all the destinations were in Japanese and I didn't know the word for Aquarium, so I had to leave without getting anywhere, but what I did see with my own eyes was how the Japanese run and jump into the already packed railway carriages during their rush hour. I'd seen it on the TV but it really does happen during the busy times.

Back at the hotel, I had another look at the map and counted how many stops to my destination and went back to the tube station the next day and made it to the Aquarium.

Sadly, the Japanese tour was coming to an end but sometime during the last week of the tour, Mr Ito, the Japanese promoter left his camera in the communal dressing room. Someone suggested taking a picture of one of us doing a moony, and being the extrovert that I am, I volunteered; so the picture was taken. As we were talking about what we'd done, someone told us it was the biggest insult you could possibly give to a Japanese person, by which time Mr Ito had retrieved his camera and panic set in.

After the concert we all started to get on the coach. One of the guys spotted that Mr Ito had gone back into the venue leaving his camera on his seat so one of the guys opened up the back of the camera to expose the last few pictures in the hope he wouldn't see what we'd done. We spoke to the lady interpreter to ask if she would be the one to take the roll of film to get it printed, without telling her exactly what we had done, we just said we'd taken a few pictures of our own, asking her to make sure that there weren't rude pictures on the film before she handed the pictures back to him. When we next saw her, we asked if everything was OK. She said,

"Yes but Mr Ito couldn't understand why two of the frames were blank."

Phew, we got away with it once again. It was all over and time to head to the Airport for our flight home, with lots of memories. The tour was repeated again the following year.

I returned back home to Bournemouth, and had a few days with Harold, to get over the travel. A couple of weeks went by before I was contacted by Frank White, who had been the tenor player sitting next to me in Grimsby some twenty years before. He was now running a continental Glenn Miller band in France.

The band was made up of mainly British and Belgium musicians who did two tours a year in France. Frank was ringing to see if I was available to play Lead Alto on the next tour. Everything was arranged. We Brits met in London to catch the train through the channel tunnel, to be met on the other side by the band coach, which was already half-full with the Belgian contingent. All meals out were provided and we were treated very well. It was during that tour that I had my first taste of horse meat. We also stayed in a château for one night.

The band was OK, considering it was basically thrown together for the tour. I didn't think much to the Belgian culture in the band; they were a bit too bombastic for my liking. The best part of the trip for me was a concert in Carcassonne, situated in South West France. It is a most beautiful ancient walled city, which is a world heritage site. If you are ever in the area and get the chance to visit, please do so; I promise you won't be disappointed. It's so well preserved; we don't have anything like it in England.

One of the best parts of being freelance for me was the chance to see all these places, and to do some exploring, while doing my job and getting paid to be there at the same time. It was all adding to my general experience both musically and worldly. I did two tours with that band but unfortunately I was unavailable when the next tour came up, so just did the two.

I mentioned one of my best friends, Dave Willis, earlier in this chapter. He put quite a lot of work my way during the next few years, including sending me to deputise for him on Baritone sax with the British Glenn Miller Band.

The leader of the band was Johnny Watson. He was working under licence from the Glenn Miller office in New York, to officially call his band the Glenn Miller Orchestra UK. This office was run to collect all the royalties from Glenn Miller's recordings and music he had written, notably "Moonlight Serenade". These royalties were payable to Glenn's remaining family. Every time the British band performed, a percentage was to be sent to America. There was also a Glenn Miller band still doing gigs in the States as well.

My first gig with the band was at the Royal Festival Hall on the South bank of the Thames in London. Apparently, Johnny Watson complained to Dave. He said I didn't sit properly but Dave persisted and I did some occasional jobs that Dave couldn't do, but more of that later, in the next chapter. In the meantime Johnny Howard was forming a big band, which was completely separate to his function gig band. He asked Dave if he thought I might be prepared to do the Lead Alto chair. I think John thought I might not want to work for him again after replacing me in his gig band with a younger model, but I didn't have an axe to grind with him, because he did the right thing for both of us at the time.

Now I had yet another couple of fingers in the pie with Johnny Watson's Glenn Miller band plus Johnny Howard's band as well.

During 1999, Johnny Howard had been asked to book a Victor Sylvester type band to take part in a Stanley Kubrick film, with Tom Cruise and Nicole Kidman. Stanley Kubrick was famous for producing the film *The Clockwork Orange* and this film was to be called *Eyes Wide Shut*. John was just acting as an agent, so he asked Peter Hughes to fix the musicians which included me, along with Dave Willis and Martin Dunsdon on saxes. First we went into the recording studio to record the music we would be playing during part the film, which was a ballroom scene to be shot on location at Luton Hoo. Before filming started, one of the things we were told was on no account must we make eye contact with Tom Cruise.

We all had to go to the wardrobe mistress to be measured for our uniforms before going onto the stage to position our music and our instrument stands which had to have tape put on the floor to make sure they were always in the exactly the same place every time we were performing. As I've already mentioned, we had pre-recorded the sound track in the studio, so all we had to do was mime to the pre-recorded track, it was a piece of cake. We were on call for about three weeks spending most of the time in our allotted room getting paid for doing very little but what a great experience it was. It would appear that it was best for freelance musicians to have fingers in lots of pies and to keep doing a few jobs with them all, to keep your face known. They refer to it as keeping all your plates spinning. You will have seen jugglers on the TV with a lot of plates spinning on sticks in a long row and having to rush from one end to the other to keep them all spinning at the same time. That's how the musicians worked it, with all the different connections they had, in order to keep their faces in the minds of their various contacts.

So I started to do the same for myself. I had Ray McVay's gig band plus his big band as well, the Joe Loss band, the French Glenn Miller band, Johnny Howard's new big band and now the official Glenn Miller Band UK, to add to the list of my contacts. Glenn Miller music seemed to be having a bit of a comeback, as I was also contacted by Glenn Miller's nephew. John who was also running a Glenn Miller band. Thereby hangs another tale to tell.

Glenn had a brother called Herb but from what I understand, the two brothers didn't get on too well, so they both went their separate ways. I don't know who it was who decided to go to America to find Herb and to bring him back to England to start a Glenn Miller band.　At the time, Herb was the Musical Director of a circus orchestra in the States, while his son, John was also the Ringmaster.

They both came to England together, where Herb proceeded to form his own Glenn Miller band. I had heard about Herb but never actually met him, as by the time John Miller called me, Herb had retired. I was asked to do some gigs with the band on Second Alto; the Lead Alto's name was Alan Beaver. My first job with that band was a short tour of Belgium, playing on wartime airfields. John Miller had a band bus in which we all travelled to the destination. Once again the drinkers were at the back of the bus all the way, including one of the sax players called Eric George.

Once we reached our destination and the hotel for the night, Eric fell off the coach in a drunken heap on the ground, wearing a black overcoat and feeling no pain. As if it was quite a normal thing to do, John Miller just picked him up, threw him over his shoulder, like a bag of potatoes and walked into the Hotel reception, with this drunken heap of a musician draped over his shoulder saying,
"We're the John Miller band. I believe we have reservations".
The receptionist's face was a picture, one I'll never forget. I began to wonder what I'd let myself in for.

After our return to England, I continued to do occasional jobs with the band, now and again, including one in the grounds of Winston Churchill's country home, Chartwell, near Westerham, Kent.

I had forgotten my black shirt, so John Miller cut holes for my head and arms in a black bin liner which I had to play in all night. It was so hot, clammy and uncomfortable, but needs must.

My good friend and mentor, Dave Willis also put me in as a deputy on Baritone sax, with another Bandleader / Lead Trumpet player, called Freddy Staff. Peter Hughes was the same Lead Alto who Johnny Howard had used to play Lead Alto on the Come Dancing TV show from South Wales, mentioned in Chapter 20. The Second Alto was a former BBC Radio Orchestra player, Tony Arnopp. Pete Warner, the Tenor sax player was the one who had recommended me to the Eric Delaney band when I was only twenty three. I hadn't seen him since then, so it was a nice reunion. The other Tenor player was Martin Dunsdon, someone I would get to know very well, along with his wife Sue, during the next few years. They had just had their first baby they called Eleanor, who herself is now an accomplished harpist.

Also in the trumpet section was Ronnie Hunt, the man who had played the original trumpet solo used for the introduction of *Coronation Street*. As many *Coronation Street* fans will already know, it was originally going to be called *Florizel Street*. An outstanding trumpet player, Stan Roderick sent Ronnie to deputise for him on a recording session one day, not appreciating that it would turn out to be the recording of the signature tune for the pilot programme *Coronation Street*. Had Stan have played the theme, he would have done so beautifully. Ronnie made another kind of job of it which you can still hear today, and, of course, it fits the show perfectly. *Coronation Street* wouldn't be the same without Ron's trembling trumpet solo.

An attempt was made in later years to re-record that solo, using Stan Roderick, but it sounded too good, and they reverted to the old one. Ronnie Hunt was asked if he would like to take the session fee for the recording, or the royalties from any other future episodes. Thinking it was only a pilot programme that wouldn't go any further, he took the session fee. If he had taken the royalties instead, it would have made him a millionaire, because the music was played four times during each episode plus repeats. The original music has since been re-recorded several times but in my opinion the original was far more authentic than any of the others that followed. Poor Ronnie!

Worldwide, many others have falsely claimed to have played that piece.

When I first set out on my musical journey, the target I set for myself was to be a competent Lead Alto in the Mecca Dance Halls, something I achieved before I was twenty five, by playing Lead Alto with Tony Evans at the Empire ballroom in Leicester Square. Now I find myself not only rubbing shoulders but playing in the same bands with most of the top musicians in the country in my particular field. No one had any big-time attitudes. I was accepted as an equal, whilst having the best time of my life so far.

24 - THE GLENN MILLER ORCHESTRA UK

I'd been doing more and more deputising on the Baritone sax for Dave Willis and was now accepted by the bandleader, Johnny Watson. For the first half of the show, the band wore their own white shirts and black trousers, plus a red jacket supplied by the bandleader. For the second half, the band wore American army uniforms. For this I was lent a shirt and trousers for the night. I wasn't too comfortable with this arrangement, as there wasn't a way of knowing who had been the last person to wear them, so I set about finding my own instead. The trousers and belt were not too much of a problem. The main difficulty was finding the correct American badges to sew onto the sleeves of the American army shirt. Johnny Watson was so strict about exactly where the badges should go, inspecting them before he would allow me to wear my own shirt.

I really enjoyed deputising in this band. There were so many of the 'old school' big band players in it. I didn't ever imagine in my wildest dreams that I would be sitting beside or playing in the same band with some of these big band legends. Bobby Orr was the drummer. The Lead Trombone was Ted Barker, from the Ted Heath Band. Ronnie Chamberlain was Lead Alto and was also from the Ted Heath Band. Peter Hughes, a top recording session Tenor Sax. I usually deputised for Dave Willis on the Baritone chair. What a great band this was. After a while, the Bandleader, John Watson asked me if I would also like to deputise on the Second Tenor sax chair, if any of the Saxes' were off doing a recording session or other more important job. Naturally, I jumped at the chance, because I would have double the jobs, covering two chairs.

After my father passed away I'd always tried to spend some of my time visiting mother in Kimberley, which meant I was trying to split my time into three different places, between my work, Harold and my mother. I usually drove to Nottingham at night, after a weekend gig. I arrived one weekend in the early hours of the morning to find the kitchen like a tip, with half eaten meals just lying round along with un-washed pots. This was most unlike my mother at all; she was usually a very house-proud woman I went into her bedroom to find her really ill in bed, so the next day I went with her to see the doctor. Apparently she had already been to see him several times before but all he'd done was to take her blood pressure. I really had to push him to give her a blood test. When we went back to get the result of the blood test he said,

"You must take your mother straight to the hospital; don't even go home to get any clothes, go right away."

I was none too pleased with the doctor; he should have given my mother a blood test before, not just have only taken her blood pressure. I did as he asked and took her to the hospital. It turned out after further tests that she had two leaking heart valves. She was told she had two options. One was to have the operation but was warned that she was so weak she probably wouldn't make it at her age. The second option was to let nature take its course which she chose.

The medical profession has improved in leaps and bounds since then; they would probably have been able to do a successful operation today, but then was then and now is now. After leaving hospital, she came to live with Harold and me, so we could keep an eye on her health and wellbeing. Harold was able to keep an eye on her health for me while I was away in London, working. I had a stair lift installed, so she could get upstairs. I also made the dining-room into a sitting-room, with her own television from Kimberley in order to make her feel as comfortable as possible but never the less, it was a big wrench for her, leaving her own home where she had lived for most of her life.

This arrangement worked very well, leaving me able to continue working as normal for the time being. Dave Willis, the Baritone player along with Johnny Evans the Tenor player from the Glenn Miller band were away doing a Japanese tour with Ray McVay. While they were away, I was deputising for Dave on the Baritone Sax, which included a concert in York, followed the next night with a gig in the concert hall in Glasgow. Neither Ronnie Chamberlain nor Peter Hughes could do the gig in Glasgow, so they were travelling back from York to London by train the next day.

Fortunately, Dave Willis and Johnny Evans, the Tenor player were both back from Japan and were travelling up to Glasgow on the train to re-join the band for the concert in Glasgow. However this meant that John Watson the Bandleader was still left without a Lead Alto player for Glasgow. It was suggested that I would play Lead Alto. John Watson hadn't ever heard me play Lead and was a bit sceptical at first but agreed that this was the best option he had under the circumstances. This may seem very complicated but it all managed to come together in the end. The band was staying in a hotel in York for the night after the concert, which gave me the opportunity to take the Lead Alto music to my hotel room and silently practise the parts before going to bed. I knew that there was one particularly difficult clarinet part to play in the tune "Sunrise Serenade" that Ronny Chamberlain had some difficulty with, owing to arthritis in some of his fingers, so I had to make sure that I was able to play it, knowing full well that as far as the Band Leader was concerned this was my test piece. I managed to get some sleep that night but was also able to catch up with some more sleep on the coach the next day on the way to Glasgow.

Unfortunately there was some problem with the coach which meant we were behind with the schedule, only arriving at the concert hall in time to set up, get changed and go straight onto the stage to do the concert without being able to even have a warm up. All went well; after all, I was by now a very experienced Lead Alto who had played most of these Glenn Miller tunes many times before throughout my career in other bands. It was just that I was a completely unknown quantity as far as Johnny Watson was concerned. When it came to the clarinet lead in "Sunrise Serenade", I could see out of the corner of my eye that Johnny Watson was hovering close by, to see if I could play that middle section which was difficult. Thank goodness I'd had the foresight to practise it in my room the night before. All went according to plan and he moved away again. During the evening as I sat there I suddenly thought, I wish my dad could be here to see me playing Lead with the Glenn Miller Orchestra UK; he would have been so proud. As I mentioned in one of my early chapters when I was learning to play the clarinet, my dad was always going on about how important it was to be able to play the clarinet. He was a big fan of Glenn Miller, whereas at that time as a young teenager, I was more interested in Rock and Roll.

No one really knew what happened to Glenn Miller during that fatal flight across the English Channel in 1944. There was a standing joke around at the time which went something like this. No one has found Glenn Miller's body, but the really bad news is that his music survived.

As we were playing "Moonlight Serenade" that night in Glasgow, the memory of my dad's words became so strong. I began to get emotional, so much so that my bottom lip began to quiver and I found it hard to control my sound. Fortunately the thoughts soon passed. At the end of the concert every single member of the band congratulated me, including the hard to please John Watson who was all over me after the concert because I hadn't let him down. That was first of many times I was called upon to play Lead. John was a lucky man; he potentially had three Lead Alto players in the one band and be able to swap around, making the saxophone section extremely flexible.

Very soon after that, Ronnie Chamberlain had to retire on health grounds so Peter Hughes moved up, onto the Lead Alto chair, so I finally got a permanent seat on the Second Tenor chair, in what was in my opinion, currently the best big band on the road in the country. All was going well as far as work was concerned but my mother's health was deteriorating quite quickly. She said she couldn't swallow properly and stopped eating the meals I cooked for us all. I tried liquefying her food but to no avail. I called the doctor, who diagnosed a urinary bladder infection and sent her to the hospital. As she began to recover, the hospital transferred her to a rehabilitation hospital where they began to encourage her to start eating again. One day while I was visiting the rehabilitation hospital they told me she could only stay there for six weeks and I had to find a nursing home for her. I managed to find a place just round the corner from us that had a room on the ground floor with a view out over the garden.

The first night, she fell out of the bed and lay on the floor until her calls brought someone to put her back. The next day I called to see her and during the conversation I had to tell her that I was working the next day so wouldn't be able to see her. She gave me a reply that haunts me to this day. She said

"Tell me I've done alright?"

I said, "What do you mean? Of course you've done alright."

She must have known she was about to die, because the very next morning the nursing home rang to tell me she had passed away in the night. As you can imagine, I was in bits. It made me realise that when your mother has gone, you're really on your own. I was an only child. Now, both my parents had passed away, along with my aunt and even my only cousin had tried to take his own life, after which, he was almost a vegetable, unable to walk, talk or look after himself. I didn't have any living family, so from then, I really was on my own. I don't know how I managed to work that night but it was too short notice to find anyone to deputise for me. Even though I am now 78 and a lot of water has gone under the bridge, I still occasionally beat myself up wondering if I could have done things differently about my Mother, but life must go on.

As far as the band was concerned, the next major change came when Johnny Watson decided to retire due to ill health. Around 1988, Ray McVay took over, and after a meeting in New York, the re-branded band became the Glenn Miller Orchestra UK. Ray, as Musical Director and Bandleader promised to keep all the existing members but it wasn't long before Jim

Paxton the Second Alto player decided to retire leaving the Second Alto chair free for me to move into, and to sit between Dave Willis and Peter Hughes. This was a chance I had been waiting for, to be able to play Alto Sax, sitting next to Peter Hughes. After doing two tours of Japan with Ray's Glenn Miller Band, I knew that he had arrangements of two favourite clarinet features that he liked to do, both of which I had managed to photo-copy while in Japan. I had learned and memorised both clarinet solos. I was able to tell Ray that I could do them. This was going to be my way of making a mark in the band. The first solo was a special Glenn Miller arrangement of Arty Shaw's "Begin the Beguine". I remember the first night I played it was at the theatre in Southend. I was very nervous standing out in the front of the band with only my memory to get me through. All went well, so it went into the programme every night.

I know my playing of the solo impressed Ray because I hadn't had the chance before to let him see what I was really capable of, just sitting on the end of the sax section playing baritone when I went to Japan with his Glenn Miller band. My next chance was soon to come, to let him see how capable I was.

It came when Peter Hughes needed to take the night off and told Ray he was putting me on the Lead chair to cover for him, as I had previously done when Johnny Watson was still running the band. I know Ray was a bit sceptical at first but he soon realised that I was more than capable of handling the Lead chair. He came up to me afterwards and said
"You played your little heart out for me tonight, thank you."

I mentioned earlier in the book that I had known Ray from the days of his very first band in the Locarno Ballroom in Derby. And I am of the opinion that he still thought of me as that boy of about 15 years of age, working in his dad's semi-professional band in Nottingham, because he said,
"You never cease to amaze me."
I could see it was going to be hard to make him realise I had actually come a very long way since then.

My next project was to memorise and perfect the second of Ray's favourite Arty Shaw's clarinet solos, which was called "Hawaiian Love Song". In this piece, I was also required to sing as well as play a long clarinet gliss at the end of the piece. In order to try to explain what a gliss sounds like, I can only mention the most famous clarinet gliss is at the beginning of Gershwin's "Rhapsody in Blue". But the gliss in "Hawaiian Love Song" goes higher and is much more difficult to play. I used to try to do a gliss in my bedroom as a little boy at home and that was the sort of messing about that would prompt my dad to come rushing up the stairs threatening to wrap that bloody thing round my neck if I didn't get on with my proper practice instead of what he considered to be messing about.

I also used to have a tutor book that explained how to make all the different trick sounds on the saxophone such as slap tonguing and the laugh. I could do both of those sounds and the laugh came in very handy when some years before, I had helped Eric Delaney out on the last two weeks of a

210

summer season with Ken Dodd because Ken required a saxophone laugh as part of his act and I was able to oblige. Sorry, I digress again.

Jeff Mason, Lead Sax

When I felt ready to perform "The Hawaiian Love Song", we rehearsed it and it went into the programme as well as 'Begin the Beguine'. Now I had two features standing out on the front of a theatre stage with a magnificent band behind me. This was much better than sitting in a function band playing for dancing where the audience were only interested in partying and having a dance whilst drinking and having a good night out as opposed to sitting in a theatre watching a performance where the band and soloists are the focus of their attention. One of my best musician friends, Simon Currie who now works with the re-formed Manfred Mann group feels the same way as I do when he said to me,

"I could never go back to working in a function band again".

You can't beat a theatre full of people showing their appreciation in response to a solo you have just performed for them.

      I think that it was in the autumn of 1999, that there was a big band cruise coming up on the *QE2* to look forward to, which involved bands from both sides of the Atlantic. There were three British big bands, including the Glenn Miller Band UK, along with a couple of smaller units and a similar contingent that had flown over from the States to join the *QE2* in Southampton. Neither Peter Hughes nor Dave Willis did the cruises, so I played Lead Alto. My pal Simon Currie deputised on Baritone and Paul Jones came in on Second Alto.

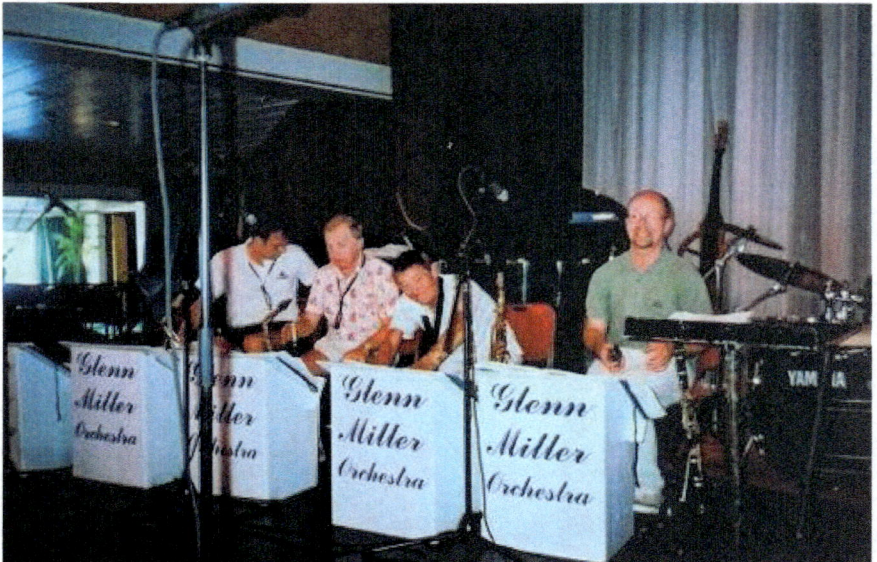

Casual rehearsal on *QE2*

      After the cruise, the Americans got off in Fort Lauderdale. Whilst they had flown over to England they were now back on home soil, we had to fly back from Fort Lauderdale. This was a great cruise; wherever you went on the ship there was music somewhere. We did a couple of these big band cruises. I enjoyed the first cruise the most, as we called in to Bermuda on the way over to Fort Lauderdale. Sailing into Bermuda was something I will never forget; the scenery was magic to my eyes.

The unfortunate part was that we didn't get enough time in Bermuda, before we were off again across the Atlantic to Fort Lauderdale. The following year, which I think was 2000, we did the same thing again, only this time it was in reverse; we flew to New York in September and sailed back to Southampton.

We had a couple of days in New York before embarkation for the return journey which gave us all chance to have a little look round some of the sights. Broadway was a 'must'.

However, my main quest was to find a famous music shop called Manny's, the shop about which I had heard so much in my youth. Manny's was the place the musicians would visit, to buy instruments and accessories they couldn't buy in England at the time. Manny Goldrich had started the business on W 48th Street in the 1930s, selling brass instruments but then moved very much into being the place where legends like Jimmy Hendrix, the Beatles, Eric Clapton and U2 bought their guitars.

I was a little disappointed with Manny's as there was not one wind instrument in the shop; the company had sold its soul to the modern musical electronics - guitars, keyboards, amplifiers and drums. However, the main object was to find the shop which is what I had achieved. Eventually, it closed down in 2009.

Too soon, it was time to board the ship for a musical extravaganza on the trip home. After returning home, we resumed the usual round of theatre venues and concert halls, playing to Glenn Miller fans before the next major overseas tour. This was in 2001, when we went to South America, visiting Argentina, Paraguay and Uruguay. We weren't allowed to tour North America, because our band was under a contract, which excluded touring the States, where there was already a Glenn Miller Orchestra, which was mainly made up of young college graduates. I heard one of their records and frankly I think the British band has a closer copy of the original sound than our American counterparts, but I would think that, wouldn't I?

In the meantime Harold's glaucoma was getting much worse and I didn't want to leave him for five weeks on his own so we decided he might be best to go into a rest home for the duration of the tour, so he could be looked after. We found a nice place near to where we lived and I think he enjoyed a little holiday himself, being waited on, hand and foot. The band flew overnight to Buenos Aires. I managed to grab three empty seats to myself, so was able to lie flat and have a reasonable night's sleep. On arrival in Buenos

Aires, we had a day to get settled in our accommodation before being taken out by the agent for a meal at a restaurant that specialised in steaks. Before the meal we were treated to some starters that were considered delicacies in Argentina various little titbits were handed round including a round flat thing a bit like a poppadum but only the size of the palm of your hand. It tasted very bitter and nobody who tried it liked it. When I asked what it was, we were told it was bull's scrotum. Needless to say, no one ate any more after that.

I suppose the Argentinians would have had to use every little piece of the animal in the past, just as the British people in decades gone by had to do the same. I remember my father eating pig's trotters (the name suggests what they are), plus tripe made from animal stomachs. Sweetbreads were also on the menu; they were made from bull's testicles; needless to say I never tried any of those old fashioned British delicacies, however we still eat oxtail soup which is made from the tails of cows and bulls. My grandfather would never eat oxtail soup; he said it was too close to the animal's rear end for his liking. I have to say I was also disappointed with the main course of steak that followed, I was expecting a nice tender juicy steak, but instead I found mine to be rather tough. Whilst touring we had the use of a marvellous modern double-decker coach to travel to some of the major cities where we played, including Cordoba, Rosario and Mendoza.

Rosario was my favourite city, as it was more like I imagine an old Victorian city would have looked like in England. Lots of British families emigrated to Argentina, along with many Germans and other Europeans. This was noticeable in Buenos Aires where you could distinguish the European descendants from the indigenous population.

The band had a luxurious double-decker coach during the tour which gave us the opportunity to see some of the country.

I had been expecting to see lots of gauchos, herding cattle, but we only came across this on one occasion. However what I did see which disturbed me somewhat, was to see a huge garbage dump just outside of one of the cities where children and horses were looking for scraps of food in order to survive. Can you imagine what sort of life they were living picking through a rubbish tip along with those horses urinating and defecating amongst the rubbish? I had seen such scenes before on the TV but it brings it home when you see it with your own eyes.

I was playing Lead Alto during the tour as Peter Hughes didn't want to come, probably because he had previously been on tour with the band to Argentina under the direction of Johnny Watson before I joined the band. I must have caught a bug during the flight over and it was one that settled on my chest. I have mentioned in previous chapters about the weakness in my chest through bronchitis in my childhood that has dogged me throughout my life. This was the worst attack I have ever had but I couldn't take time off work because there wasn't anyone who could cover for me. On days off, I would just lie in bed trying to sleep it off. As the saying goes, "the show must go on" and being the true trouper that I am, I just got on with it as best as I could.

However I did manage to do a bit of sightseeing in Buenos Aries, including visiting the Pink Palace, where Eva Peron (Evita) made her famous speech on the balcony.

Also a few of us found the mausoleum where she is buried.

As well as Argentina, we also played in Montevideo, the capital of Uruguay. We took the ferry across the river Plate where the German ship *Admiral Graf Spee* was scuttled by captain Langsdorff in 1939 during World War II. It was possible for us to just see the top of the upper structure when the tide was low but I believe it has now been blown up as it was a possible danger to shipping.

216

A lot of the crew of the *Graf Spee* were taken to Montevideo, where some stayed and continued to live in Uruguay after the war. Three days after he scuttled the ship, Captain Langsdorff shot himself in a hotel room in Buenos Aries.

Ted Barker at the grave of Captain Langsdorff
La Chacarita Cemetery in Buenos Aires, Argentina

However, our tour, like all good things, had to come to an end; it was time to fly back to The UK for another round of the British theatres. Soon after we returned home, Johnny Evans the First Tenor sax player decided to retire and we were joined by a young tenor player called Paul Booth, who had just finished touring the world with the Irish musical, *River Dance*. Paul is an exceptionally talented musician and was an asset to the band. He arranged a piece from *River Dance* especially for the band which he played on the soprano sax. (I mentioned the soprano sax in Chapter 9 – 'About The Saxophone Family'.)

Unfortunately for the band but fortunately for Paul, he wasn't with us for long, as he was recalled to the *River Dance* show, to do a tour of China for a fee he just couldn't afford to turn down. After he left, I decided to learn the soprano part for myself and to add another solo feature to my repertoire. There were a few technically difficult bars to overcome but the biggest problem was that the piece is very repetitive and remembering where I was in the music at any one time was the greatest difficulty.

With my tenacity and a few pointers from my partner Harold, I worked hard with it. He who would occasionally come into my practice room and say,

"That section needs to be smoother and less stiff"

I eventually managed to perfect it and put myself forward to perform it in front of the audiences, which prompted Ray to say once again,

"You never cease to amaze me".

During one of the British tours, building up to the Christmas period, I decided to visit one of these fancy dress hire shops to see if I could hire a Leprechaun outfit with the intention of wearing it to play "River Dance". I didn't let on to anyone in the band except for Ray's wife Sue, who helped me to change behind the stage. When I knew "River Dance" was coming up, I slipped off the stage to get changed and hid behind the curtain waiting, when Ray turned to look for me and I wasn't there he didn't know what to do but Sue gave him the thumbs up and he announced it and counted the band into the introduction. I pranced on the stage, trying to look like a Leprechaun. The band members were in stitches of laughter and could hardly play their parts, which was the reaction I was hoping for. However, it was the sort of stunt you can only perform once.

One heart-stopping moment was during a tour of the British Isles. We had played a concert in Glasgow and were flying to Dublin the next day. I could only take one piece of luggage into the cabin which was my alto sax. My clarinet was packed into my suitcase in the hold and I also had to put the soprano into the hold, as a separate item in its own case. I had packed the soprano very carefully and wrapped it in bubble wrap for extra protection, but when I got it out of the case in Dublin, I could see it had been opened at the airport and not put back in its case properly. Maybe the security had thought it could have been a gun of some sort as it was in a long case, I'll never know but the top and bottom of it was that I couldn't get a note out of it. I must say that I was in quite a panic, but after closer inspection the only option I had was to try to bend it back over my knee, which I did and so was able to do my "River Dance" as usual.

After I had finished, to my absolute amazement the whole theatre gave me a standing ovation. This was something I have never seen before or since for any other musician I have ever worked with and for it to be for "River Dance", in the home country was most extraordinary, to say the very least. The best part was that the audience didn't have any idea of the panic I had gone through just a few hours before. That has to go down as one of my best moments of my playing career ever.

Not even Paul Booth achieved that. Some months ago in 2019, which was 16 years after I retired, the band came to Christchurch Dorset to do a concert. I went to see the guys. The sax player Andy Potts, who is now playing Lead Alto said to me,
"How did you ever manage to play *River Dance*"?
All I could say was, "With great difficulty!"

It was becoming clear to me that Harold's eyesight difficulty was becoming more acute through his glaucoma. It was also clear that it wouldn't be long before I had to retire, in order to look after him, but there was one last trip I had to do with the band, which was a three day trip to Moscow in November 2000.

One of Glenn Miller's most popular tunes was "American Patrol", which we played at every concert but Glenn also had a tune called "Russian Patrol" which I hadn't heard of until I played with John Miller (Glenn's Nephew). I knew John had an arrangement of it, so asked if he would let me copy it for us to play in Moscow, With reluctance that it wasn't his band going instead of us, he agreed, so we were able to play that as well, along with a rendition of Kenny Ball's "Midnight in Moscow" which I believe was originally a Russian Folk song.

When we arrived in the capital, there was a banner across the main street which said, in Russian, of course:

Welcome The Glenn Miller Orchestra.

First, we were taken to our hotel which was a modern Marriott Hotel. I was quite surprised as I had heard stories of dark Victorian-style hotels with an old lady on each corridor watching every movement you made, The Marriott wasn't like that at all it was just the same as any modern hotel, in any Western city. Once we were settled into our hotel, we had the rest of the day to explore. I made a bee-line for Red Square. Previously, I had only seen Red Square on the TV, with the endless displays of armoured vehicles passing through. I also had a jigsaw puzzle of St Basil's Cathedral which was somewhere I hadn't ever expected to see, never mind to go inside. To stand in Red Square was a moment I will never forget; something I'd never expected to do.

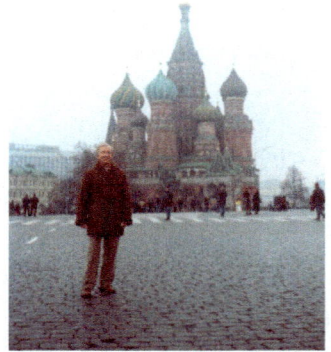

Quite a few of us took our sheep-skin coats, expecting it to be really cold but there wasn't a snow flake to be seen until the last morning before we left, when I rushed down to take picture of the square with snow.

The venue where the band was to be playing was called the Kremlin Palace Theatre. We all thought we would be playing inside the Kremlin but it turned out to be a huge theatre which appeared to have been used for the huge communist rallies in the past. It was certainly the biggest theatre I have ever seen, with four tiered balconies. The theatre was built on the outside edge of the Kremlin and the public access was from the road. However we had to go inside the walls of the Kremlin in order to get to the stage door. The coach was stopped by the gates and guards got onto the coach to inspect all our passports before we were allowed through the gates. Talk about security! During the time the stage was being set up for the band, some of us took the opportunity to go outside, into the grounds of the Kremlin to have a little peek but all the blinds were down so there was nothing to see, but I was able to take a few pictures from the outside.

We did two concerts, both of which were full, which received a very good reaction from the audience, although I seem to remember they were not too impressed by our rendition of Kenny Ball's "Midnight in Moscow", a jazzed up version of their traditional folk song.

On the fourth morning of our trip to Moscow, it was time to head for the airport and our flight back to London. Just before we took off, the trumpet players talked their way into the cockpit of the British Airways plane and played to the two pilots.

Trumpet players entertain the British Airways pilots

I knew it wouldn't be long now before I had to retire and stay home to look after Harold but as we didn't have any more foreign trips on the horizon, I was able to continue with the band until the summer break. My last professional concert was an outdoor performance in Southsea.

My last performance with the Glenn Miller Orchestra, in Southsea

After that concert, I told myself I would put my instruments away and never play again. After all, when most people retire from their job, they walk away to enjoy their retirement, so that's what I intended to do.

My job now was to look after Harold, which became more and more difficult, as his dementia crept in and he became very confused. I fully understand anyone that has to go through that, and in the end I was on the point of a nervous breakdown myself and was put on anti-depressants by my doctor. Eventually, I couldn't cope any more and he had to go into a nursing home, where at the age of 95, he sadly passed away. That meant I was now alone in the world for the first time in my life, as everyone in my family had previously passed away.

Some time after Harold's passing, I bumped into an old friend, Bill, who I had known from my school instrumental teaching days. He had since lost his wife and was also living on his own. We started going for a coffee in the mornings and maybe a drink in the evenings, with an occasional meal out. We were both lonely, but under different circumstances. As neither of us was looking forward to Christmases alone, we talked about maybe getting away together on a cruise for Christmas, which we did on numerous occasions. Mediterranean cruises included ports in Spain. Once we called into Gibraltar, which gave us a chance to climb the rock, see the monkeys etc. However, the best was a three-week cruise to the Caribbean where amongst many great sights. We were also able to swim in the Caribbean. Not only did we go on the cruises at Christmas but we also spent summer holidays in Tenerife, sharing an apartment owned by a mutual friend of ours. As Bill's age and general health began to deteriorate, it was decided that maybe we should stay closer to home from now on, and instead we should spend Christmases in a British hotel in Torquay, which we did for a few years.

Bill is now living in a rest home at the grand old age of 96 going on 97 in February 2021. Owing to the present lock-down situation with the COVID-19 outbreak, he is currently confined to his room, with no visitors allowed, which is pretty barbaric, but that's just how bad things are at the moment.

25 - RETIREMENT BUCKET LIST

For anyone who is not acquainted with the term, the 'Bucket List' comprises those things that one would like to do before 'kicking the bucket' - a colloquial expression for dying, which itself has various alternative supposed origins.

One of the first things on my bucket list was to visit a friend in Italy, in April during the spring of 2010. I booked my return flight and set off. All started well, my Italian friend met me at the airport and took me back to his house. During my short stay, he also took me on a few sight-seeing trips which I enjoyed. There we received news of a volcanic eruption in Iceland which was causing all flights in Europe to be cancelled, owing to the danger of ash and other pollutants getting into the engines.

This meant my chance of getting back to England in time for the next holiday which I had booked for the Scilly Isles was looking unlikely. I had to start making plans for alternative ways back to England other than flying. I decided to investigate getting back by train. There had been an extra over-night train put on from Venice to Paris so I set off from my friend's house to catch the train. There were so many other people in the same position as me, trying to get back to their own countries, that the queues at the booking offices stretched a very long way back. I knew if I got in at the end of the line, I wouldn't get to the ticket office soon enough to make the train on time. Therefore I walked to the platform where the train was standing and explained that I hadn't got a ticket yet. The man in charge told me I could get on the train and they would come round later for the fare, which they did. The carriages were similar to our old British carriages with a corridor down one side and separate compartments with doors. I found an empty compartment and settled down for the long trip.

It wasn't long before another English man joined me in the compartment, so we began to chat and get acquainted. He introduced himself as Peter and told me he was returning home from visiting suppliers for his British company. Eventually the train set off with still just the two of us in the compartment, so we locked the door, pulled the blinds down and stretched out on opposite seats to try to get some sleep. What we didn't know was that the train was also stopping in Milan. The platform in Milan was heaving with passengers waiting to get onto the train.

We tried to keep the door locked, but the guards came round and threatened to break the door down and throw us off the train if we didn't open the door. We didn't have much choice, so opened the door, only to be

224

quickly invaded by five other people. That was the end of a peaceful journey to Paris, but it was only the start of Peter's and my bizarre journey back home. We discovered that the Eurostar was fully booked for the next 5 days, and realising how much it would cost to stay in an hotel for 5 days we opted for 'plan B' which was to try to get a train to the coast, in order to board a ferry back home.

As we stood staring at the departure board at Gare Du Nord station, looking for a train, a young Asian man approached us, asking if we were looking for a lift back to England. He explained that he and three of his friends had come up with the idea of booking return fares for their individual cars on the car ferry with the idea of picking up stranded paying passengers to take back to England. He was asking
£350 pounds each to get us back. We haggled a bit got it reduced to £300 each and sat back, to be driven home. This was pure luxury. I was in the back seat and managed to get some sleep, which was just as well, given what was to happen later.

It was evening when we arrived in London. The driver dropped Peter off at his son's London flat but I still had to get to Bournemouth. The driver offered to take me home to Bournemouth for an extra £200, so we set off. He pulled into a petrol station on the outskirts of London to fill up but I realised that he was dead beat after his long day driving from London to Paris and back and that it wasn't safe for him to drive, so I suggested that I drive his car for the next two hours to Bournemouth, with him asleep in the passenger seat all the way. When I got home, I paid him his £200 and he drove away. I was now home safe and sound but that wasn't something I wouldn't like to do again.

Just like many other young boys of my age, I used to like watching the cowboy films and had always wanted to visit America, in particular to meet a real live Native American. I had heard of an American gay dating site called Silver Daddies, so, as I preferred older partners, I decided to join, after which I was able to look through the picture profiles and eventually came across a gentleman from Hollywood, California. His name was Rial (as in 'trial'). After a lot of emails to and fro, we got onto Skype where we could chat face to face, and eventually it was decided I would go over to America for two weeks and he would show me around. Rial had also recently lost his lifelong partner, so we were both in a similar situation. He was a really nice man and we got on well together, enjoying one another's company. Over a long period of time and many trips to the States, he took me to all the sights I wanted to see and more. Rial was an exceptional host, who was only too pleased to take me to see the best sights in California. On the way to our first destination, we passed the set where the TV series *Bonanza* had been filmed, that being one of my favourite series when I was young. I couldn't believe how small the actual set was; there must have been some very clever filming, to make the homestead look as big as it was on the show.

Having stopped for a while, we continued to our next destination, which was the Sequoia National Park, to see the giant redwood trees - the largest trees in the world. The largest of them all is called The General Sherman.

In the past, I had seen a picture of one particular tree which was large enough at the base to drive a horse and cart through it. That tree was in Yosemite National Park and was called the Wawona Tree. It fell down in 1969.

On that same trip we also took in Yosemite National Park.

Later during that same visit he said,

"I'm taking you to see a castle tomorrow."

I thought to myself, "I don't need to come to America to see a castle, we have plenty of those in England" but what I was about to see was a very special castle, Hearst Castle which was built in the 1920s by the famous New York newspaper publisher, Randolph Hearst, about whom the classic film was made, called *Citizen Kane,* starring Orson Welles. This castle was a stunning example of the decadent lavish lifestyle of the 1920s, where Randolph Hearst invited notable and famous film stars of the time.

Hearst Castle

I was particularly taken by the indoor swimming pool.

The day before I was due to come home we visited the Universal Studios in Los Angeles to see the sets of *Jaws* and *Back to The Future* plus the scenes of a plane crash, a flood and more.

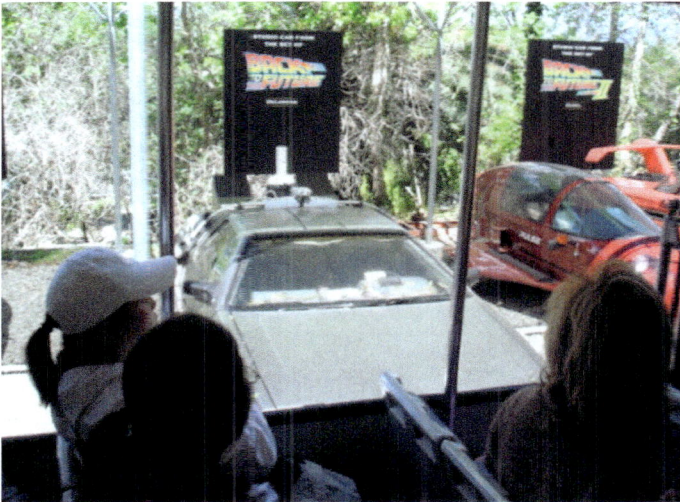

What I also enjoyed about being in Hollywood was visiting the sites of some of the streets I had known from my teenage years like Sunset Boulevard, 77 Sunset Strip, and Hollywood Boulevard, where all the film stars have their names in stars on the pavement (side walk). I walked the whole length from end to end, looking at the famous names.

On my next visit, we travelled over the Hoover dam, named after Herbert Hoover the 31st president of the USA, on our way to our destination, which was Las Vegas. En route, we drove through Death Valley where, during the summer of 2020, as I was writing this book, Death Valley was the hottest place on Earth. Some of the rock formations were stunning and my pictures don't do them justice.

The open road through Death Valley was long and straight; it went on for miles and miles.

All you could see in the distance was the next mountain range to be conquered, which made me think how disheartening it must have been for the early settlers with their covered wagons, having to navigate through mountain range after mountain range.

We finally made it to Las Vegas, where we spent a few days seeing the sites and sumptuous hotels, but didn't do any gambling, as I'm not a gambling man. We stayed in the Venetian Hotel, complete with gondolas. From there we could see many other luxury hotels.

231

On the way back, we stopped at the Hoover Dam again, in order to take a tour down into the bowels of the dam, to see the giant turbines generating electricity.

233

I was so grateful to have Rial as my guide; I would never have seen all these sights without him. On my next visit to see Rial, we took a trip to view the Grand Canyon from the ground.

We then took a helicopter trip over the canyon. Before the helicopter was allowed to take off, everyone had to be weighed for equal weight distribution.

I was the lightest one in the group, so got to ride up front, in the passenger seat, so to speak, next to the pilot - a woman who was also very light. All of us had to wear head phones, to hear the commentary given by the pilot.

We were flying low, over the top of a forest of trees when suddenly we came to the rim of the canyon with a sudden drop over the side. It was so breathtaking, being in the front seat, so much so, that I said out loud "F***ing hell!"

234

It was a good job everyone had their head phones over their ears, so they didn't hear my expletive. That experience was definitely up there with the best.

The best trip of all with Rial was definitely on my wish list. It was a trip through the Panama Canal.

We boarded the *Carnival Pride* at Long Beach, California, but before boarding, we had lunch in the dining room of the original RMS *Queen Mary* which is now permanently moored in Long Beach.

I took several photos inside the well-maintained liner.

We cruised down the west coast of America, calling at ports in Mexico, including experiencing a traditional Mexican dinner, accompanied by musicians playing traditional songs. We eventually reached the entrance to the canal early one morning, so most of the passengers were up on deck in the semi-darkness to catch their first glimpses of the canal. As we neared our first lock, some of the crew were also out on deck to catch their first glimpses.

Once through the canal, we called at a couple of Caribbean islands one of which had a turtle farm raising young turtles. I was able to hold one of the baby turtles for a photo opportunity. However, the sad part is that they are being bred in captivity to provide meat for such things as turtle soup and for Turtle-shell which was very popular in Victorian times. Because it is now illegal to kill wild turtles, they just farm them instead.

Turtle Farm

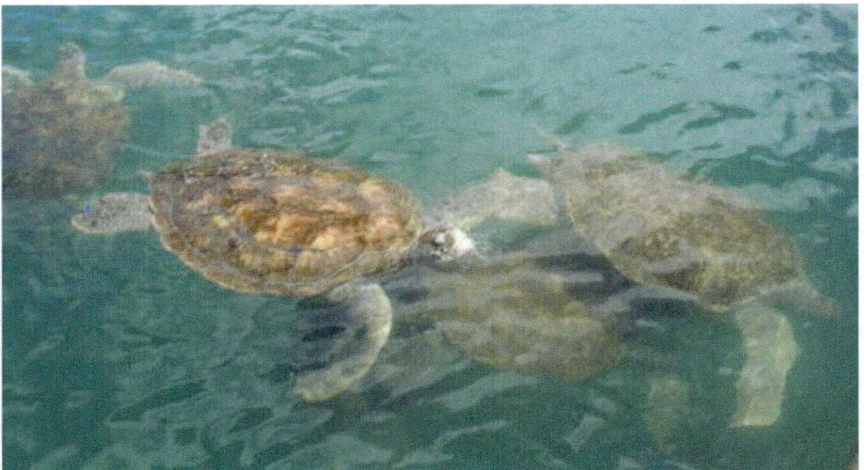

The most exciting stop for me was in the Cayman Isles, where we were taken on a boat trip, quite a fair way out into the ocean, to a sand bar where the sea was only up to the waist and you could feed wild Sting Rays. We all were given some squid with which to feed them and told to keep our thumbs in, as they suck the food from your hands. There were already other boats there before us, but as soon as they saw a new boat with more food, they all swarmed towards us. We all had to stand in a circle facing inwards. (The Australian zoo presenter, Steve Irwin, the crocodile hunter was killed by a sting ray.) We were all told that unless anyone inadvertently trod on the tail of one you were safe, as you will see from one of the pictures of our guide kissing a Sting Ray.

Rial also visited me here in England a few times. I reciprocated by taking him on a tour of Scotland as well as of South East England, as he wanted to see the white cliffs of Dover plus, of course, London, where we did the Buckingham Palace tour, a boat trip down the Thames including the Tower of London, and visits to Ascot, Windsor Castle and Runnymede, where the Magna Carta was signed in 1215.

The last time he came to see me, he wanted to go to Austria. We set off, getting as far as Frankfurt, where he went into a diabetic coma, ending up in hospital. He recovered from that, but after he got back to the States he started to get worse and eventually was found in his apartment by the police.

239

He was taken to the hospital but unfortunately never recovered consciousness. This was a sad time for me, as I had already booked a flight to go over to see him. If I had been there, I could possibly have saved him. Unfortunately I had lost another good friend, someone I will be eternally grateful for.

Soon after Rial passed away and totally out of the blue, I received an email from another American called Bud. We had met years before, when Harold and I used to sell antiques in London. He and his wife would to come over to England to buy antiques to ship back to the States. I hadn't heard from them in years. He was writing to tell me that his wife had since passed away. He was coming over to England again, staying in London for a few days before returning to America on the new *Queen Mary 2*. He asked if we could meet up in London for old time's sake.

To cut a long story short, I met him at his hotel, stayed the night and drove him to Southampton the next morning to catch the ship back to New York, as Southampton is on my way home to Bournemouth. We kept in touch on Skype and eventually agreed that I should go over to New Jersey, where he lived and he would drive me up to see Niagara Falls, which was on my bucket list.

Niagara Falls

After that, we stayed in touch and I went over again because I had read extensively about the Everglades which had been added to my bucket list, mainly because I wanted to see a Manatee and to ride on one of those air boats (hydrofoils) that skim over the water, driven by a huge fan at the back of the boat. We flew from New York, hiring a car in Florida.

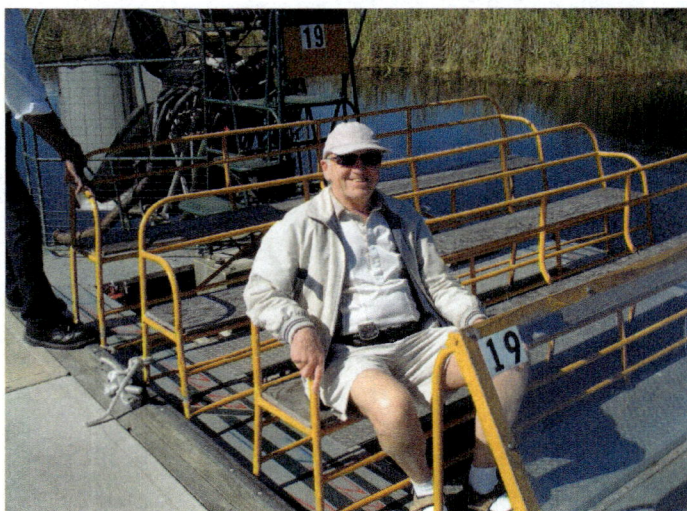

I got my wish to ride on the air boat, and while there, we visited an alligator farm, where I handled a young alligator and ate an alligator steak across the street in a restaurant.

WARNING
WILD ALLIGATORS
DO NOT FEED
OR ENTICE
VIOLATORS WILL BE PROSECUTED
BY THE MICCOSUKEE POLICE
FLORIDA STATE STATUTE.372.067

      While still in Florida, we travelled north, in order to visit the Epcot Center and Water World. There I saw Manatees, which were on my wish list.

Epcot

Manatees

During my next visit, Bud & I spent a week in San Francisco and we took a boat trip around the harbour and under the Golden Gate Bridge, which also took us round the Alcatraz, the notorious rock where the hardest criminals were imprisoned.

However, we did get to ride on the famous trams, where I managed to get a picture, hanging onto the outside of a packed tram.

Although I have been to visit Bud a few time since San Francisco, that was the last of our road trips, as I have now completed most of my wish list and much more The only two things left on my bucket list are Machu Picchu in Peru, and New Zealand, neither of which I expect to see, as at 77 years old, I am content to be at home, but who knows what's around the corner?

During the past ten years, I have started playing music again on clarinet, joining a local community band called the Christchurch & District Band, where I am enjoying playing again on a social level, making a few new friends on the way. I have also gone back to my roots by buying a caravan and travelling around Britain on caravan rallies, where I have made many friends and one particular buddy with whom to share meals and time.

I started writing this book in March 2020. By December 2020, we were still in a lockdown situation, which had lasted for most of the year, which has been a year out of everyone's life. However, there is some hope on the horizon, as just today (2nd January 2021) it has been announced that they are starting vaccinations in one week's time, in the hope that everyone will be vaccinated by spring next year.

I have enjoyed sharing my adventures and hope that you have also enjoyed reading about them.

EPILOGUE

In planning to help Jeff with his book, the original idea was that he would come to visit us and we would enjoy a long period of working together, as the book evolved. That did not allow for the pandemic and being locked down, 300 miles apart.

Late February 2021, almost a year since Jeff started working on his book we reached a milestone of the first complete draft. As he progressed, he had been emailing me each chapter, accompanied by scanned old photographs and more recent digital camera images. Later, he mailed me all the photos, so I could scan at a higher resolution. We then reached the pivotal moment for me to print, bind and mail to him something resembling the finished product.

I have really enjoyed reading all of his tales and am in awe of his amazing talent that has taken him around much of the world. He responded to many opportunities and wisely declined some others. Too many people work hard all their lives yet don't manage to survive to enjoy an active retirement. Here is a guy who has grabbed life by the balls and lived the dream.

Some of the reasons we have been able to work well together are sharing the same positive attitudes, having easy-going temperaments and a thirst for fun. Following our initial chance meeting we did not see each other again for over two years, in April 2022 and again in June. From the outset, an enduring friendship quickly developed. It has been an unusual project involving over 870 emails and numerous telephone conversations.

On tour, Jeff and the band would often move on, without seeing any reviews. However, one review that he had never seen has come to light, and it is fitting to include it here.

Chris

Another full house for the Glenn Miller Band was no surprise, bearing as it does the biggest name in the big band business. To a backdrop of stars and stripes the band played Miller music and with a superb sax section to boot. Their programme wasn't limited to Miller music only, the bands of Dorsey (T), James, Shaw and Herman were musically acknowledged. Glenn's arrangement of "Begin The Beguine" featured Jeff Mason on clarinet to warm applause. Leading the reeds was Peter Hughes and his clarinet added polish to a strong section which produced the Miller sound to perfection. The brass was unamplified ensuring that they never overblew the beautiful reeds.

MUSICIANS

Here is a list of the names of many of the musicians featuring in this book. They include those who have taught me, those with whom I have played, some of those I have taught and those in whose bands I have worked.

Alan Beaver	alto sax	
Alan Boynton	drums	
Alan	organ	
Alan Dilly	tenor sax	
Alan Skidmore	tenor sax	
Ally Thorn	guitar	
Arthur "Art" Lester	sax teacher	bandleader
Barbara White	trumpet	
Baz	trumpet	
Benny Daniels	alto sax	bandleader
Bobby Byrne	trombone	
Bobby Orr	drums	
Brian Ling	tenor sax	
Dave McQuater	guitar	
Dave Smith	organ	
Dave Willis	baritone sax	
Don Fay		bandleader
Don Jones	tenor sax	bandleader
Duane Eddy	guitar	
Eric Delaney	drums	bandleader
Frank White	tenor sax	
Freddy Staff	trumpet	
Gene Mayo	drums	bandleader
Glyn 'Black'	guitar	
Glyn Thomas	drums	
Graham Jarvis	drums	
Harold Fisher	drums	
Hilson Hatley	drums	
Ian Fenby	trumpet	
Ian Spencer	trumpet	

Isaac "Ike" Cole	piano	bandleader	
Jim Roberts	tenor sax		
Johnny Evans	tenor sax		
Johnny Francis	tenor sax		
Johnny Hilton		bandleader	
Johnny Howard	sax	bandleader	
Johnny Watson	trombone	bandleader	
Jos Taylor	tenor sax		
Keith Monk	piano	bandleader	
Lionel Lowe	clarinet		
Louie Bellson	drums		
Martin Dunsdon	tenor sax		
Maurice (Mo) Robinson	guitar		
Melt Kingston	bass		
Mike Grigg	drums		mikegrigg.com
Paul Booth	tenor sax		paulboothmusic.com
Paul Jones	alto sax		
Paul Woodburn	baritone sax		
Pete Warner	tenor sax		
Peter Hughes	alto sax		
Phil Chapman	tenor sax		
Ray McVay	sax	musical director	glennmillerorchestra.co.uk
Ronnie Asprey	alto sax		
Ronnie Chamberlain	clarinet, sax		
Ronnie Hunt	trumpet		
Roy Bell	guitar		
Sam Watmough	trombone	bandleader	
Sandy Nelson	drums		
Sarah Bolter	clarinet, sax		sarahbolter.co.uk
Scott Povey	alto sax		
Simon Currie	sax		simoncurrie.co.uk
Ted Barker	trombone		
Tony Arnopp	alto sax		
Tony Evans		bandleader	
Tony Wally	trumpet		
Wink Meer	clarinet		
Zeke Zarchy	trumpet		

Printed in Great Britain
by Amazon

84630641R00149